ANALYTICS FOR MANAGERS

Analytics, the data-driven approach to management, is an essential managerial tool. The objective of *Analytics for Managers* is to introduce analytics from the perspective of a corporation's general manager. Rather than examining the details or attempting an encyclopedic review of the field, this text emphasizes the strategic role that analytics plays in globally competitive corporations today. Each chapter introduces a potential issue in the field, and then presents some basic analytical concepts that have been successfully used to address that problem. This innovative presentation of material provides the student, the manager of the future, with a well-rounded understanding of the analyst's tools and techniques. This book will appeal to upper-level undergraduate and MBA level students.

Peter C. Bell earned BA and MA degrees from Oxford University and MBA and PhD degrees from the Graduate School of Business, the University of Chicago, and is a Professor of Management Science at Ivey. He is a Fellow of INFORMS and was awarded the 2005 *INFORMS Prize for the Teaching of OR/MS Practice.*

Gregory S. Zaric earned a BSc degree from the University of Western Ontario, an MASc from the University of Waterloo, and MS and PhD degrees from Stanford University. He is an Associate Professor of Management Science at Ivey and holds a Canada Research Chair in Health Care Management Science.

ANALYTICS FOR MANAGERS

WITH EXCEL

Peter C. Bell & Gregory S. Zaric

Routledge
Taylor & Francis Group

NEW YORK AND LONDON

First published 2013
by Routledge
711 Third Avenue, New York, NY 10017

Simultaneously published in the UK
by Routledge
2 Park Square, Milton Park, Abingdon, Oxon OX14 4RN

Routledge is an imprint of the Taylor & Francis Group, an informa business

The author/editor and publisher gratefully acknowledge the permission granted to reproduce the copyright material in this book. Every effort has been made to trace copyright holders and to obtain their permission for the use of copyright material. The publisher apologizes for any errors or omissions and would be grateful if notified of any corrections that should be incorporated in future reprints or editions of this book.

Library of Congress Cataloging-in-Publication Data

Bell, Peter.
Analytics for managers : with Excel / Peter Bell & Gregory Zaric. — 1st ed.
   p. cm.
  Includes bibliographical references and index.
  1. Management. I. Zaric, Gregory. II. Title.
HD30.19.B345 2012
003'.54024658—dc23   2012016360

ISBN: 978-0-415-62269-1 (hbk)
ISBN: 978-0-415-62268-4 (pbk)
ISBN: 978-0-203-10581-8 (ebk)

Typeset in StoneSerif
by Apex CoVantage, LLC

Printed and bound in the United States of America by Edwards Brothers Malloy, Inc.

CONTENTS

ANALYTICS FOR MANAGERS

The objective of this book is to introduce analytics from the perspective of the general manager of a corporation. Rather than examine the details or attempt an encyclopedic review of the field, this text will emphasize the strategic role that analytics is playing in globally competitive corporations today.

Analytics is one of a number of terms used to describe a data-driven, more-scientific approach to management. Analytics is multifaceted:

- Ability in analytics is *an essential management skill*: knowledge of data and analytics helps the manager to analyze decision situations, prevent problem situations from arising, and identify new opportunities, and often enables many millions of dollars to be added to the bottom line for the organization.

- Analytics is *a vital functional area* in many organizations, although the function is not always known as "analytics." "Management Science," "Decision Technologies," "Decision Sciences," and "Operational Research" are some other names used for the analytics function. Some firms have very large "analytics" functions: "Decision Technologies" at American Airlines was a separate division employing several hundred engineers and scientists providing analytical services to American Airlines and many other organizations before being divested as part of Sabre Technology Holdings. Other organizations seek to distribute analytical services throughout the organization by offering courses, training sessions, and support services.

- Analytics is *a source of competitive advantage* that, under the right conditions, can be sustainable over a long period of time. Organizations that are good at analytics can create a cost or revenue advantage over their competitors. Many documented cases exist where this advantage equals hundreds of millions of dollars.

- Analytics is an *industry* made up of hundreds of firms and individuals who provide services to business, government, and individuals.

- Analytics is also *an academic discipline*, where many leading-edge ideas in management first appear. This discipline insists that ideas be theoretically sound or proven effective (unlike many other areas where new concepts, often expressed as buzz words, appear and disappear according to the rumblings of the "Guru-of-the-Month").

The Institute for Operations Research and the Management Sciences (INFORMS) provides support for analytics practitioners in industry and also for many academics who are teaching analytics in universities and colleges. INFORMS publishes *Analytics* magazine and sees three levels of analytics:

Descriptive analytics: Describing and analyzing historical data identifying patterns from samples. Example: finding and reporting trends.

Predictive analytics: Estimating probabilities of future events and trends and finding relationships in data that may not be readily apparent with descriptive analysis.

Prescriptive analytics: Evaluating and determining new ways to operate to achieve business objectives while balancing all constraints

_____

Source: http://www.informs.org/Community/Analytics/About-Us

SAS, a corporation that is a major player in the analytics marketplace, has published a more-detailed list of *Eight Levels of Analytics* to describe the role of analytics within the firm (full details at http://www.sas.com/news/sascom/2008q4/column_8levels.html). The eight SAS levels can be used to assess where the firm is in terms of its analytical competencies, and also at what level the individual manager is capable of performing analytically. In abridged form, the eight levels are:

Eight Levels of Analytics from SAS (abridged)

1. STANDARD REPORTS

    Answer the questions: What happened? When did it happen?

    Example: Monthly or quarterly financial reports generated on a regular basis.

2. AD HOC REPORTS

   Answer the questions: How many? How often? Where?

   Example: Custom reports that describe the number of hospital patients for every diagnosis code for each day of the week.

3. QUERY DRILLDOWN

   Answers the questions: Where exactly is the problem? How do I find the answers?

   Example: Sort and explore data about different types of cell phone users and their calling behaviors, allowing for a little bit of discovery.

4. ALERTS

   Answer the questions: When should I react? What actions are needed now?

   Example: Sales executives receive alerts when sales targets are falling behind.

5. STATISTICAL ANALYSIS

   Answers the questions: Why is this happening? What opportunities am I missing?

   Example: Banks can discover why an increasing number of customers are refinancing their homes . . . (including some) complex analytics, such as frequency models and regression analysis. We can begin to look at why things are happening by using the stored data, and then begin to answer questions based on the data.

6. FORECASTING

   Answers the questions: What if these trends continue? How much is needed? When will it be needed?

   Example: Retailers can predict how demand for individual products will vary from store to store.

   Forecasting is one of the hottest markets—and hottest analytical applications—right now. It applies everywhere. In particular, forecasting demand helps supply just enough inventory, so you don't run out or have too much.

7. PREDICTIVE MODELING

   Answers the questions: What will happen next? How will it affect my business?

   Example: Hotels and casinos can predict which VIP customers will be more interested in particular vacation packages.

8. OPTIMIZATION

Answers the question: How do we do things better? What is the best decision for a complex problem?

Example: Given business priorities, resource constraints, and available technology, determine the best way to optimize your IT platform to satisfy the needs of every user. Optimization supports innovation. It takes your resources and needs into consideration and helps you find the best possible way to accomplish your goals.

Source: SAS website: www.sas.com/news/sascom/2008q4/column_8levels.html. Copyright © 2008, SAS Institute Inc. All Rights Reserved. Reproduced with permission of SAS Institute Inc., Cary, NC, USA.

SAS points out that most of the analytics offerings in the marketplace relate to the first four levels and that increasing the firm's business intelligence involves moving the firm up to higher levels of analytics competency.

The SAS *Eight Levels* and the INFORMS three levels of analytics are frameworks that help to integrate the materials in this book. As you read further, you will learn more about the various kinds of analytics and see the advantage associated with moving your personal skill set up to higher levels of analytical competence. You will also read many examples of firms that have prospered by integrating higher levels of analytics skills throughout their operations. Additional motivation should come from the fact that analytics is hot right now. Just a few of the current trend highlights:

- The bestseller *Supercrunchers* by Ian Ayres and *The Numerati* by Stephen Baker have introduced analytics to a wide audience.

- *60 Minutes* on CBS television broadcast a piece on Bill James and the analytics he has brought to the Boston Red Sox (view online at http://www.cbsnews.com/video/watch/?id=4541230n%3E%3Cimg%20src=; and also available on YouTube: search for *Red Sox Bill James*.)

- An article in Canada's major newspaper in January listed eight big trends that you should be thinking about in preparing for 2008 and beyond. The first trend identified was reprinted from futurist Jim Carroll's "What Comes Next?" think-piece (http://media4.jimcarroll.com/wp-content/uploads/2010/04/FutureTrends.pdf).

REVENGE OF THE MATH GEEKS

Analytics is Hot

Remember those kids in school who were really good at math? They own the future . . . The 21st century is all about math: some of the most unique, innovative ideas are emerging with these types of analytic projects. This is where the next billion dollar industries are being born.

- *Business Week* had an article on a similar theme: "A generation ago, quants turned finance upside down. Now they're mapping out ad campaigns and building new businesses from mountains of personal data" (Stephen Baker, "Math Will Rock Your World," *BusinessWeek*, January 23, 2006).

- Following the successful use of analytics in baseball (Michael M. Lewis, *Moneyball: The Art of Winning an Unfair Game,* W. W. Norton & Co., 2004; and Jeff Passan, "Royals' Bannister Unafraid to Do the Math," *Yahoo! Sports*, March 8, 2008). Analytics has even found its way into hockey (Iain Macintyre, "Number Cruncher Courts Canucks," *Vancouver Sun*, May 6, 2008).

- INFORMS and SAS have started publishing *Analytics* online magazines (http://www.analytics-digital.com/analytics/2008spring/?pg=4, and http://www.sas.com/news/).

- Research by MGI and McKinsey's Business Technology Office finds that "the amount of data in our world has been exploding, and analyzing large data sets—so-called big data—will become a key basis of competition, underpinning new waves of productivity growth, innovation, and consumer surplus. Leaders in every sector will have to grapple with the implications of big data, not just a few data-oriented managers" (http://www.mckinsey.com/Insights/MGI/Research/Technology_and_Innovation/Big_data_The_next_frontier_for_innovation).

- These same researchers also report: "There will be a shortage of talent necessary for organizations to take advantage of big data. By 2018, the United States alone could face a shortage of 140,000 to 190,000 people with deep analytical skills, as well as 1.5 million managers and analysts with the know-how to use the analysis of big data to make effective decisions" (http://www.mckinsey.com/Insights/MGI/Research/Technology_and_Innovation/Big_data_The_next_frontier_for_innovation).

We share this view of the importance of business analytics as a competitive strength, and throughout this book we will examine a number of firms that have been successful using analytics. San Miguel Corporation of the Philippines saw its very successful Operations Research Group as a functional area providing vital help to the general management of the corporation:

"Operations Research plays a big role in the five-year, approximately one billion dollar-expansion and modernization program that we launched in 1987. Under the program, we have built 22 manufacturing plants—we would not have dared to undertake the expansion at all without Operations Research. In our strategic planning meetings every year, whenever a division or business unit manager presents a project, we always make sure that Operations Research has gone through the proposal . . .

"San Miguel's Senior Management appreciates the vital role of Operations Research in attaining our corporate goals, and in implementing the strategies that enable us to achieve adequate growth and satisfactory returns for our various stakeholders."

Source: Francisco Eizmendi Jr., President, San Miguel Corporation, the Philippines, quoted in E. Del Rosario, *OR/MS Today*, 21, 5.

In contrast, Daniel Elwing, Chief Executive Officer of ABB Electric, emphasized analytics as an essential management skill:

"[Analytics] is not a project or a set of techniques; it is a process, a way of thinking and managing."

Source: Daniel Elwing, President and CEO of ABB Electric, quoted in D.H. Gensch, et al., *Interfaces*, 20, 1.

Both ABB Electric and San Miguel Corporation have effectively used analytics to create and sustain a strategic advantage. Fully understanding the strategic use of analytics involves learning some essential skills that all general managers must have in their tool bag, coupled with achieving an understanding of how these skills can be mobilized to bring advantage to the competitive firm (to the disadvantage of the competition).

Thomas H. Davenport in his pioneering article "Competing on Analytics" emphasizes the role of analytics in winning in a highly competitive environment: "Organizations such as Amazon, Harrah's, Capital One, and the Boston Red Sox have dominated their fields by deploying industrial-strength analytics across a wide variety of activities."

The field of analytics is extensive and fast growing. We hope in this text to convey some of the excitement and opportunities that the adoption of analytics is creating for the manager of today.

The Organization of the Book

The chapters of this book are organized in two main parts. The first part introduces a problem area and presents some basic analytical concepts that have been successfully used to address the problem area. The objective of this material is to provide you, the manager of the future, with a general understanding of the tools and techniques used by the analyst.

This general understanding is very important: Felix Rohatyn of the New York investment banking firm Lazard Freres & Co., quoted in the *New Yorker* magazine, provides a rationale for achieving a basic level of understanding:

> "Too many high-level executives are prisoners of their staffs. They have never really done the nitty-gritty stuff, which is not terribly mysterious once you tackle it. And if you haven't done these things, the technicians can absolutely wrap you up in the details, and you never find your way out."

The second part of each chapter is a series of short descriptions of organizations that have effectively used the tools described. These readings are designed to demonstrate that the tools introduced in the chapter are not some obscure theory, but rather have been used, are being used, and will continue to be used by corporations and other organizations in seeking to enhance profits or improve effectiveness or productivity.

We recommend that you work through some cases to help you improve your understanding of the basic concepts and their use, and at the end of the book, we provide a list of cases we have used to teach these materials. These cases describe real-world situations where the use of the concepts may be challenging and, usually, not definitive: many of these cases have no "correct" answer, although some answers are always better than others. Working these cases can provide an experience similar to that found "on-the-job": you may have to cope with ambiguity and extraneous or missing data. You may feel that you do not have enough information to proceed, but the situation demands action. The emphasis in these cases is to derive a recommendation for sensible action: what should the decision maker do? How should the action be implemented? Working some cases will provide an opportunity to learn about the concepts presented in the chapters and also, importantly, how to achieve useful results by applying these concepts in the real world.

The Challenge

The recurring theme of this text is that managers who understand analytics are better trained and better equipped to manage the modern corporation than are those who do not. Of course, there is much more to management training than analytics, but as we move into the twenty-first century, managers who understand analytics have been instrumental in pushing forward the leading edge of management practice in many industries. The challenge is to understand how and where this is happening, so that analytics can provide our firm, not our competition, with a competitive advantage.

CHAPTER 1

AN INTRODUCTION TO ANALYTICS

Recent years have seen the emergence of a new type of corporation. These firms have prospered as a direct consequence of developing and exploiting special skills in analytics, allowing them to gain and hold a competitive advantage in their marketplaces. In certain industries, a high level of analytical sophistication has emerged; the very existence of firms in these industries depends not only on their marketing, financial, and human resource skills, but also on their ability to use the concepts and tools of business analytics on a day-to-day basis.

A View of the Corporation

In thinking about the strategic use of analytics, it is helpful to have a common view or "model" of the corporation. The model used in this book is one of global competition. Competition is a familiar concept to us through the world of sports but, at its extreme, competition can be a matter of life or death. A metaphor from the animal world illustrates this point:

Every morning when the sun comes, up a gazelle wakes. It knows that it must outrun the fastest lion or it will be eaten.

When the sun comes up, the lion also wakes. The lion knows that it must outrun the slowest gazelle, or it will starve.

In the end, it doesn't really matter whether you are a lion or a gazelle; when the sun comes up, you had better be prepared to run for your life.

Major global corporations often exist in an environment of intense competition where comparisons with warfare are common. Some corporations "win" and others "lose." Some win local skirmishes, or achieve a temporary advantage, while others move more slowly, conquer new territories gradually, and consolidate and hold positions for long periods of time.

Comparisons between global competition and warfare may not be too far-fetched. Here is the view from the head of Matsushita Electric Corporation of Japan, one of the world's leading manufacturers of electronic equipment, with brand names that include Panasonic and Quasar:

> "We are going to win and the industrial west is going to lose; there's nothing much you can do about it . . . business, we know, is now so complex and difficult, the survival of firms so hazardous in an environment increasingly competitive and fraught with danger, that their continued existence depends on the day-to-day mobilization of every ounce of intelligence."
>
> _____
> *Source*: Konosuke Matsushita of Matsushita Electric Industrial Company, *Not For Bread Alone*, Berkeley Publishing, 1994.

Robert Cross, who has spent his career at the leading edge of developments in the practice of management, is also comfortable with the warfare metaphor:

> "War—that's really what it's all about in today's business world. The generals, captains, and lieutenants may wear gray flannel suits and carry black leather briefcases, but they're still fighting a war. Every day, they march off to a new battle over some piece of turf, and the headlines of the *Wall Street Journal* scream about bombs being dropped, predators swooping down on their prey, winners and losers, bloody battles in the boardroom, and wounded companies . . . For some, this new kind of cold war is exciting as hell. For others, it *is* hell. But make no mistake about it—it's war all right."
>
> _____
> *Source*: Robert G. Cross, *Revenue Management*, Broadway Books, 1997.

All corporations engaged in global competition possess certain advantages and disadvantages. For example, corporations located in China have the advantages of a cooperative and well-trained workforce and a supportive government structure with few environmental rules, but also have the disadvantages of being a long distance from both their major markets and their supplies of raw materials. North American firms are closer to resources and markets, but have more expensive labor, more costly regulations and environmental rules, and less support from governments.

An innovative new product, a particularly appealing advertising campaign, or a cost savings resulting from an innovation in production methods may create a temporary victory for a corporation in the battle against the competition. But a temporary victory is just one battle won: the war goes on and new combatants will appear. To survive in the long term, the corporation must create and maintain a *sustainable competitive advantage*.

Often, a sustainable competitive advantage results from structural considerations which prevent or discourage the competition. For example, locating a plant in a major market may create a niche that competitors choose to allow to continue. Another example is a patent awarded by the government that may prevent direct competition. But for firms in most markets, the only way to sustain a competitive advantage is by keeping one step ahead of the competition: a process of *continuous improvement*. A successful advertising campaign must be followed by an even more successful campaign: the firm must continuously improve its marketing. Production innovation must be ongoing as the firm continuously improves its production systems.

Analytics can help this process of continuous improvement through constantly striving to improve the corporation's decision making. Can the corporation choose to ignore the potential benefits of analytics? Almost certainly not, since others are already gaining advantages from using analytics as a competitive weapon.

In short, in order to survive in the intensely competitive marketplaces of today, the firm must be good at everything. Certainly marketing is important, certainly human resources management is important, certainly finance is important, but if the firm is to survive, it must be as good as, or better than, its competitors at decision making. If two firms face the same decision problem and one makes a more profitable decision, then it has won a local skirmish. In the long term, battles are won by stringing together victories in local skirmishes.

Decision Making

The emphasis of this book is on *decision making* in the context of the corporation. Making decisions is just one of many things that corporations do, but it is a critical activity. The epochs at which decisions are taken differentiate successful organizations from unsuccessful ones. The successful organization has a history of making decisions that are timely, opportunistic, and that generally "work out."

Decision making in a corporation is a carefully controlled activity, where responsibility for decisions is formally assigned to particular individuals or groups (or committees). The human resources or personnel group generally have responsibility for hiring and terminating decisions; the marketing group for decisions about sales force planning and advertising spending; the financial manager has the responsibility for making decisions relating to investing surplus funds. These individuals, however, do not set their own decision-making rules, but rather make decisions within a framework which originates from the highest levels of management and ownership (the Board of Directors, or the shareholders). This framework is articulated through statements about the corporation's *vision*, *mission*, and *strategy*.

While these statements can be criticized on the grounds that they don't vary much from corporation to corporation, and that the statements appear to be largely aimed at an outside audience, they do generally define the objectives of the corporation and set guidelines for decision making within the corporation. As an example, here is a statement of "Mission, Values, and Guiding Principles" from the Ford Motor Company:

Statement of Mission, Values, and Guiding Principles by Ford Motor Company

Mission

Ford Motor Company is a worldwide leader in automotive and automotive-related products and services as well as in newer industries such as aerospace, communications, and technical services. Our mission is to improve continually our products and services to meet our customers' needs, allowing us to prosper as a business and to provide a reasonable return for our stockholders, the owners of our business.

Values

How we accomplish our mission is as important as the mission itself. Fundamental to success for the Company are these basic values:

- **People** Our people are the source of our strength. They provide our corporate intelligence and determine our reputation and vitality. Involvement and teamwork are our core human values.

- **Products** Our products are the end result of our efforts, and they should be the best in serving customer needs worldwide. As our products are viewed, so are we viewed.

- **Profits** Profits are the ultimate measure of how efficiently we provide customers with the best products for their needs. Profits are required to survive and grow.

Guiding Principles

- **Quality comes first** To achieve customer satisfaction, the quality of our products and services must be our number-one priority.

- **Customers are the focus of everything we do** Our work must be done with our customers in mind, providing better products and services than our competition.

- **Continuous improvement is essential to our success** We must strive for excellence in everything we do: in our products, in their safety and value, and in our services, our human relations, our competitiveness, and our profitability.

- **Employee involvement is our way of life** We are a team. We must treat each other with trust and respect.

- **Dealers and suppliers are our partners** The company must maintain mutually beneficial relationships with dealers, suppliers, and other business associates.
- **Integrity is never compromised** The conduct of our company worldwide must be pursued in a manner that is socially responsible and commands respect for its integrity and for its positive contributions to society. Our doors are open to men and women alike without discrimination and without regard to ethnic origin or personal beliefs.

Source: Ford Motor Company, *Annual Report,* 1994.

Note the recurring themes of profitability, competitiveness, and continuous improvement. Ford Motor Company sees itself in a highly competitive industry in which it must continuously improve "everything we do" in order to generate the profits required to "survive and grow." Decision making at Ford is expected to take place within this framework.

At a large corporation such as Ford, hundreds of decisions are made every day. In many cases, decisions are taken deliberately but, perhaps more often, decisions are a consequence of inaction resulting in opportunities being missed because the corporation failed to recognize them. Decisions not made explicitly are often made anyway. There is little difference in result between a firm that carefully considers a new business opportunity but decides not to proceed, and a firm that did not identify the opportunity in the first place. To use an example closer to home, this business class will neither include students who carefully thought about taking a business degree, but who decided not to, nor will it include students who didn't even think of taking a business degree, but who would have benefited from (and enjoyed!) the program.

Consistently good decision making results when the corporation has processes in place to identify and evaluate decision situations. This is what analytics is all about: Analytics provides the vehicle for the systematic improvement of decision-making processes in organizations. Through analytics, organizations can improve the way they make decisions.

Analytics should not, however, be seen as an isolated activity; the greatest benefits accrue when analytics is highly integrated with the other business functions. For example:

> After the financial specialists have arrived at the desired financial characteristics for a portfolio, the analytics specialist can help choose the best stocks to include. Having an "optimal" portfolio provides an immediate advantage over the competition.

or

> Analysis of customer purchasing behavior can lead to insights that enable managers to design products and advertising that better meet the needs of the customer.

or

> After the marketing group has decided which markets to enter, the analytics specialist can provide advice on how many warehouses to build, which cities to build them in, and how to ship products around the distribution system. A low-cost or high-response distribution system provides a competitive advantage.

One objective of this book is to make you, the manager of tomorrow, a better decision maker. Developing individual decision-making skills is one path to improved organizational performance, and much of what you will learn is taken from real life and contains lessons immediately transferable to your future work. However, improving individual decision-making skills is not enough: there are organizational issues that must also be addressed. A second objective is to understand the organizational issues: What can we learn by examining some of the many examples of corporations that have flourished by excelling at analytics? Which corporations appear to have very good decision-making processes? How does a corporation organize to do analytics well? How do successful organizations transfer analytics technology into improved decision making?

Analytics as a Source of Competitive Advantage

Can a corporation use analytics to achieve a sustainable competitive advantage? The answer to this critical question is a definite "Yes." (We address this question in more detail in Chapter 9.) We can document numerous examples of firms that are both very good at analytics and very successful in their competitive marketplaces. While it is difficult to

A Major Corporation

DIRECTOR, OPERATIONAL ANALYTICS: North America

POSITION SUMMARY

There is key advantage to a business where its decisions are made through the careful use of system understanding, advanced analytic techniques, complete data, and assessment of risk. xxx invests significant resources in developing, maintaining, and providing access to a rich data and analytics environment and it is imperative that xxx fully leverage the uniqueness and power of this environment.

The fundamental job function of Director, Operational Analytics is to manage the development, integration, and strategy for analytics for xxx. The successful candidate will have an operational view of key xxx systems and their data and the dynamic behaviour in these systems over time. The foundation for the function will be through understanding xxx's distinctive capabilities that can be supported by analytics, planning and guiding high-impact analytics, considering evolution of systems and their data, and identifying new opportunities for data and analytics. He/she will manage a team that specializes in statistical methods, data mining, Operations Research, reporting applications, and data management and will be responsible for setting strategic direction in each of these areas.

This position was posted April, 2009. To see others visit:
http://lionhrtpub.com/orms/classifieds/ORMS-classifieds.html

Figure 1.1 Example of an Analytics Position

conclude that their competitive success is the result of their skill at analytics, there are many people both inside and outside the firms who are making this claim, including CEOs and members of Boards. In some cases, spectacular growth in the number of people employed in the analytics area has occurred: American Airlines had eight people employed in analytics in 1982, but by 1993 this had risen to almost 400.

The actions of other corporations in hiring analytics specialists (a recent example is shown in Figure 1.1) also support a view that analytics can support business strategy at the highest level of the firm.

In their bestseller *Competing on Analytics: The New Science of Winning* (Harvard Business Press Books, 2007), authors Thomas Davenport and Jeanne Harris state, "Any competitive advantage needs to be a moving target, with continued improvement and reinvestment. Analytics are particularly well suited to continuous innovation and renewal" (p. 49).

The Future for Analytics

Information technologies grounded by corporate Enterprise Resource Planning (ERP) systems are now ubiquitous in management. The great majority of management decision making now involves extracting information from mountains of data: the issue is no longer whether data should be used to inform the decision maker, but rather how data can be used to help the human decision maker(s) to make better decisions.

Barry Beracha, the former chief executive of the Sara Lee Bakery Group, emphasizes the importance of data as an input to management decisions:

"In God we trust. All others bring data."[1]

Since data-driven decision making is the domain of analytics, the future for analytics specialists looks bright. The press has picked up this trend:

Trends to watch for in 2008

In preparing for this year and beyond, there are eight big "trends that you should be thinking about," according to Toronto-based innovation consultant and futurist Jim Carroll:

"Revenge of the Math Geeks"

Analytics is hot

> Remember those kids in school who were really good at math? They own the future. Our world is faced with a tremendous number of complex challenges and fascinating opportunities, and it's the math experts who will figure it all out. That's because they have mastered the skill of processing complex analytical algorithms with massive computing horsepower, and solving some of world's most complicated issues by doing so . . . The 21st century is all about math: some of the most unique, innovative ideas are emerging with these types of analytic projects. This is where the next billion dollar industries are being born. (http://media4.jimcarroll.com/wp-content/uploads/2010/04/FutureTrends.pdf)

Companies will need to learn to match the price of their service or product with the immediate, second-by-second need of the consumer who wishes to purchase it. The supplier will gather data on the customer's use of the product in real time and then set prices accordingly, trying to induce or gain from certain behaviours.

Insurers, for example, can put data recorders in cars and give lower rates to people who drive less frequently or at lower speeds, while cola vendors could charge higher rates for pop in vending machines in hotter weather.

———
Source: "Storm Signals: Future Shock, Here and Now," *The Globe and Mail*, May 7, 2008.

Business analytics and optimization

Business consulting: **Business analytics and optimization**

Can you predict and respond to opportunities and threats? Optimize operations to capitalize on new sources of revenue? Proactively manage risk while ensuring efficiency? IBM Business Analytics and Optimization capabilities are your most powerful ally in the new economic environment.

Globalization, massive interconnections and increased risk, combined with an explosion of information, results in a challenging and continuous cycle of inefficiency and operational complexity. Unfortunately, many leaders are making crucial business decisions based almost entirely on intuition and personal experience rather than intelligent information.

A fundamental shift to a smarter, fact-based enterprise should be on your information agenda. How can this help your organization? A more predictive information strategy paves the way for more intelligent decisions.

Leading edge algorithms, and advanced mathematic assets, methods and capabilities help you develop predictive analytics and business optimization to create new solutions for unique challenges. Discover predictive insights and turn them into operational reality to close the gap between strategy and execution. Harness the power of analytics to help you survive and thrive in these challenging conditions.

The smarter enterprise and the age of analytics

http://www-935.ibm.com/services/us/gbs/bus/html/bcs_centeroptimization.html April 26, 2009

Figure 1.2 IBM Center for Analytics and Optimization. Reprinted by permission from IBM.

IBM, a leading provider of business information technology consulting services, recently bought ILOG®, the owner of the CPLEX® suite of optimization software. Following this acquisition, IBM launched a "Business Analytics and Optimization" center to expand their offerings of analytics consulting (Figure 1.2). IBM has emerged as a leading supplier of analytics to corporations and has also developed strong internal analytics capabilities.

This promising future is not limited to Western economies. Chinese Vice-President Rong Yiren has said that "administrative systems based on scientific theory are important for economic development and social progress in both developed and developing countries" (Cao Min, "Officials Improve Efficiency," *China Daily*, October 9, 1996).

One reason for the expected growth in analytics is the increasing competitiveness and increasingly global nature of business. In order to survive, firms and countries must continually seek sources of competitive advantage that they can sustain over periods of time. In addition, the use of analytics has been facilitated by significant advance in the technology for doing analytics, including computers and spreadsheets, which now provide a powerful and convenient platform for the business analyst.

In seeking a sustainable advantage, it is important to concentrate on the *process* of decision making rather than on individual decisions. An organization with effective decision-making processes will make some decisions which turn out badly; the organization was simply unlucky. It is important to distinguish between *decisions* and *outcomes*; a good decision can produce a bad result, and vice versa. Consider the following example:

> You are offered a chance to play the following game: a coin (selected at random from those in your pocket) will be flipped by a disinterested third party. If the coin shows "Heads," you will receive $1,000, but if it comes down "Tails," you will have to pay $1.

Choosing to play this game is a correct decision for most of us. If we could play it over and over again, we would become very rich, but if we were only able to play the game once, we could end up losing a dollar. A spectator seeing us lose a dollar might conclude that our decision to play was a poor one. However, they would be incorrect. We made a good decision—we were simply unlucky as to the outcome. Of course, the reverse is also true: firms that make bad decisions sometimes "get lucky" and experience a good outcome.

An organization cannot avoid bad outcomes, but it can control the risks that it takes and act in a way that enhances its chances of survival. To do this, the organization must continuously work to improve the *processes* by which its decisions are made.

Four decisions that did not work out so well:

In August 1981, IBM launched the IBM Personal Computer (PC) and, in this one bold move, seized control of the PC market. For a few short months, IBM dominated this market, but in a series of decisions made over about a ten-year period, IBM handed the PC market to Microsoft. Based on the capitalized value of Microsoft in 1991, the cumulative result of these decisions was a "gift" of about $1 billion from IBM to Microsoft—IBM may well be the only company which has given $1 billion to a competitor and survived!

In the movie *ET*, Elliot lures the cute extraterrestrial into his house with Reese's Pieces candy. The director, Steven Spielberg, had tried to get Mars Corporation to let him use M&Ms in the film at this point, but Mars decided not to allow this. After the release of *ET*, sales of Reese's Pieces rocketed by more than 65%.

Kentucky Fried Chicken (KFC) had a successful ad campaign on their hands in 2009. Oprah Winfrey had promoted a giveaway of free grilled chicken via a web coupon. However, KFC hadn't anticipated the huge number of coupon downloads. After giving away 4 million meals, the fast food chain had to start turning away coupon holders. Coupon holders were furious and staged sit-ins, and a few even sued KFC, who quickly backpedaled and offered a free chicken meal plus a soft drink to those turned away from the promotion.

In 1961, Decca Records auditioned an unknown Liverpool group but decided that the group had little promise and did not sign them to a contract. Very soon after that audition, the group signed with EMI. The group's name? The Beatles.

. . . and two of the most successful business decisions in history:

Microsoft purchased all rights to a fledgling personal computer operating system called 86-DOS in July 1981 for two payments, which totaled $75,000. 86-DOS had been developed by the Seattle Computer Products Company in response to the need they perceived for a general-purpose PC operating system. Development began in April 1980 and the first version (called QDOS 0.10 for "Quick and Dirty Operating System") was released in August, having been thrown together in two people months (although it worked surprisingly well). Version 0.3, now known as 86-DOS, was released in the last few days of 1980. Seattle passed this new version on to Microsoft, which initially purchased non-exclusive marketing rights: it had just one customer at the time.

In April 1981, Seattle released version 1.0, which was essentially MS-DOS as used on the first IBM PCs. In July 1981, Microsoft purchased all rights to the DOS outright. Shortly afterwards, IBM announced the IBM PC using essentially this operating system, now bearing the Microsoft name.

The McDonald brothers opened their first restaurant in 1940, expecting nothing unusual. Ray Kroc, a Multimixer Milkshake machine salesman, hoped to sell one milkshake machine to any given customer, but the McDonald brothers needed eight machines! Intrigued at how a restaurant could be so busy as to need eight milkshake machines (each producing five milkshakes at a time), Kroc met the brothers, convinced them to sell him the McDonalds name, and started franchising food "factories" that amassed $28.8 billion in sales in 2008 alone.

Richard Caldwell, executive vice president of Harris Trust and Savings Bank, gave an interesting example of the partnership between analytics and the other business functions leading to improved decision making:

> "We became familiar with some of the academic work on decision making only after we discovered that a simple computer program could in some cases outperform our experts."

Caldwell continued, emphasizing the process of continuous improvement:

> "Puzzled by this phenomenon, we turned to the literature and were able to fine tune our decision process and use the knowledge of our experts more effectively."

Presumably, with more effective experts, even more effective "simple computer programs" can be developed, leading to even more effective experts, and the cycle continues.

The first step toward implementing sound decision making is to examine the decision-making process itself.

The Decision-Making Process

Decision making requires that three basic tasks be performed: *pathfinding, analysis,* and *managerial review and action* (Figure 1.3).

Figure 1.3 The Management Decision-Making Process

Pathfinding is the step at which possible acts that can be taken are identified. Pathfinding involves answering questions such as:

- What alternatives (or options) do we have?
- If we have a problem, what can we do about it? What are the possible solutions?
- The organization is not doing as well as we feel it should; what can we change?
- The competition is killing us. What can we do?
- How do we get to where we want to be from where we are?

Pathfinding requires managerial expertise and experience coupled, sometimes, with creativity and intuition. "Thinking outside the box" is a pathfinding activity from which "creative" options may emerge, but in other cases, the options may be straightforward. There may be a large number of options, or few. There may be some that, while strictly possible, are easily discarded. As an example, one option is almost always to close down the business, but in most instances this is not worth spending much time analyzing.

Analysis involves "laying out" the possible acts in some way, and comparing and contrasting them. Typical questions include:

- What are the consequences of each act?
- How can we choose one act over some other act?
- What relevant data are available?
- Is there some further data that we can collect?

- Can expert opinion help us decide?
- What "number crunching" or other analysis should be done?
- Can some type of "model" help us decide?

Analysis usually concentrates on the "harder" facts and the quantitative aspects of the decision, since these are easier to analyze, to draws conclusions based on data, calculations, and perhaps some theory (particularly economic theory).

An analytics specialist or trained analyst can often provide assistance at the analysis stage, but the manager cannot stand completely aside. Many "management issues" emerge and must be addressed early. For example, what are our goals? What are appropriate criteria? Do we face any constraints? What are the sources of data?

Managerial Review and Action follow the analysis step. The manager must review both the pathfinding step (Were the "right" actions considered? Were there others that were missed?), and the analysis step (Was the analysis valid? What conclusions were reached? What was learned from the analysis?).

At this stage, other managerial issues might emerge. The analysis may suggest one route forward, but management may feel that some other action may be more consistent with the organization's long-term strategy. The review stage brings in the "softer" intangible issues that could not be adequately addressed during the analysis but which are critical to making a good decision.

Finally, after management becomes comfortable with a decision, steps must be taken to implement the required action. This may include testing the decision in some way (one form of testing is to try out the new system in parallel with the old system; another is to do some form of simulations using a computer model), and may also include monitoring and reviewing the results of the action. Implementing decisions is one of the basic tasks of line management. Implementation requires skill and perseverance, coupled with attention to the process by which the decision is implemented.

The Strategic/Tactical/Operation Framework

The *Strategic/Tactical/Operational framework* identifies different *types* of decision making at different levels in the organization. In the Strategic/Tactical/Operational framework, the organization is thought of as having a pyramid structure (Figure 1.4). At the bottom of the pyramid is the *operational* layer, while the top of the pyramid represents the *strategic* layer. Between these two are the middle management or *tactical* layers.

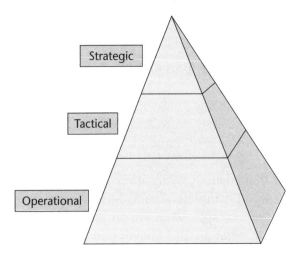

Figure 1.4 Decision-Making Levels

Operational decision making takes place at the lower levels of the firm. These decisions are required for the day-to-day running of the corporation, and have mainly short-term consequences; they can be changed fairly easily, often at low cost. Examples include: how much of a product to order when the stock has (or is about to) run out, how much fuel to load into an airplane, and what route to take to deliver our packages. Despite the fact that operational decisions happen at the lowest levels of the firm, they can be of great importance. Firms such as Wal-Mart have thrived by mastering operational-level decision making.

Tactical decision making takes place in the middle, managerial levels of the organization. These decisions have longer-lasting effects than do operational decisions and are more costly to change. Examples include: deriving the manufacturer's master production schedule, deciding on the organization's operating budget, and hiring management staff.

Strategic decision making is the task of top management, often including the Board of Directors. Strategic decisions affect the long-term direction and vitality of the organization. Generally, strategic decisions, once taken, are very costly and difficult to change. Examples include: leasing or buying a new building, launching a major new product, acquiring another company, and selecting the Chief Executive Officer for the organization.

Knowing whether a decision is strategic, tactical, or operational says much about the process of making the decision. Clearly, each individual strategic decision is worth time and effort, since the cost of a mistake here is generally very high. Operational decisions, on the other hand, may not justify as great an expenditure of effort on each decision individually, since these are easier and less expensive to change if a poor choice is made. Operational decisions, however, often recur: each time an airplane lands, the airline must decide how much fuel to load on board. While each individual operational decision may not have great consequences, the total of all the operational decisions may lead to a source of significant competitive advantage. The airline that can implement a set of refueling decisions which takes best advantage of fuel price differences at different airports avoids the cost of flying excess fuel around the skies, arranges refueling so as not to interfere with its flight timetable, and, importantly, ensures that no plane runs out of fuel while flying, will have lower fuel costs than the competition. Implementing a good solution to the "refueling problem" is, therefore, of strategic importance. (Fuel costs are the single-largest cost item for the major airlines, amounting to some $2 billion/year for a major carrier.)

The Data, Models, and Knowledge Framework

The Strategic/Tactical/Operational framework looks at where decisions are made, while the *Data, Models and Knowledge Framework* characterizes the inputs in a decision process.

Data is an important input to decision making: there are few decision situations that can be resolved in an informed way without reference to data. Organizations contain vast amounts of *data*. Some is specific to the organization (e.g., payroll numbers), while other data is public (e.g., today's stock prices). Some data is captured in the organization's databases (in libraries and in data warehouses), while other data exists in the minds of employees, or is available externally (e.g., through public, electronic databases). Managing the organization's data is often a multimillion-dollar activity in which providing access to the data is as important as managing the entry of new data.

Looking at data, however, is rarely sufficient. The data must be compiled, abstracted, and manipulated in some way in order to be relevant to the decision. This is the role of the *model*: a model is a construct that *adds value* to data. The use of a model allows for an informed analysis of a decision situation, bringing relevant data and structure to the decision-making task. Taking care of the models within the organization includes providing access, model maintenance and updating, and developing new models, and these tasks provide many managerial challenges.

Few decisions are made without *knowledge*. Organizations contain vast amounts of knowledge, most of it in the minds of employees. Increasingly, knowledge can be extracted from humans, represented in some structured way, and stored in a *knowledge base*. For the most part, however, knowledge relevant to today's decisions comes from the people involved in the decision-making process. This includes knowledge about the data, knowledge about models and model building, and managerial knowledge about this decision and similar situations that have occurred in the past (Figure 1.5).

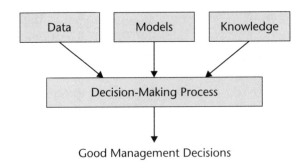

Figure 1.5 The "DMK" Framework

Knowledge of the Data-Models-Knowledge (DMK) framework prompts many probing questions about how a decision was made. For example:

- What data was used to make this decision? Where did it come from? Was it reliable?
- Was current data used? If forecasts were used, how were these obtained?
- What model was used?
- Was this a valid model?
- What knowledge went into the decision making? Whose knowledge was it? Does this individual have this knowledge?
- How do we know?

Successful decision making requires that appropriate data, useful models, and relevant knowledge be mobilized in the decision-making process.

Summary

To survive in the long term, the corporation must create and maintain a *sustainable competitive advantage*. For most firms, in most markets, the only way to sustain a competitive advantage is by keeping one step ahead of the competition: a process of *continuous improvement*. Analytics can help this process of continuous improvement through contributing to continually improving the corporation's *decision making*.

Two frameworks were presented that are useful in analyzing decision-making processes. The "Strategic, Tactical, Operational" framework identifies decisions according to their importance in the organization, while the "DMK" framework looks at the inputs to each decision. The manager who understands these two simple frameworks is well equipped to ask many probing questions about the firm's decision-making.

What the Manager Must Know

- Analysis is an essential step in decision making: after the decision options have been identified, analysis is performed, with the objective of thoroughly understanding the options and their implications, and to compare and contrast the options to try to identify the best path forward.

- The persons performing the analysis, be they managers or trained analysts, usually make use of broad set of quantitative techniques to construct some form of model of the decision. Good, effective analysis of decisions leading the firm to implement better decisions can provide the firm with a sustained competitive advantage.

- Maintaining a competitive advantage over time will require continuous improvement in the firm's analytical processes.

- The frameworks presented are useful aids to working through the decision-making process, but also for asking useful questions when others make decision recommendations.

- Many companies have become leaders in their industry through mastery of analytics.

CHAPTER 2

MODELS AND MODEL BUILDING

In Chapter 1, we introduced the notion of the model. The use of models is the distinguishing feature of business analytics. In this chapter, we present more details on models, model building, and the role of models in management decision making.

We are all familiar with models of various kinds. Architects use small-scale models to help them to design new buildings, automobile designers build models of new cars to test out design features, and crash-test dummies are used to model the effects of automobile accidents on car occupants. These are all examples of physical models that can be seen and touched.

Analytics models, however, are *logical*, *mathematical*, or *computer models* in which relationships from the real world are approximated by mathematical equations or logical statements.

Models in Management Decision Making

The development and use of models to aid management decision making began during World War II when a group of scientists was assembled at Royal Air Force Fighter Command in England. This group was asked to provide a scientific point-of-view on various operational problems to do with fighter aircraft. The first problem investigated was how to translate data on approaching aircraft from the air defense warning system into an organized fighter response. In May 1940, however, this group was involved in some very critical strategic decision making. As Harold Larnder recounts:

> When the Germans opened their offensive against France and the Low Countries, Fighter Command was quickly involved to the extent of ten of its Home Defence squadrons . . . maintained and operated from airfields on the Continent. (By May, 1940) British losses were running at a rate of some three squadrons every two days . . . On 14 May, (Air Chief Marshal Sir Hugh) Dowding learned that the French Premier was asking for

an additional ten squadrons and that Churchill, because of his strong sense of loyalty to Britain's ally, was determined to accede to the request. On the morning of May 15, (Dowding) invited Larnder to see him and . . . finished by saying, ". . . is there anything you scientists can suggest bearing on this matter?" Anything that could be done had to be done before he would leave for the Cabinet meeting two hours later.

So, at the suggestion of E. C. Williams, a rapid study was carried out based on current daily losses and replacement rates, to show how much more rapid this would become if additional squadrons were sent. For ease of presentation, Larnder converted Williams' findings from numerical to graph form. (At the Cabinet meeting) Dowding, feeling that he was making little headway in dissuading the Prime Minister from his determination to reinforce France, got up, walked round the table and said to Churchill, "If the present rate of wastage continues for another fortnight, we shall not have a single Hurricane left in France <u>or</u> in this country" . . . he laid his graphs in front of the Prime Minister. In Dowding's considered view, "That did the trick." Not only were the requested ten additional squadrons not sent to France, but of those already there all but three were returned to the United Kingdom within a matter of days. (K. B. Haley (Ed.), *Operational Research '78*, North Holland, Amsterdam, 1978)

This was clearly a pivotal decision. The Battle of Britain, which began about two months later, was fought with an average strength of 650–700 fighter aircraft: with twenty squadrons of fighters in France for a single week, the loss of 250–260 aircraft was expected.

This incident from the early history of analytics exemplifies three characteristics of the strategic use of analytics. First, the decision maker (the prime minister) was in the upper ranks of the organization; second, the model was produced in timely fashion and was appropriate to the problem; and third, some effort was made to present the results in a way that the decision maker could understand.

In this example, the model was a *mathematical* model: the loss of aircraft was approximated by a mathematical function (in fact, an exponential decay curve). The mathematical model, solved by hand, was the mainstay of analytics prior to the arrival of the computer. Often, solving the model was a time-consuming and laborious task involving rooms full of people with calculators, working long hours, often overnight. The new electronic computers were first seen as particularly good calculators to solve this computational problem (their accuracy was an important benefit), but it was soon recognized that the computer could drive other kinds of models, particularly *simulations* which emulate the function of the real world in the computer.

The early computers were batch-processing devices: the modeler produced a program that was submitted to the computer, and the output was returned some time after the job was submitted. The appearance of *interactivity* has had a profound impact, with managers now routinely using spreadsheet programs (such as Microsoft Excel). For the model builder, we now have sophisticated environments that permit the interactive construction of highly graphic and interactive models that make extensive use of color and graphics to aid communication between user and model.

Type of Models

Different types of models are appropriate for particular decision issues:

- **Decision analysis** models (Chapter 3) provide a useful vehicle for exploring sequential decision situations involving uncertainty. These models have been widely used for the analysis and management of risk and uncertainty.

- **Statistical models** (Chapters 4 and 5) are useful for understanding and summarizing *data*, and for using data to *forecast* and *predict*.

- **Simulation** modeling (Chapter 6) has become a very big business. Computer simulation is now routinely used to review the operation of manufacturing plants before construction begins, to design warehousing and materials handling systems, in military operations and gaming, and in a broad range of service sector applications (including airports, banks, etc.). Simulation models are *descriptive models*, in that they describe the way things are (versus *normative*, which describe the way things should be). Descriptive models are used to evaluate different alternatives; however, since a descriptive analysis examines only a given set of alternatives (and not all possible alternatives), the result of this kind of modeling may be a good solution but not necessarily the best solution.

- **Optimization** models (also known as mathematical programming models) (Chapter 7) maximize or minimize an objective, while keeping within a number of constraints. Optimization models that provide the solution having the maximum profit, minimum cost, or maximum rate of return have been widely applied to structured operational problems such as the day-to-day operation of an oil refinery, planning maintenance, transportation, and production scheduling. Small examples of such models can now be solved in a spreadsheet with standard tools. Larger models require special purpose software (often in the form of spreadsheet add-ins) and are embedded in an interactive system that permits the data to be easily entered or modified, and allows the results to be viewed from several different perspectives. Optimizing models are also referred to as *normative* models, since they seek to find the best possible solution: what ought to be done in a normal situation?

Other types of models commonly use in analytics generally require the manager to seek the help of an analytics specialist. While these types of models will not be discussed in detail in this book, they include:

- **Expert systems**, also known as knowledge-based or rules-based models. These models attempt to solve problems using the same kind of logic that humans would use.

- **Data mining models** apply advanced statistical and non-statistical techniques to search for patterns in very large data sets. Such data sets can now easily be produced by recording real-time point-of-sale or customer behavior (e.g., web page visits).

- **Stochastic processes models** are formal analytical models that incorporate uncertainty. Two common types of stochastic process models are Markov models and queuing models. The stochastic simulation models that will be discussed in Chapter 6 provide one tool for examining stochastic processes.

The Model-Building Process

The basic steps in the use of a model to address a decision problem are illustrated in Figure 2.1.

These steps are described in more detail below:

1. **Building the model:** The *model builder* studies the real world where the decision issue exists, and *abstracts* from the real world to construct a model. The model is designed to allow the *model user* to vary the decision variables (the *inputs* to the model) and to see how the decision criteria (the *outputs* from the model) vary in response. The *logic* of the model, while much simpler than that of the real world, is designed to accurately reflect the real-world relationships between the decision variables and the decision criteria.

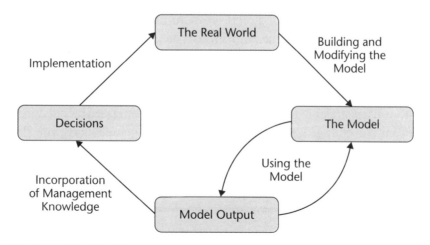

Figure 2.1 The Role of the Model

2. **Using the model:** The *model user* (who may be an individual or a group, or may be the decision maker or the *model builder*) works with the model and gains an understanding of the decision issue. After a period of time, the *model user* is able to identify values for the input variables (the decision variables) that produce "good," or perhaps even "the best," values for the decision criteria. These modeling results are then translated into recommendations for change.

3. **Decisions:** With experience gained from the model, along with real-world management knowledge, the model user is better equipped to make effective decisions. For example, a pilot who has logged many flight hours (e.g., real-world experience) and trained extensively in a flight simulator (e.g., use of a model) is well equipped to make good decisions in a wide variety of situations.

4. **Implementation:** Translating the results of the modeling effort into effective change in the real world is the final step. Considerable management skill may be required to do this in some instances, since implementation may affect the way people work. Often, implementation may also require software to be designed or modified, equipment purchased, or factories built.

5. **Modifying the model:** The entire process is presented as a continuous loop. Initially, the user or analyst builds the model. However, as experience with the model is gained, the user will also modify the model. Model modifications could be the result of experience gained by using the model or by changes caused by decisions that were implemented. For example, if the implementation suggested that new factories be built, then the model would need to be modified to account for the presence of these new factories.

In general, these steps are iterative rather than sequential. Model building and model use often follow an iterative design or "prototyping" methodology in which a simple "prototype" model is built quickly and made available to the model-user. The user experiments with the model and determines the direction for future model development jointly with the model builder. This leads to a second prototype, and the process is repeated until a final model, if there is one, emerges as an advanced "prototype."

The effective use of analytics within the organization requires that appropriate models be constructed, that users are able to use these models to investigate the need for change and the direction that the change should take, and that management have the skills, and perhaps the courage, to translate the results from the modeling into action.

Management Issues Surrounding the Modeling Process

A manager equipped with a spreadsheet can perform much useful modeling, but in many situations, where substantial returns are available, analytics models are highly complex and are developed and operated by specialists. For example, the optimization models, which are the heart of the operation of a supply chain, are built and maintained by groups of technicians who report to senior management. While actual model construction or model use can be delegated to the analytics specialist, there are many issues where management must be involved in the modeling effort:

- **Problem formulation** is the process of studying the real world and deciding which decision issue (or problem) should be addressed. Sometimes, problem formulation is straightforward: we are going to build a new factory and must come up with a design. On other occasions, problem formulation may be very difficult: our production process does not seem to be operating as well as that of our competitors. Deciding what problem to address, and, hence, what model to construct, is an important management issue within the analytics approach.

- **Model validation** is the process of ensuring that the mathematical model adequately captures the relationships between the model inputs and outputs. Modeling the past is often a useful aid to model validation, even though the model's purpose is to predict future behavior. Management should play a key role in model validation, since they have the best understanding of how the real process works. A useful model is one that supports the manager's understanding of the decision, not one that contradicts this understanding.

- **Sensitivity analysis** addresses the sensitivity of the results of the modeling to the values used for the inputs, or to the assumptions made in the modeling. If sales increase by 15% instead of the 10% that we assumed, what effect does that have? If the rate of inflation were 4% instead of the 6% that was used in our model, would we make a different decision? Management should be sure that any decision is sufficiently *robust*: that is, it is a good (perhaps the best) decision for the assumptions that have been made, but it is not a disastrous decision if reality differs a bit from what was assumed.

- **The design of the model interface** may also be an important management issue. Modelers are paying increasing attention to the displays produced by the model and how the user interacts with the model. Color and graphics are now widely used to communicate model results to the user, and, in some cases, a soundtrack adds to the multi-sensory impact of the model. Microsoft Excel provides the ability to design a sophisticated user interface using Visual Basic for Applications (VBA), the programming language embedded in Excel. Management should ensure that the model interface is useful and sufficiently user-friendly, particularly if the model is designed to be used by the manager. A good interface can do much to help the user understand both the model and the real decision issue that it addresses.

To conclude this introductory section on the managerial issues around modeling, it is useful to reinforce the reasons why models are proving useful to senior managers. Frederick W. Smith, chairman, CEO, and founder of Federal Express Corporation (FedEx), which is one of the world's largest air-package transportation companies, is convinced of the benefits analytics models have provided FedEx. Smith has said:

> By modelling various alternatives for future system design, FedEx has, in effect, made its mistakes on paper. Computer modeling works; it allows us to examine many different alternatives and it forces the examination of the entire problem. (P. Horner, "Eyes on the Prize," *OR/MS Today*, 1991)

Decision Making with a Spreadsheet Model: An Example

Development of an understanding of models and modeling must necessarily begin with a simple example. Here is an example of a decision consumers often must make:

"New Convenient Monthly-Pay Plan"

An auto insurance renewal offers the following three payment options:

OPTION 1: Pay the annual premium ($1,500) in full by the beginning of the month.

OPTION 2: Pay in three equal installments: the first by the beginning of the month, with the remaining installments paid at two-month intervals. A $3.50 service charge is added to each payment.

This year, for the first time, a third "convenient monthly-pay plan" is offered.

OPTION 3: Under this plan, the first two months are paid immediately, and the remaining payments are made monthly for the balance of the year. A 3% service charge is added to each payment.

Which plan is best?

At first, it appears that Option 1 represents the best deal, since Option 2 costs $10.50 extra (three service charges of $3.50), and Option 3 costs 3% extra (3% of $1,500 is $45). However, there is a tradeoff: under Options 2 and 3, some payments can be postponed until later and this postponement has value, in that the money can be invested until it is needed. If the interest earned on the invested money is included, the decision might be different.

To simplify the problem, let us assume that we have $2,000 (i.e., enough to pay with Option 1) invested in an account that pays interest at a rate of 0.5% monthly (approx. 6% annually).

We can now use Microsoft Excel to model the three options. Under each option, we compute the amount in the bank at the beginning of each month. Figures 2.2 and 2.2a show screen captures of the Excel model used to evaluate each of these plans.

For Option 1, we pay $1,500 immediately, resulting in a balance of $500. We then earn interest at a rate of 0.5% per month on this $500 balance, resulting in $528.28 at the end of the year.

	A	B	C	D
1	Month	Option 1	Option 2	Option 3
2	1	=2000-1500	=2000-1500/3-3.5	=2000-2*1500/12*1.03
3	2	=B2*1.005	=C2*1.005	=D2*1.005-1500/12*1.03
4	3	=B3*1.005	=C3*1.005-1500/3-3.5	=D3*1.005-1500/12*1.03
5	4	=B4*1.005	=C4*1.005	=D4*1.005-1500/12*1.03
6	5	=B5*1.005	=C5*1.005-1500/3-3.5	=D5*1.005-1500/12*1.03
7	6	=B6*1.005	=C6*1.005	=D6*1.005-1500/12*1.03
8	7	=B7*1.005	=C7*1.005	=D7*1.005-1500/12*1.03
9	8	=B8*1.005	=C8*1.005	=D8*1.005-1500/12*1.03
10	9	=B9*1.005	=C9*1.005	=D9*1.005-1500/12*1.03
11	10	=B10*1.005	=C10*1.005	=D10*1.005-1500/12*1.03
12	11	=B11*1.005	=C11*1.005	=D11*1.005-1500/12*1.03
13	12	=B12*1.005	=C12*1.005	=D12*1.005
14				

Figure 2.2 Screen Capture of Insurance Plans Model Showing Excel Formulas

	A	B	C	D	E
1	Month	Option 1	Option 2	Option 3	
2	1	500.00	1,496.50	1,742.50	
3	2	502.50	1,503.98	1,622.46	
4	3	505.01	1,008.00	1,501.82	
5	4	507.54	1,013.04	1,380.58	
6	5	510.08	514.61	1,258.74	
7	6	512.63	517.18	1,136.28	
8	7	515.19	519.77	1,013.21	
9	8	517.76	522.37	889.53	
10	9	520.35	524.98	765.23	
11	10	522.96	527.60	640.30	
12	11	525.57	530.24	514.75	
13	12	528.20	532.89	517.33	
14					

Figure 2.2a Screen Capture of Insurance Plans Model Showing the Resulting Numerical Values

For Option 2, the initial balance is $2,000 less the first payment of $503.50, or $1496.50. This amount earns interest for the first month and the account is credited with interest of 0.5% of $1496.5, or $7.48, leaving a balance at the beginning of month 2 of $1,503.98. This now earns interest for month 2 (0.5% of $1,503.98), but then the second installment of $503.50 must be paid, leaving a balance at the start of month 3 of $1,008.00. Interest is earned in months 3 and 4, with the third installment due at the end of month 4. Finally, the remaining balance earns interest to the end of the year.

For Option 3, the monthly payment is $1,500/12 plus 3%, or $128.75. The initial balance is $2,000, less two monthly payments (or $257.50). For the next ten months, interest is earned on the balance and payment of $128.75 is made each month.

The lowest-cost option is the three-payment plan (Option 2), which saves $4.69 over the single-payment plan (shown in this case by a final balance that is higher by $4.69). The monthly payment plan (Option 3) costs $10.87 more than does the single payment and $15.56 more than does the three-payment plan. Under Option 2, the interest earned by delaying the second payment for two months, and the third payment for four months more than covers the $3.50 service charge added to each payment.

The model constructed above is a type of *simulation* model, since in the model we have simulated making payments under each of the payment options and then compared the results. In building this simulation model, we have made several assumptions. For example, we have assumed that the interest rate on our savings account will not change during the year, and that there is no postage or other cost of making the payments. We have also assumed that we receive interest for the full month for payments that are due at the insurance company by the first of the following month.

One of the great benefits of modeling decision problems such as this is the *precision* that the modeling task imposes. Constructing a model raises many issues that must be addressed, and requires assumptions to be made and challenged. Constructing a useful model requires a precise and detailed understanding of the problem, which can rarely be achieved by any other means.

Building Useful Models

The model constructed above provides an answer, but is unsatisfactory in several respects. For example, suppose that we checked with the bank and found that the interest rate was 0.6% per month (about 7.2% annually) rather than the 0.5% month that we had assumed. To modify the model, we must change the 1.005 (which appears in 33 different cells) to 1.006. This requires editing 22 formulas, one at a time. To avoid this, it is useful to parameterize the model.

Parameterizing the model means that we take those parameters that appear in several places in the model and place them in labeled locations. When the parameters are needed in formulas, they are referred to by address (i.e., the address of the Excel cell containing their assumed value) rather than by value.

We can start by constructing a new version of the model shown in Figure 2.2 as a fully parameterized model. Every number used in the model has been listed as a parameter, and every equation refers to one of these parameters. The resulting model, with equations, is shown in Figure 2.3.

It is easy to verify that the final numerical results here are the same as in the previous model. However, this setup has some advantages. We can now change the value of the interest rate by changing only a single cell (A4). One immediate benefit of this paramaterization is the ability to quickly and easily perform a *validation* check: if the monthly interest rate were zero, the only difference between the payment plans should be the service charges. If the logic of the model is correct, it should reflect this result (Figure 2.4).

Indeed, as seen in Figure 2.4, the difference between Option 1 and Option 2 is $10.50 (= 3 × $3.50), and the difference between Option 1 and Option 3 is $45 (= 3% × $1,500).

	A	B	C	D
1	Initial Balance:		Insurance Premium	
2	2000		1500	
3	Monthly Interest:		Service Charge - Option 2:	
4	0.005		3.5	
5			Service Charge - Option 3:	
6			0.03	
7				
8	Month	Option 1	Option 2	Option 3
9	1	=A2-C2	=A2-C2/3-C4	=A2-2*$C$2/12*(1+$C$6)
10	2	=B9*(1+$A$4)	=C9*(1+$A$4)	=D9*(1+$A$4)-$C$2/12*(1+$C$6)
11	3	=B10*(1+$A$4)	=C10*(1+$A$4)-C2/3-C4	=D10*(1+$A$4)-$C$2/12*(1+$C$6)
12	4	=B11*(1+$A$4)	=C11*(1+$A$4)	=D11*(1+$A$4)-$C$2/12*(1+$C$6)
13	5	=B12*(1+$A$4)	=C12*(1+$A$4)-C2/3-C4	=D12*(1+$A$4)-$C$2/12*(1+$C$6)
14	6	=B13*(1+$A$4)	=C13*(1+$A$4)	=D13*(1+$A$4)-$C$2/12*(1+$C$6)
15	7	=B14*(1+$A$4)	=C14*(1+$A$4)	=D14*(1+$A$4)-$C$2/12*(1+$C$6)
16	8	=B15*(1+$A$4)	=C15*(1+$A$4)	=D15*(1+$A$4)-$C$2/12*(1+$C$6)
17	9	=B16*(1+$A$4)	=C16*(1+$A$4)	=D16*(1+$A$4)-$C$2/12*(1+$C$6)
18	10	=B17*(1+$A$4)	=C17*(1+$A$4)	=D17*(1+$A$4)-$C$2/12*(1+$C$6)
19	11	=B18*(1+$A$4)	=C18*(1+$A$4)	=D18*(1+$A$4)-$C$2/12*(1+$C$6)
20	12	=B19*(1+$A$4)	=C19*(1+$A$4)	=D19*(1+$A$4)
21				

Figure 2.3 Screen Capture of a Parameterized Version of the Insurance Plans Model Showing Excel Formulas

	A	B	C	D
	I9		*fx*	
1	Initial Balance:		Insurance Premium	
2	2000		1500	
3	Monthly Interest:		Service Charge - Option 2:	
4	0.00%		3.50	
5			Service Charge - Option 3:	
6			3%	
7				
8	Month	Option 1	Option 2	Option 3
9	1	500.00	1,496.50	1,742.50
10	2	500.00	1,496.50	1,613.75
11	3	500.00	993.00	1,485.00
12	4	500.00	993.00	1,356.25
13	5	500.00	489.50	1,227.50
14	6	500.00	489.50	1,098.75
15	7	500.00	489.50	970.00
16	8	500.00	489.50	841.25
17	9	500.00	489.50	712.50
18	10	500.00	489.50	583.75
19	11	500.00	489.50	455.00
20	12	500.00	489.50	455.00

Figure 2.4 Screen Capture of the Auto Insurance Example Showing the Impact of Setting the Monthly Interest Rate to Zero

By varying the interest rate in the modified model, we can begin to understand the *sensitivity* of the decision to the value of the interest rate. At low interest rates, Option 1 is preferred, since the interest earned does not cover the service charges. Through trial and error, we can quickly determine the interest rate at which we are indifferent between Options 1 and 2. This rate is 0.003502 monthly and we call this an *indifference point*, since at this parameter value we are indifferent between Options 1 and 2 (since they both have the same cost; see Figure 2.5).

Indifference points can be found through trial and error or by using the Excel Goalseek tool (see Appendix for details).

For high interest rates, we might expect that Option 3 becomes the best deal (since under Option 3, we postpone payment the longest). We can quickly determine whether this is the case by searching for the indifference point between options 2 and 3 (Figure 2.6):

We can now "solve" our decision problem without knowing the exact interest rate:

	A5		f_x		
	A	B	C	D
1	Initial Balance:		Insurance Premium	
2	2000		1500	
3	Monthly Interest:		Service Charge - Option 2:	
4	0.350200%		3.50	
5			Service Charge - Option 3:	
6			3%	
7				
8	Month	Option 1	Option 2	Option 3
9	1	500.00	1,496.50	1,742.50
10	2	501.75	1,501.74	1,619.85
11	3	503.51	1,003.50	1,496.77
12	4	505.27	1,007.01	1,373.27
13	5	507.04	507.04	1,249.33
14	6	508.82	508.82	1,124.95
15	7	510.60	510.60	1,000.14
16	8	512.39	512.39	874.89
17	9	514.18	514.18	749.21
18	10	515.98	515.98	623.08
19	11	517.79	517.79	496.51
20	12	519.60	519.60	498.25

Figure 2.5 Screen Capture of the Insurance Model Showing the Monthly Interest Rate for Which a Policyholder Would Be Indifferent Between Options 1 and 2

	A4		f_x 0.8909%		
	A	B	C	D
1	Initial Balance:		Insurance Premium	
2	2000		1500	
3	Monthly Interest:		Service Charge - Option 2:	
4	0.8909%		3.50	
5			Service Charge - Option 3:	
6			3%	
7				
8	Month	Option 1	Option 2	Option 3
9	1	500.00	1,496.50	1,742.50
10	2	504.45	1,509.83	1,629.27
11	3	508.95	1,019.78	1,515.04
12	4	513.48	1,028.87	1,399.79
13	5	518.06	534.53	1,283.51
14	6	522.67	539.30	1,166.19
15	7	527.33	544.10	1,047.83
16	8	532.03	548.95	928.42
17	9	536.77	553.84	807.94
18	10	541.55	558.77	686.39
19	11	546.37	563.75	563.75
20	12	551.24	568.77	568.77

Figure 2.6 Screen Capture of the Insurance Model Showing the Monthly Interest Rate for Which a Policyholder Would Be Indifferent Between Options 2 and 3

Option 1 is preferred for monthly interest rates less than 0.3502%,

Option 2 is preferred for monthly rates between 0.3502% and 0.8909%, and

Option 3 is preferred for monthly rates greater than 0.8909%.

This is called a *contingency solution*: the decision has been stated as being *contingent* on the value of an important parameter. To determine our best decision, it may be sufficient to know a reasonable range for our interest rate rather than its exact value. Of course, if we think the interest rate is close to one of the indifference points, we may need to know its exact value in order to make the right decision. However, since the total cost is approximately the same at the indifference points, for interest rates close to the indifference points, the extra cost incurred as a result of making the wrong choice will be quite small. For example, if the interest rate is around 0.35% monthly, it really doesn't matter whether you choose Option 1 or Option 2: the total cost is about the same. The solution makes sense—when the interest rate is high, there is value to deferring payments.

We can do further sensitivity analysis on all parameters to determine how they affect the optimal decision. We could conduct one-way sensitivity analysis, varying one parameter at a time, or two-way sensitivity analysis, systematically varying two parameters at a time. One result of this type of analysis is that the optimal decision is completely insensitive to our assumptions about the initial balance. That is, when all other parameters are set at their "base case values," for any assumption about the initial balance, Option 2 results in the highest end-of-year balance. Further, the ending balance for Option 1 is $4.69 lower than for Option 2, and the ending balance for Option 3 is $15.56 lower than for Option 2. This type analysis can be complex and considerable searching and plotting may be required. However, it can be done quickly using the Excel Data Tables tool (see Appendix for details).

Communicating the Results

Communicating the results from the modeling to an end user who was not involved in building the model requires some skill and an understanding of the user. The model (above) is fine for us, since we developed it and we understand the terminology (for example: 1.005 for the "interest rate"). Some minor changes would make the model much more user-friendly for a user who was familiar with the problem but not the details of the model. First, we "hide" all the details of the model by moving them to an area of the spreadsheet away from the list of parameters and assumptions screen. Second, we add a title, some friendly labels, and we display the parameter values and the results (both

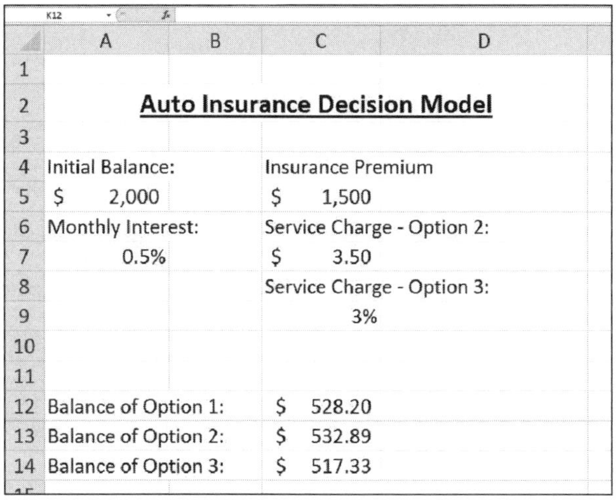

K12				
	A	**B**	**C**	**D**
1				
2		**Auto Insurance Decision Model**		
3				
4	Initial Balance:		Insurance Premium	
5	$ 2,000		$ 1,500	
6	Monthly Interest:		Service Charge - Option 2:	
7	0.5%		$ 3.50	
8			Service Charge - Option 3:	
9			3%	
10				
11				
12	Balance of Option 1:		$ 528.20	
13	Balance of Option 2:		$ 532.89	
14	Balance of Option 3:		$ 517.33	

Figure 2.7 Screen Capture of a "User Friendly" Version of the Auto Insurance Decision Model

linked to the model through the cell formulae) in the terms that the user understands (Figure 2.7).

We now have a screen display that clearly presents the annual premium and the interest rate (the *inputs* to the model) in a way that the decision maker understands. It also provides for easy changes to these inputs, and presents the cost of the various options (the *outputs* from the model) in terms familiar to the user. Nontechnical users could work with this screen to explore their personal decision situations and make informed decisions.

A second approach for communicating the results of the modeling effort is to develop some form of *decision aid*. A decision aid is a device that presents a summary of the dependence between the decision criteria and the decision variable(s) in a user-friendly form. Decision aids come in many forms, including formal reports (which may include recommendations from the modeler to the decision maker), and various kinds of charts and graphs.

For the auto insurance example, the modeling results can be summarized in a series of graphs. For each Premium Amount, we can vary the interest rate per month over a reasonable range (from zero to 2% per month) and plot the cost of the three payment options. (This can be done by setting up an Excel data table over the desired range of values, and then drawing a graph of the results.) This graph is a very useful decision aid for this problem: for any interest rate the optimal plan can quickly be determined (by choosing the highest line; see Figure 2.8).

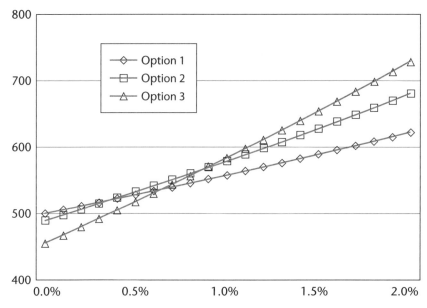

Figure 2.8 Chart Showing the End of Year Balance for Any Interest Rate

Analytics at Work

1. The Mexico Stock Exchange Settlement Model

   In November 2008, *Institución para el Depósito de Valores, S.A. de C.V.* (INDEVAL) [or Mexico's central securities depository for all financial securities (or Stock Exchange)] successfully launched a new model to settle securities transactions according to international best practices. This followed three years of business process design and programming and nine months of exhaustive daily tests. In excess of 12,000 man-hours were invested in the design and documentation of the new model-based system. INDEVAL's clearing and settlement model cycles about every five minutes and settles securities transactions that average over $250 billion daily. Implementation of this model has reduced the liquidity requirements for the members of the exchange by 52% and the volume of securities required for settlement by 26%. Intraday financing costs for market participants have been reduced by more than $150 million annually. (*Source*: *Interfaces*, 41, 1, January–February 2011, pp. 8–17)

2. Treating Prostrate Cancer

   Memorial Sloan-Kettering Cancer Center (MSKCC), the world's oldest private cancer center, uses sophisticated models and analytical techniques to control the real-time (intraoperative) treatment of prostate cancer using brachytherapy (the placement of radioactive "seeds" inside a tumor). The models produce significantly safer and more reliable treatment outcomes and eliminate the need for preoperative simulation and postimplant dosimetric analysis, resulting in savings of hundreds of millions of dollars per year in the United States alone.

Use of these analytical tools has drastically reduced (up to 45–60%) postoperative complications, because the treatment plans produced using the models deliver less radiation to adjacent healthy structures, and also facilitate the more accurate placement of the seeds in the target. Use of the models has reduced seed use by 20–30% and needle use (used to place seeds inside the prostate gland) by about 15%, resulting in reduced operating-room times and less-invasive procedures. (*Source*: *Interfaces*, *38*, 1, January–February 2008, pp 5–25)

3.   Bombardier versus Transmanche Link

Bombardier, Inc., was a Canadian-owned company that specialized in manufacturing railroad rolling stock, airplanes, and snowmobiles. Transmanche Link (TML) was the consortium behind the construction of the Channel Tunnel linking England and France.

TML contracted with Bombardier's Euro Shuttle Consortium Wagon division (ESCW) to supply 254 double- and single-deck wagons for *Le Shuttle*, the railway system that was to carry cars, buses, and heavy goods vehicles through the Channel Tunnel. The single-deck wagons were built at BN in Bruges, Belgium, and the double-deck wagons at ANF-Industrie at Valanciennes, France. ESCW subcontracted the manufacture of 19 single-deck loader wagons to Fiat Ferroviaria in Turin, Italy.

The contract between Bombardier and TML was signed in 1989 for C$820 million. Unfortunately, after the contract had been signed, and manufacturing had begun, a large number of changes, some major and some minor, were made to the design of the wagons by British and French government safety inspectors. As a result of these changes, Bombardier's projected final cost of completing the wagons was about double the original contracted price. Bombardier wanted reimbursement for the cost overrun, but TML balked at the amount requested. Bombardier held up delivery of the wagons, leading to the prospect of a delay in the opening of *Le Shuttle* service through the Chunnel. Both parties were anxious to settle, but were uncertain as to how an agreement on the amount could be reached.

Enter the international commercial lawyers, who began to document a large, detailed claim based on ESCW's cost of responding to TML's requests for design changes. A team of Dutch engineers went through every document that had passed between the parties and obtained evidence that TML had been slow to respond to design-documentation, and that this had imposed delay and disruption on ESCW. The problem remained of how to quantify the effect of design-documentation delays and the other elements of the claim.

ESCW called in Colin Eden, professor and head of the Management Science Department at the University of Strathclyde, Glasgow, Scotland, and three of his colleagues. The team began by interviewing a large number of senior members of ESCW's project team to find out what management perceived the problems to have been. From these interviews, the management scientists began to build a model of the project. This model was validated with groups of senior managers and lawyers.

As work progressed, the model was refined and expanded and became the repository of all knowledge about the project. The final model used the Bombardier-TML interactions as exogenous variables: when these were switched off (corresponding to completion of the contact as originally specified), the model provided a cost of completing the contract without disruption, but when switched on, provided an estimate of Bombardier's actual completion cost. The model was designed to be used within a court situation: if the judge upheld some parts of the claim and not others, the model could be rerun to provide new cost estimates.

The completed model acted as a structure for discussions, became the communications mechanism by which the management scientists and ESCW exchanged ideas, and provided a rich history of the project's progress. The management scientists became convinced of the validity of the cost estimates produced by the model and believed ESCW management was also convinced. The model and the results of the modeling were shown to TML.

The claim was settled out of court at a value that (presumably) was satisfactory to both parties. ESCW received FFr700 million in phased payments, while Bombardier received up to 25 million Eurotunnel shares. (*Sources*: T. Williams, "Shuttler's COPE with Delay and Disruption," *OR Newsletter*, May 1994, and "The Channel Tunnel," *Financial Times Survey*, May 6, 1994.)

Summary

This chapter has introduced the concept of the management model, and some of the issues surrounding the development and use of models in management decision making. In the following chapters, several different types of management models will be examined in more detail, as will examples of organizations that have used these models to their competitive advantage.

What the Manager Must Know

- Models provide a useful decision tool for managers.

- The model-building process is an iterative one that involves abstraction from the real world, model building, model usage, and implementation.

- Useful models should be parameterized and follow guidelines for "Good Model-Building Practice." This typically includes separating data from models, and documenting all assumptions.

- Models have been used extensively and with great impact in many organizations and industries.

Appendix to Chapter 2 Technical Details

Absolute vs. Relative References in Excel

You may have noticed in Figure 2.3 that some of the cell references in the Excel formulas had dollar signs ($) and some did not (i.e., there were some cell references of the form A2, and others of the form $A$2). What's the difference? Excel uses *relative referencing* in formulas. Thus, a formula of the form A2 is interpreted as meaning "a cell that is in the position of A2 relative to the current cell." For example, if the current cell is B3, then the formula "=A2" would mean "the cell that is 1 column to the left and 1 column above the current cell." If you copied this cell somewhere else on the spreadsheet, the result would be a new formula that preserved the relative referencing, and would, thus, no longer refer to cell A2. If you want to always refer to cell A2, then you must insert the $ symbol in front of the column (A) and row (2). When written in this way, the row and column become frozen, and $A$2 is said to be an *absolute reference*. If a formula with $A$2 is copied somewhere else on the sheet, it will always refer to the contents of A2. Note that you can also freeze only the row (as in A$2) and only the column (as in $A2), depending on the desired use.

Keyboard shortcut: On PCs, you can create an absolute reference by hitting the "F4" key immediately after entering a cell reference. If you hit F4 repeatedly, it will toggle through all possibilities for absolute references.

Hard Coding vs. Soft Coding in Excel

When introducing the auto insurance example, we presented a revised model in which all of the parameters were listed separately. The difference between the original model and the parameterized model is sometimes referred to as "hard coding" vs. "soft coding." In a hard-coded model, all of the numbers used are embedded in the formulas. In a soft-coded model, there should be no numbers embedded in cell formulas. Rather, all cells containing formulas would refer to cells containing numbers (as was the case in the parameterized version of the insurance model).

The advantages of soft coding in a spreadsheet model include:

- Each cell with a number can be labeled. The label can be descriptive (i.e., a name of the particular parameter), or it could also contain additional information on the assumptions required to produce that number. This labeling is very helpful to users of the model, since without this information, it might be difficult for someone to interpret the model.

- If you need to change your assumptions, you only need to change a single cell in a soft-coded model. The result of the change will carry through the entire model. In a hard-coded model, you would need to change *every cell containing that particular number*. In the example in the text, changing the interest rate would involve manually editing 33 cells—quite a bit more tedious than changing a single cell. Note that spreadsheet models with several thousand cells over multiple worksheets within a large workbook are common in practice. Clearly, a hard-coded model of that size would present several challenges.

- Soft coding facilitates sensitivity analysis, and, in particular, allows you to use Excel tools such as Goal Seek and Data Tables.

- Soft coding aids model debugging and reduces the possibility of errors: if you entered the value 1.06 instead of 1.05 in one of the 33 cells requiring the interest rate, this error would be difficult to find.

Good Model-Building Practice

The following represent good spreadsheet model-building practices:

- Separate the model into separate different sections. A common, useful way to separate the model is to have separate sections for "Data and Assumptions," "Decisions," "Model and Calculations," and "Results."

- Provide meaningful labels for all data values.

- Include the units for all data (e.g., meters, $/kg, and so on). For Imperial units, it may be necessary to specify whether they are U.S. or UK standards.

- Provide additional information to document assumptions. This could include the source of the assumption (such as a report, a web site, or expert opinion), or any additional calculations that were done to generate the assumed value. When citing a web site, it is consider best practice to include the date the page was accessed, since web pages can change.

- Include descriptions in the model section for anything that might not be immediately obvious.

Modeling Tip: Validation Checks

It is useful to perform as many validation checks as possible while building the model. This can be done by choosing parameter values where you know what the result should be, and checking whether the result from the model is correct. We saw an example of this in the insurance model: when the interest rate was set to zero, the only difference between the three options was the cost of the service charges. Performing these sorts of validation checks will give you confidence that your model is correct and it will help to catch small problems before they become big problems.

Finding Indifference Points with Goalseek

The Goal Seek tool is useful for finding indifference points. The Goal Seek tool is found by selecting the "Data" tab, then choosing "What-If Analysis" from the Data tools block, and selecting Goal Seek from the resulting drop-down menu. To use Goal Seek, you will need to specify three values:

1. The address of the cell that is being modified (called "Set cell" in the Goal Seek dialog box). This must be a cell with a formula that refers to other cells. Note that it is often necessary to create an additional cell in your model for use as the Set cell. For example, when finding indifference points, it is common to create a new cell with a formula that is the difference between two existing cells.

2. The desired value of the cell that is being modified. This will be a number entered into the Goal Seek dialog box.

3. The address of a single cell whose value must change in order to make the "Set cell" achieve the desired value.

We illustrate using the auto insurance model (Figure 2.A.1). Our goal is to find the value of the interest rate for which a consumer would be indifferent between Options 1 and 2. We first add a cell that is the difference in the final balance for Option 1 vs. Option 2 (in C17). We then apply Goal Seek, with the aim of setting the difference in final balance between the two options (C17) equal to zero (an indifference point) by changing the value of the interest rate (A7).

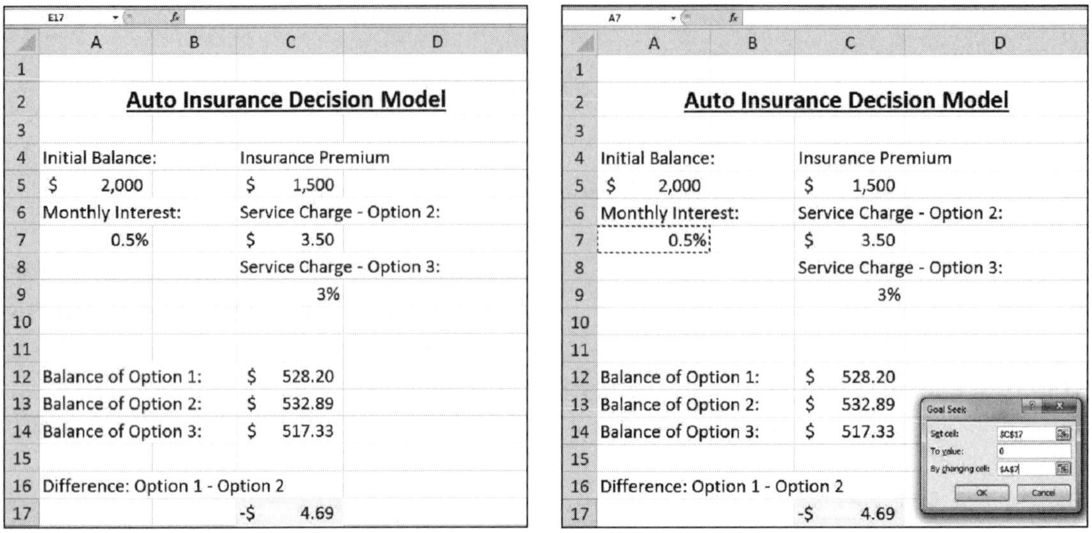

Figure 2.A.1 Example of Use of Goal Seek. When we hit "OK" we find that the indifference point is a monthly interest rate of 0.3502%. Note that it would not have been possible to do this using Goalseek without a parameterized model.

Using Data Tables in Excel

Data Tables provide a tool to systematically change a parameter in a model and observe what happens to a calculated value. The Data Table tool is found by selecting the "Data" tab, then choosing "What-If Analysis" from the Data Tools block, and selecting Data Table from the resulting drop-down menu. After building a parameterized model, the steps involved in building a one-way data table are as follows:

1. Set up a column with values of the parameter that you wish to consider.
2. In the cell that is one column to the right and one row above the top entry in the column, enter "=" and refer to the cell that contains the final calculated value.
3. Highlight both columns.
4. Select the Data Table tool.
5. Leave the "Row input cell" field blank (since the data range has been listed in a row, not a column). In the "Column input cell," enter the address of the cell that contains the parameter that is being varied.

We illustrate with an example in which we vary the interest rate between 0 and 1.0% per month and record the final balance under Option 1 (Figures 2.A.2 and 2.A.3).

Sometimes when you hit "OK," all numbers in the table will be the same. If this happens, press the "F9" key. In Excel, "F9" recalculates the spreadsheet, and pressing "F9" will

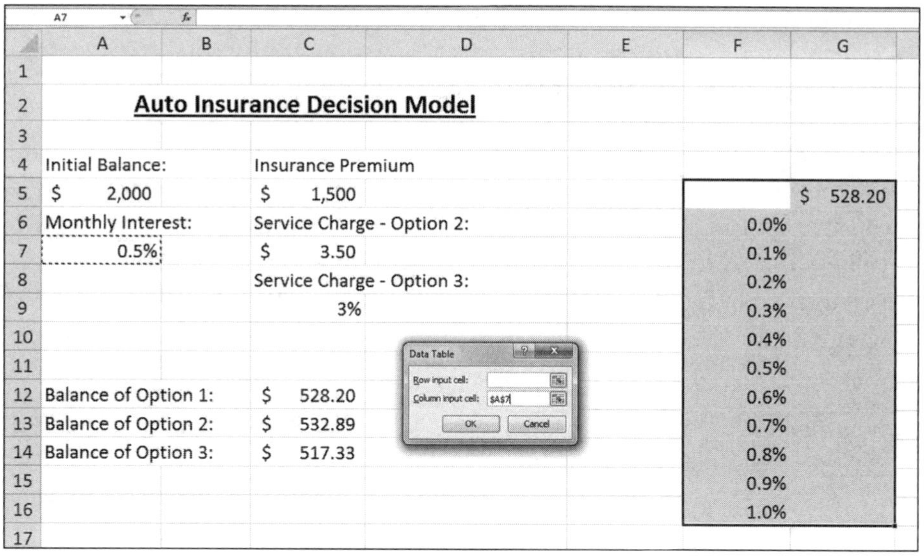

	A	B	C	D	E	F	G
1							
2	**Auto Insurance Decision Model**						
3							
4	Initial Balance:		Insurance Premium				
5	$ 2,000		$ 1,500				$ 528.20
6	Monthly Interest:		Service Charge - Option 2:			0.0%	
7	0.5%		$ 3.50			0.1%	
8			Service Charge - Option 3:			0.2%	
9			3%			0.3%	
10						0.4%	
11						0.5%	
12	Balance of Option 1:		$ 528.20			0.6%	
13	Balance of Option 2:		$ 532.89			0.7%	
14	Balance of Option 3:		$ 517.33			0.8%	
15						0.9%	
16						1.0%	
17							

Figure 2.A.2 Screen Capture of the Setup of a 1-Way Data Table

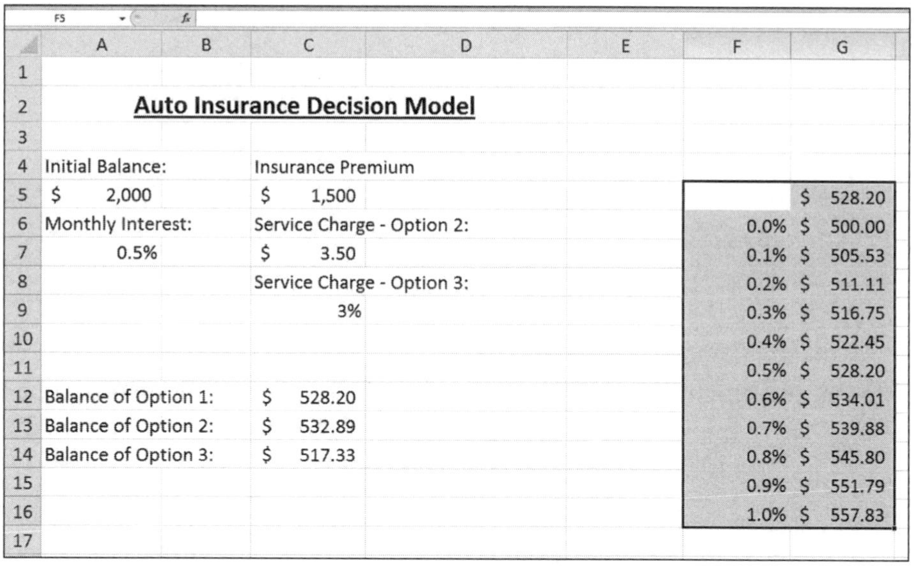

	A	B	C	D	E	F	G
1							
2	**Auto Insurance Decision Model**						
3							
4	Initial Balance:		Insurance Premium				
5	$ 2,000		$ 1,500				$ 528.20
6	Monthly Interest:		Service Charge - Option 2:			0.0%	$ 500.00
7	0.5%		$ 3.50			0.1%	$ 505.53
8			Service Charge - Option 3:			0.2%	$ 511.11
9			3%			0.3%	$ 516.75
10						0.4%	$ 522.45
11						0.5%	$ 528.20
12	Balance of Option 1:		$ 528.20			0.6%	$ 534.01
13	Balance of Option 2:		$ 532.89			0.7%	$ 539.88
14	Balance of Option 3:		$ 517.33			0.8%	$ 545.80
15						0.9%	$ 551.79
16						1.0%	$ 557.83
17							

Figure 2.A.3 Screen Capture of the Data Table Example After Hitting "OK"

update the table. This can be set to happen automatically by adjusting your calculation options, although sometimes it is desirable for tables to not update automatically.

It is also possible to create a two-way data table in which two parameters are varied simultaneously. To do this, you would create a column with all of the desired values of one parameter and a row with all of the desired values of the other parameter. Figure 2.A.4 shows a screen capture of the set up for a two-way table of the final balance for Option 3, varying the interest rate and the monthly service charge.

It is sometimes possible to switch up the row and column input cells. One way to verify that you have set up the data table properly is to check if the base case value appears in the appropriate spot in the table. In this example, after hitting "OK," we would expect to see the value $517.33 in the 7th row (for monthly interest of 0.5%) and 5th column (for a service charge of 3%) of the table. If this is not the case, then you have made an error in setting up the table.

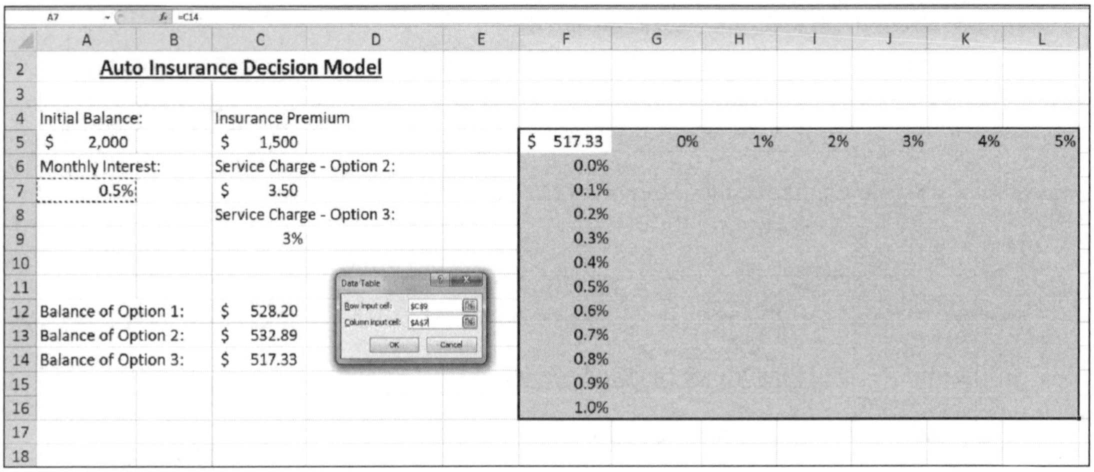

Figure 2.A.4 Screen Capture of the Setup of a 2-Way Data Table

List of Useful Excel Functions

In addition to the functions and techniques described through this chapter, the functions shown below are often helpful in building good Excel models.

Type of Function	Function Name	Usage
Calculation	EXP	Exponentiation of a number (the inverse of LN)
	LN	Natural log of a number
	MAX	Returns the maximum of a list or array of numbers
	MIN	Returns the minimum of a list or array of numbers
	SQRT	Square root of a number
	SUM	Returns the sum of a list or array of numbers

	SUMPRODUCT	Given 2 arrays of equal length, multiplies all corresponding terms together and returns the total (i.e., the sum of the products).
Database	INDEX	
	MATCH	
	VLOOKUP	
Logic	IF	Evaluates a test condition Returns one value if the test condition is true and another if false
	AND	Evaluates a set of test conditions Returns "TRUE" if all test conditions are satisfied and "FALSE" otherwise
	OR	Evaluates a set of test conditions Returns "TRUE" if at least one test condition is satisfied and "FALSE" otherwise

Exercises

Problem 2–1

We have acquired new furniture for the office. The invoice for $6,000 offers two ways to pay: we can pay the entire amount by September 1, or we can pay $3,060 by September 1 and $3,000 by January 1. How does our decision depend on the interest rate at which we can invest our funds?

Problem 2–2

An auction house has accepted an item for auction where the owner has placed a reserve price of $100,000: that is, if the item sells, the owner must receive at least $100,000, less a seller's commission of 9%. On sale of an item, the buyer pays a "buyer's premium" of 10% to the auction house. If the item does not sell, the seller must pay a listing fee of $2,500 to the house.

What is the break-even sale price for the auction house?

Problem 2–3

An underground depository for the disposal of medium-level nuclear waste can be built in 2010 for a cost of £3,000 million, but construction of the facility can be deferred for 50 years, when the construction cost will be £7,000 million. Additional interim "storage" costing £160 million per annum will be required if construction is deferred (all costs in

2010 £). Assume a 6% real interest rate. Which option is preferred? Does your answer change if a 2% real interest rate is assumed?

(This is a simplified version of the Nirex Ltd. decision discussed in *Review of Radioactive Waste Management Policy Preliminary Conclusions: A Consultative Document*, Department of the Environment August 1994, as presented by Chapman and Howden, July 1995).

Problem 2–4

Your corporate office is in New York. You must visit the distribution centers in Boston, Chicago, Cleveland, Detroit, and Toronto. The available airfares between these cities are shown below:

From:	To: New York	Boston	Chicago	Cleveland	Detroit	Toronto
New York	–	$79	$179	$115	$165	$195
Boston	$99	–	199	129	105	199
Chicago	195	155	–	55	59	175
Cleveland	137	149	79	–	45	65
Detroit	165	135	55	55	–	65
Toronto	285	255	295	79	125	–

Use a spreadsheet to determine the minimum cost "tour" which begins and ends in New York and visits each city once.

Recommended Cases

The following cases provide an opportunity to apply and practice the topics in this chapter:

Williams Coffee Pub: The Franchising Opportunity (Ivey)

The Video Mart, Inc. (Ivey)

Professional Media Inc. (Ivey)

Dollar Thrifty Automotive Group Online Discounting (Ivey)

Tridev Realty Partners (Ivey)

CHAPTER 3

ANALYZING SEQUENTIAL DECISIONS

How many units to manufacture? What price to charge? How many workers to hire? Should the offer be accepted? Which ad should be run? Managers make a host of decisions such as these every day of their working lives.

Management is about making decisions. To be an effective manager, you must be able to make *good* decisions. You must also be able to explain to others why your recommendations constitute good decisions.

From the perspective of the organization, it is essential that decision making be handled throughout all levels of management in a way that encourages good decisions and controls risk. In extreme cases, just one bad decision can put a firm out of business. The successful organization has good control of its decision making and has processes in place to ensure that important decisions are made in a timely way after appropriate analysis and discussion.

The Basic Elements of a Decision

Every decision involves a choice between a number of *alternatives* or *options*. There may be hundreds of alternatives (such as, what list price do we set for our new product?) or just two (Should we accept their offer, or not?).

In order to make an intelligent choice, there must be some *criterion* (or several *criteria*) associated with each alternative that provides a basis for making a choice. In the world of business, the decision criterion is often money (for example: the government generally awards contracts to the lowest bidder, the one that will fulfill the contract for the least money), but multiple criteria are also common (Should we hire contractor A who is cheaper than contractor B but will take longer to complete the job?).

Decision situations usually involve *uncertainty* and *risk*. (If there was no uncertainty, many decisions would be very easy!) The future, after we have chosen a particular alternative, may not be entirely known (If we set our product price at $6.95, how many will we sell?). Elimination of uncertainty is rarely possible, although effective *forecasting* and planning can reduce uncertainty and help to control risk.

Finally, there is an important *timeliness to decision making*. If a decision is taken too late, the chosen option may no longer be available, while a decision made too early may result in vital, but late-arriving, information being missed.

A Useful Model for Helping to Understand Decision Situations

Important decision situations are rarely simple. The first step in intelligent decision making is to attempt to understand the decision situation. A useful vehicle to assist grappling with the complexities of a decision is the *decision tree*. A decision tree is a *model* (or abstraction) of a decision situation that helps to lay out a sequence of decisions and uncertain events. The tree does not "make" the decision or "solve" the problem, but rather lays out the situation in a way that makes the choices and their ramifications more easily understood. Decision trees have proved useful time and time again in providing a basis for a group of managers to talk about a decision (leading to more effective group choice).

A decision tree is constructed from a few simple icons. A square, or "decision node," is used to denote a decision point (Figure 3.1).

A decision to be made from five alternatives (A, B, C, D, E) would be shown, as in Figure 3.2.

A circle, or "chance node," is used to denote a point of uncertainty or an *event*. At these points, there is no choice to be made, rather, one of a number of *outcomes*, over which we have no control, occurs. For example: a flip of a coin is an event with outcomes "heads" and "tails," and would be indicated on a decision tree, as in Figure 3.3:

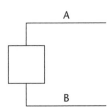

Figure 3.1 A Decision Tree Representation of a Choice Between Alternative A and Alternative B

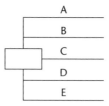

Figure 3.2 A Decision Tree Representation of a Choice Between Five Alternatives (A–E)

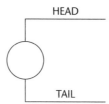

Figure 3.3 A Decision Tree Representation of a Coin Toss

Figure 3.4 A Decision Tree Showing the Time Sequence of Two Decisions

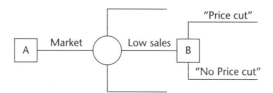

Figure 3.5 A Decision Tree Showing the Time Sequence of Events and Decisions

In assembling a decision tree, the horizontal axis represents time: e.g., Figure 3.4 denotes that decision B is made *after* decision A.

The sequence shown in Figure 3.5 indicates that if we choose decision "market," and if the outcome of the next event turns out to be "low sales," then we are faced with decision B between "price cut" or "no price cut." Note the importance of sequence, as illustrated in Figure 3.5: the impact of a price cut following low sales would likely be different than that following high sales.

The basic building blocks of the decision tree allow very complex decision situations to be laid out on paper. The process of doing this significantly improves understanding of the decision and is often a useful and worthwhile way to improve managerial decision making. The exercise of constructing the tree often raises questions and issues that would not emerge in a less-rigorous analysis.

An Example: Testing an Athlete for Drug Use

Whether or not to test athletes for the illegal use of performance enhancing drugs is an issue of concern to many involved in athletics and sports. Why are the issues surrounding testing so complex? Perhaps laying out a decision tree will provide some hints.

We begin with a discussion about how to structure a decision tree for this issue. The first decision is straightforward: should we test an athlete for illegal drug use or not? The decision tree, therefore, begins as shown in Figure 3.6.

Now, consider what happens if we decide to test the athlete. The *event* of conducting the test produces two possible *outcomes* (we cannot control which occurs): a "positive" test result or a "negative" test result. This event is added to the tree (Figure 3.7).

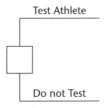

Figure 3.6 First Step in Decision Tree for Athlete Drug Test

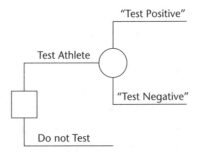

Figure 3.7 Addition of Test Outcome to Drug-Testing Decision Tree

After we find out the result of the test, we must decide what to do with the athlete. If the test is "negative," this is presumably straightforward: the athlete is pronounced "clean" and allowed to compete. If the test is "positive," the decision is more difficult: what are the *alternatives*? To keep the tree manageable, only two of the sanctions often mentioned will be examined: a two-year suspension or a lifetime suspension for the offender. The type of sanction to be imposed is a decision that must be made. Adding this decision to the tree leads to Figure 3.8.

We now look at the "Do Not Test" option. If we decide not to test, what happens? We have athletes competing who are drug users and others who are not (if no athletes used

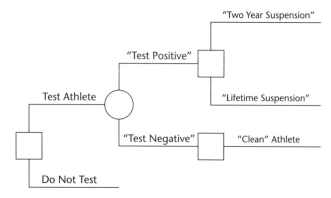

Figure 3.8 Addition of Sanction Decision to Drug-Testing Decision Tree

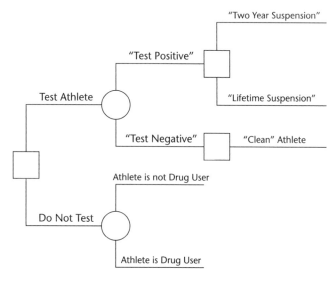

Figure 3.9 Decision Tree with "Do Not Test" Outcomes

illegal drugs, there would be no reason to test). We, therefore, add this *event* to the tree (Figure 3.9).

We now raise a critical issue: How good is the test? Most medical tests are not perfect, since sometimes the test indicates a condition that is not present (a *false positive*), while other times fails to pick up a condition that really is present (a *false negative*). In medical diagnostics, the terms "sensitivity" and "specificity" are often used to describe the ability of tests to discriminate between positive and negative cases.

The inclusion of these events produces the tree shown in Figure 3.10.

We can now label the end points of the tree according to final result (Figure 3.11).

Not all of the final outcomes are ideal. Outcomes 6 and 7 (non-user allowed to compete) are ideal, while outcomes 2 and 4 (suspension of an offender) achieve the implied objective of identifying and punishing illegal drug users. Outcomes 1 and 3 are of concern because they raise the possibility (perhaps, probability) that non-users will be labeled as users and suspended, perhaps for life. Outcome 5 raises the issue that some users will probably "escape" the drug testing and still end up competing, which could undermine the credibility of any testing program. The final outcome on the tree (number 8, "Offender

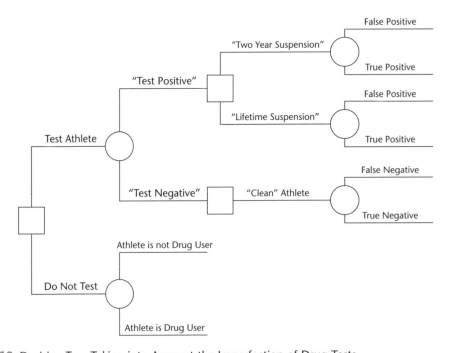

Figure 3.10 Decision Tree Taking into Account the Imperfection of Drug Tests

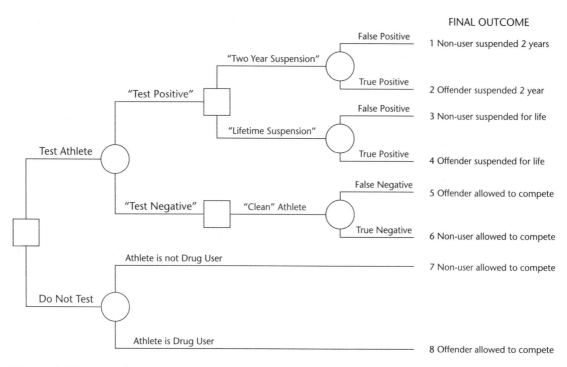

Figure 3.11 Final Labeled Decision Tree

allowed to compete") points out the reality that if no testing is done, there will be illegal drug users competing.

The analysis raises important issues that should be addressed before decisions are taken. These include:

- How many drug users are competing? (Alternately, what is the extent of the problem?)

- How accurate is the proposed test? The number of false positives that occur is critically important, but the number of false negatives is also important.

- How do we handle the very undesirable outcome where an innocent athlete may be identified as a drug user and suspended?

The decision analysis helps to identify the *risks* of different policies. The risk of not testing is that an offender may be allowed to compete. The major risk of a testing policy is that a nonuser may be suspended, perhaps for life.

An informed group could discuss these issues, weigh the alternatives, and reach a set of decisions. Note that before considering the decision whether or not athletes should be tested, the group would have to decide what to do with an athlete who tested "positive."

Coping with Uncertainty Using Probabilities

In considering alternatives, it is often necessary to talk about *probabilities*. Uncertainties exist in most business decision situations. This is inevitable, since most decisions are concerned with the future. Uncertainty can rarely be assumed away, but rather must be "coped with" somehow. One way of doing this is through *probabilities*.

The use of probabilities enables us to cope with uncertain events in the decision tree. Recall that an event denotes a situation that we cannot control and that generates several outcomes. The example of flipping a coin (Figure 3.3) has some probability of producing "HEADS," and some probability of producing "TAILS." If the coin is fair, these outcomes are equally likely. There are several equivalent ways of making a probability statement about this event. We could say that if we flipped the coin 100 times, we would expect to see 50 HEADS and 50 TAILS. We could say that, on average, half the flips will produce HEADS (or TAILS). Or we could say that if we flip the coin, the probability of the outcome HEADS is 50% (or 0.5).

The Axioms of Probabilities

In assigning probabilities, there are certain rules or "axioms" that we must follow if our numbers are to have meaning to others. A probability is a number associated with an event that satisfies the following three axioms:

- Probabilities cannot be less than 0.
- Probabilities cannot be greater than 1.
- The sum of the probabilities for a set of events that are mutually exclusive and collectively exhaustive is 1.

The axioms can be described in more detail. An outcome is *certain* if the probability of occurrence is one (or 100%); therefore, probabilities cannot be greater than one (or 100%). An outcome is *impossible* if the probability of occurrence is zero; therefore, probabilities cannot be less than zero. If we define a set of outcomes for an event in such a way that no two outcomes can occur simultaneously (i.e., the events are mutually exclusive), and if the set of defined outcomes covers every possible result (i.e., the events are collectively exhaustive), then the sum of the probabilities assigned to this set of outcomes must equal one.

We can often choose how to define the outcomes from an event. For example, consider a single roll of a die. Some of the possible outcomes are:

"1," "2," "3," "4," "5," or "6,"

"Odd," "Even," "Not 1," "Not 5," "less than 3," and so on.

There are many outcomes that are not *mutually exclusive* (example, "even" and "2," since a "2" would belong to both outcomes). We can also define many sets of outcomes that are not *exhaustive* (example: the set "Odd," "2," and "4," since this set of outcomes does not include "6").

Sources of Probability Estimates

There are three general approaches to obtaining probability estimates:

1. **Classical approaches**. These methods typically involve enumerating all the possibilities for outcomes that can occur and counting how many of these include the outcome of interest. The probability of that outcome is then the proportion of the total outcomes that include the one of interest. Such methods are often used to derive probabilities for outcomes of coin tosses, card games, lotteries, and other games of chance.

2. **Statistical analysis of databases**. These methods are often used to derive probabilities for outcomes when there is an available database of past occurrences of the same event: for example, the probability of rain on July 1 next year could be estimated using a sample of previous July firsts and counting how many days in the sample there was rain. Expressing the count of rain days as a percentage of the number of days in the sample provides an estimate of the probability of rain. More advanced statistical methods (including fitting known distributions to sample data and regression) can also be useful in extracting probabilities from data. We have more on this topic in Chapters 4 and 5.

3. **Using subjective probabilities** or **expert opinions** from individuals who have extensive knowledge of the situation.

In the past, probabilities could rarely be measured precisely. Instead, someone with a good understanding of the situation and the uncertainties usually assigned these probabilities. For example, your stockbroker might tell you, "There is a 70% probability that the market will go up today." Assigned probabilities such as these are called *subjective probabilities*. A subjective probability is an informed opinion of the likelihood of the occurrence of some outcome given by a knowledgeable individual or group. The assignment of useful subjective probabilities requires a close familiarity with the uncertain events, and with whatever data that has a bearing on the uncertainties is available. A familiar example is the weather forecast, which usually includes "probabilities of precipitation." These are subjective probabilities, usually assigned by a trained weather forecaster who possesses a great deal of experience with weather systems and armed with the most recent data on current weather conditions.

Now, however, many companies maintain vast databases of relevant data that they use, for example, to help to explain and predict customer behavior. Some companies have been able to exploit these databases as a competitive weapon.

Defining a set of *mutually exclusive* and *exhaustive* outcomes is important if we are to compute an *expected value* for an event.

Expected Value

The *expected value* of an event can be interpreted as a long-run average: if we were to observe an event a very large number of times and average the outcomes, we would arrive at an average outcome very close to the expected value. But, remember that in many management decision situations, particularly many of the important ones, events occur only once. When the outcomes of an event have a numerical value, the *expected value* of the event can be computed. Consider the event shown in Figure 3.12, where the three outcomes constitute a set of mutually exclusive and exhaustive outcomes (with probability sum equal to one).

The *expected value* of event A is computed as:

$(0.1 \times 1,000,000) + (0.3 \times 1,000) + (0.6 \times 0) = 100,300$

In general, the expected value of an event is the value of each outcome multiplied by the probability of that outcome, summed over all outcomes. Or:

$E(A) = p_1 \times x_1 + p_2 \times x_2 + p_3 \times x_3 + \ldots + p_n \times x_n$

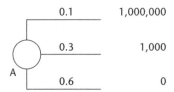

Figure 3.12 Decision Tree for Example Event

where:

E(A) is the expected value of event A,

n is a number of mutually exclusive and collectively exhaustive outcomes for event A,

p_i is the probability outcome i occurs, and

x_i is the value of outcome i.

The expected value is important in analyzing decisions, since it provides a guide as to the "average" value of the event. Other characteristics of events are also important, notably their *riskiness*. Managerial decision making involves balancing expected values and risks. The decision illustrated in Figure 3.13 would not be easy for most of us.

Choice A has an expected value of $(0.9 \times 1000 + 0.1 \times (-1000))$, or $800, which suggests that it is a better choice than $600 for certain, but A is also riskier, since we could end up losing $1,000 (but with 90% probability, could end up gaining $1,000). The final decision depends on whether the individual will give up $200 in expected value to avoid the risk of losing $1,000 or to accept the risk of winning an extra $400. There is no correct answer here; different individuals will make this decision differently.

Expected value is, therefore, only a guideline for individual decision making. However, large firms make a great number of decisions; consequently, the firm that acts to maximize expected value will, on average, come out the best. While acting to maximize expected value, however, it is important that management control the risks accepted and consider very carefully any decision that may catastrophically affect the firm. As an example of this kind of behavior, airline operators carry insurance to cover the civil liabilities that would result from the crash of one of their planes. In doing so, they give up expected value (the insurance companies profit from these policies, on average), but avoid the catastrophic impact on the firm should this unlikely event occur.

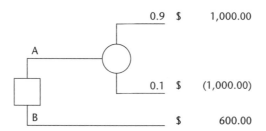

Figure 3.13 Decision Tree Showing a Difficult Personal Choice

Incorporating Expected Values into the Decision Tree—Roll-Back

Expected values can be used to assist in the analysis of the decision tree. Consider the following decision situation:

> We have $10,000,000 in "spare cash" in our corporate account. We don't need these funds for 48 hours. We know that we can invest these funds through our bankers in overnight commercial paper and receive an annual interest rate of 7% (the interest rate for 48 hours will be approximately .07 × 2/365, which yields interest of $3,835.62). Our second choice is to offer these funds to a broker who, for a fee of $100, will try to place them in the premium overnight market for 48 hours, where we will receive an 8% annual interest rate (or $4,383.56 less the $100 commission). The broker tells us that these placements can be successfully negotiated 90% of the time. If placement in the premium market is not successful, we will be too late to go to the overnight market and the funds will be idle for 24 hours but, tomorrow, we will have the same options: that is, we can go to the 7% overnight market for 24 hours (interest of $1,917.81) or pay the broker another $100 commission to try for a 24-hour premium placement at 8% (interest of $2,191.78).

The decision tree for this decision situation is illustrated in Figure 3.14.

Note that at the end of the branches, we have computed the actual conditional payoffs (in dollars) if the decisions and events lead us to that result. While other approaches are possible, this approach minimizes the possibility of confusing real dollars and opportunity dollars.

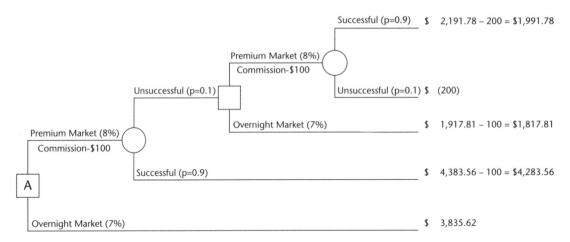

Figure 3.14 Decision Tree for Investment Problem

The decision of immediate concern is today's decision: *whether to try for a 48-hour premium placement or stay with the certain overnight investment at 7%?* This decision has been labeled "A" in the tree (Figure 3.14). We cannot, however, make this decision until we understand the conditional decision (labeled "B" in Figure 3.14) concerning what we should do if our broker fails to find us a 48-hour premium placement. Therefore, in order to analyze the decision tree, we must examine the decisions, moving backward in time (from right to left in the tree). This process is called *roll-back*.

In rolling-back through the tree, we first address the conditional decision at "B" (Figure 3.15) if decisions are made and events unfold such that we arrive at point "B," what is our best plan of action?

The choice we have is between $1,817.81 for certain in the 24-hour overnight market, or an event with a 90% chance at $1,991.78 in the premium market, coupled with a 10% chance at negative $200 (we pay two commissions but receive no interest) (Figure 3.15). The expected value of this event is 0.9 × $1,991.78 + 0.1 × (–200), or $1,772.60. On an expected value basis, we prefer the overnight market ($1,817.81 versus $1,772.60). Since the option with the higher expected value is also less risky, we can be confident that the 24-hour overnight market is the best decision at "B."

The branch of the tree beyond "B" can, therefore, be eliminated and replaced by the expected payoff from the best decision at point "B" ($1,817.81) (Figure 3.16).

We can now resolve the immediate decision "A":

We must choose between $3,835.62 for certain in the 48-hour overnight market, or an event having a 90% chance of a payoff of $4,283.56 and a 10% chance of an expected payoff of $1,817.81. The expected value of this event is 0.9 × $4,283.56 + 0.1 × $1,817.81 or $4,037. If our decision criterion is to maximize expected value, then the optimum decision is to try the 48-hour market ($4,037 versus $3,835.62).

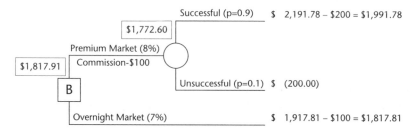

Figure 3.15 Decision Tree for Analysis of Decision B

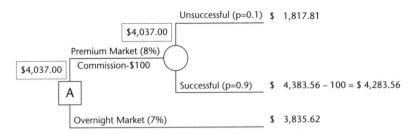

Figure 3.16 Investment Problem with Decision B Removed

We have now resolved our decision situation: our best decision strategy is to first try the 48-hour premium market; if this is unsuccessful, and if nothing changes during the next 24 hours, then tomorrow we place the funds in the 24-hour overnight market.

Note that expected value is a reasonable tool to use in this situation, as there is no risk of financial ruin in either of the strategies. If these are the only two options available, and we repeat the process every two days, this strategy will maximize our long-term expected value.

Contingency Analysis

A decision often depends critically on the value assigned as a subjective probability. In these situations, it is often helpful to conduct a contingency analysis. The contingency analysis seeks to determine the critical value(s) of the probability, that is, the value(s) that *change the decision*. We saw an example of a contingency analysis in Chapter 2, where the insurance decision depends on the interest rate used. The same principal will be applied here—that is, trying to find *threshold values* where the optimal decision changes.

As an example, consider the following decision: as a result of a supplier error, we incurred extra costs of $1,000,000. Should we sue to recover these costs? The lawsuit will cost us $50,000. This decision depends critically on our perceived probability of winning the suit.

The decision tree is shown in Figure 3.17.

Note that we have entered the probability of winning the suit as the unknown "p" and the probability of losing the suit as $(1-p)$. To roll-back the tree, we compute the expected value of the "SUE" option:

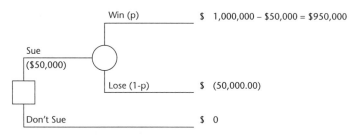

Figure 3.17 Decision Tree for Possible Legal Action

Expected value = $950,000 p + (-50,000)(1 - p)$

$$= \$1,000,000 \, p - 50,000$$

The expected value of "DON'T SUE" is $0, so, based on expected values, we prefer "SUE" if:

$1,000,000 \, p - 50,000 > 0$

or: $p > 50,000/1,000,000$

or: $p > 0.05$

The expected value maximizing decision is, therefore, *contingent upon the value assigned to the subjective probability p*. We do not need to know an exact value for p, we only need a range. If we think p is greater than 0.05, we sue: if we think $p < 0.05$, we do not.

Risk Analysis and Risk Management

Since business decisions are made into the future, almost all decisions involve uncertainties and risks:

> "All business is risk. As any chief executive will testify, running a company involves grappling with a string of uncertainties. The skill of a company lies in anticipating and managing those risks."
>
> *Source*: Peter Thal Larsen, *Financial Times*, Nov. 29, 2006.

Business decisions involve a trade-off between return and risk: the firm can generally achieve a higher return if it takes on more risk. Investing in U.S. Treasury Bills is generally seen as the risk-free option: the firm can therefore achieve the "T-Bill rate" of return at zero risk. Higher returns than the T-Bill rate can be obtained by investing in high-grade corporate bonds, but the risk of default increases along with the return. Other investments, such as equities, yield still higher average returns at even greater risk. Running a business requires the firm to take on risk in an attempt to achieve additional returns to the owners.

- **Risk analysis** involves identifying the various types of risk that the firm is exposed to and quantifying those risks.
- **Risk management** is the process of managing to reduce the known risks.
- **Risk mitigation** is taking concrete steps, such as buying insurance, to limit the firm's exposure if any of the various risks materialize.

Before risks can be managed, the specific risks facing the firm must be identified and quantified, and the management actions that can modify each specific risk spelled out. For example, if the risk item is identified as exposure to claims arising from injuries to workers on the job, then the kinds of management tools available to manage this risk include training programs, on-the-job supervision, and investment in safety equipment. Purchasing insurance is a risk mitigation tool that could limit the cost to the firm in the event that an injury to a worker does occur.

In terms of probabilities, risk analysis, risk management, and risk mitigation can be described as follows:

Let $P[x]$ be the probability that an undesirable outcome x occurs,

Let $C[x]$ be the cost to the firm if x occurs.

Then the expected value of the risk is: $P[x]C[x]$.

In general, x will occur when any one or more of a number of different "elementary" events occurs. Thus, $P[x]$ is a complex probability made up from accumulating the probabilities of several independent and dependent "elementary" events.

- The *risk analysis* task is to identify the elementary events and probabilities that make up $P[x]$.
- The *risk management* task is to take actions to reduce the expected value of the risk (that is, $P[x]C[x]$), either by reducing the probabilities of the elementary events occurring, and hence reducing $P[x]$, or by reducing the cost, $C[x]$, to the firm if x occurs.
- *Risk mitigation* involves looking at possible ways to give up some return in order to reduce $P[x]C[x]$ or eliminate it altogether.

As an example, consider the case of a natural gas distribution utility. An outcome that is particularly unsatisfactory for such a utility is being unable to supply gas to residents in

Table 3.1: Risk Factors Contributing to a Residential Gas Shortage

Sources of Risk	Possible Controlling Actions
Weather—a long, very cold, spell.	• Build more storage facilities in order to begin the season with larger inventories; • Develop a priority allocation scheme; • Install larger pipes from gas suppliers to utility.
Transmission pipe failures.	• Build redundancy into transmission system; • Maintain strategic inventories close to residential centers.
Supply shortages—suppliers cannot meet contracts.	• Diversify purchases—use many suppliers; • Include penalty clauses in contracts.
Labor disputes.	• Build/maintain adequate inventories; • Train management to operate key facilities.

the distribution area. There is some probability "$P[x]$" that such a shortage will occur. A shortage, however, is a consequence of one or more "elementary" events occurring, each of which can produce a residential gas shortage. For each of these specific events (or risks), there are possible actions that the utility could take to modify that risk and thereby reduce the probability of a residential gas shortage occurring. (Table 3.1 provides examples of some of these). The risk management task facing the utility is to choose which specific risks to address and which actions to implement as part of a balanced, cost-effective strategy aimed at controlling the probability and cost of residential gas shortages. Finally, there exists a risk mitigation strategy based on the possibility of purchasing an insurance policy to reduce the cost of claims against the utility (that is: $C[x]$) in the event that a residential gas shortage does actually occur.

Decision Analysis in Action

The S.S. *Kuniang*

The S.S. *Kuniang* ran aground on April 9, 1981, off the coast of Florida. The ship was declared a total loss by its owners, who offered to sell the salvage rights to the vessel by way of a sealed bid auction. Anyone wishing to acquire the salvage rights could submit a sealed offer to the auctioneer, who would sell the rights to the vessel to the highest bidder.

The New England Electric System (NEES) served more than one million customers in Massachusetts, Rhode Island, and New Hampshire, and required colliers to transport coal from Virginia to its power stations in New England. A NEES subsidiary, New England Energy Incorporated (NEEI), had already purchased a 36,250-ton self-loading ship, at a cost of $70 million for this purpose. If the *Kuniang* could be repaired, its coal-carrying capacity would be 51,000 tons, although the shallowness of Brayton Point harbor would limit its capacity to 45,750 tons. This was sufficient to accommodate NEES's remaining collier needs. NEEI used a decision tree to help decide whether to bid, and how much to bid, for the *Kuniang*.

The Importance of the "Jones Act"

The Jones Act, passed by the U.S. Congress in 1920, gave significant priority in U.S. ports to U.S. manufactured and crewed ships ("Jones Act" ships). These priorities were important: the wait for coal loading at ports such as Newport News and Norfolk sometimes reached 45 days, while a round trip for NEEI took only eight days if there was no wait for loading. The *Kuniang* was not American built, but there was a possibility under a 1852 statute for it to be declared a "Jones Act" ship. For this to happen, the cost of repairs to the ship had to be more than three times its "salvage value," as estimated by the U.S. Coast Guard.

NEEI had an estimate that the cost of salvaging the ship was around $15 million. Would the U.S. Coast Guard estimate the salvage value of the ship at its value as scrap (clearly less than $5 million) or would they consider the winning bid as an indication of the ship's true salvage value? Qualifying the *Kuniang* as a "Jones Act" vessel was so important that if NEEI bid more than $5 million, they would have to find some way of increasing the cost of repairs to meet the Act's requirements. One way to do this was to install self-loading equipment on the vessel, at an extra cost of $21 million. This equipment would reduce the round trip time from eight days to five, but the extra weight of the equipment would reduce the coal-carrying capacity of the *Kuniang* from 51,000 tons to 40,000 tons.

The Decision

Three million tons of coal per year were required for NEES's existing coal-burning plants. An additional 750,000 tons would be required at Salem Harbor if the environmental hearings on an additional plant conversion went successfully. Some years down the road, an additional 250,000 tons of coal might be required for the Providence plant, making a coal requirement of 4 million tons of coal per year, although this level might not be reached for several years, if ever. The General Dynamics vessel already pur-chased could move 2,250,000 tons/year. A sister to this vessel could be purchased, or chartered barges could be hired. The four options for the additional vessel are summarized in Table 3.2.

Table 3.2: Data for the Four Options

	General Dynamics	Tug/Barge	Kuniang (Gearless)	Kuniang (Self-loader)
Capital Cost	$70 million	$32 million	Bid + $15 million	Bid + $36 million
Capacity	36,250 tons	30,000 tons	45,750 tons	40,000 tons
Round Trip (coal)	5.15 days	7.15 days	8.18 days (as Jones Act vessel)	5.39 days
Round Trip (Egypt)	79 days	134 days	90 days	84 days
Operating cost/day	$18,670	$12,000	$23,000	$24,300
Fixed cost/day	$2,400	$2,400	$2,400	$2,700
Revenue/ Trip Coal	$304,500	$222,000	$329,400	$336,000
Revenue/ Trip Egypt	$2,540,000	$2,100,000	$3,570,000	$2,800,000

Any excess shipping capacity acquired by NEEI would have to find open market business, likely grain transportation, which was substantial and almost always available.

The Decision Analysis

NEEI used a decision tree to evaluate this decision. There were a number of additional complications. The *Kuniang* was already 15 years old, and it was not clear how long it would last, and the dates of conversion of the Salem and Providence plants to coal-burning were unknown. Appropriate discount rates were not easy to estimate. NEES was a large enough organization that the dollar amounts involved in the *Kuniang* decisions, although large, did not create any unacceptable financial risk and, therefore, maximizing expected value provided an appropriate guideline for bidding. Part of a decision tree representation of the problem (from David E. Bell, "Bidding for the S.S. *Kuniang*," *Interfaces, 14*, 2) is shown in Figure 3.18.

Some of the probabilities assessed were as follows:

- The Coast Guard was thought likely to assess the salvage value at the bid price with probability 0.7, and at scrap value with probability 0.3.

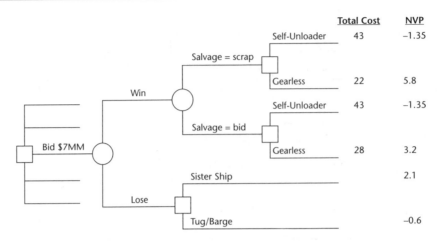

Figure 3.18 A Decision Tree Representation of How Much to Bid for the Kuniang

- NEES was sure that a bid of $10 million would win the auction, and that a bid of $3 million would definitely not win. A bid of $5 million was assessed a 1/6 chance of winning, $6 million 2/6ths, $7 million 3/6ths, $8 million 4/6ths, $9 million 5/6ths, and $10 million 6/6ths.

The analysis showed that using the *Kuniang* initially as a gearless ship and converting it to a self-loader only if the demand for coal materialized was worth about $500,000 in expected value terms.

The Results

NEES bid $6.7 million for the S.S. *Kuniang* but lost the auction to a bid of $10 million. The Coast Guard valued the vessel at its scrap value. The winning bidder had the option of operating the vessel as a full-time grain ship, which, for regulatory reasons, NEES could not do.

The decision analysis proved a remarkably effective tool for structuring this complex problem, lending insight into the most relevant information to collect, and developing a rationale for the eventual solution. Ed Brown, chairman and CEO of the New England Power Service Company, stated: "The analysis was a useful contribution to our deliberations and to our decision regarding an appropriate bid for the ship. The process was both interesting and valuable as well as being an excellent learning experience" (*Source*: Bell, "Bidding for the S.S. *Kuniang*").

Using Decision and Risk Analysis to Evaluate the United States and Russian Plutonium Disposition Options

At the end of the Cold War, the United States and Russia agreed to reduce their nuclear arsenals. Weapons-grade plutonium is highly radioactive and extremely toxic, and also needed to be kept away from terrorist groups, so it was critical that the United States and Russia dispose of the surplus plutonium in a safe and secure manner. A team of analysts from the Office of Fissile Materials Disposition within the U.S. Department of Energy developed a decision analysis model to evaluate 13 U.S. disposition alternatives, involving using the surplus plutonium to make mixed-oxide fuel for commercial nuclear power stations, immobilizing the plutonium in ceramics or glass and burying it in a nuclear waste site, or burying the plutonium in boreholes at a depth of four to six kilometers. The estimated costs of these 13 alternatives ranged from $1.1 billion to $3.6 billion. The need for the United States and Russia to wind down nuclear weapons in parallel led to Russian scientists to modify the model with the aid of the U.S. team and use it to evaluate Russia's disposition alternatives (*Source*: J. C. Butler et al., *Interfaces*, *35*, 1, January–February 2005, pp 88–101).

Bank Stress Tests

Stress tests of banks and the banking system have been conducted routinely since the financial crisis of 2009. Stress tests seek to investigate the impact of extreme situations on the banks and financial institutions to determine their robustness to various external shocks, and identify needed changes to the financial system as a whole.

The basic idea of a stress test is to build a simulation model of a bank or financial system and then simulate unlikely but possible sets of conditions ("scenarios") and examine the survivability of the institution. Stress testing differs from the routine risk exposure simulations that many banks perform regularly, in that the stress test is performed by an outside agency and may result in new rules or regulations being imposed on the bank, while routine risk management simulations help the bank's management with internal investment and asset management decision making.

The International Monetary Fund (IMF) has stress tested banks extensively to try to ensure that the banking system can survive unusual major adverse developments. The IMF tests for credit and market risks (how do potential losses from defaults on loans and mortgages or interest rate or exchange rate changes affect a bank's profits and solvency) and liquidity risk (can the bank survive if it is unable to borrow money at reasonable interest rates from other banks or sell assets to other banks.)

Recently, the IMF has developed new risk-modeling techniques and stress-testing methods to investigate the links between banks and other financial institutions and to identify the risks that local banking instabilities could spread globally, resulting in widespread economic and financial instability.

Bank simulation models used in stress testing are at the forefront of efforts to maintain the health of the global financial system. Banks, regulatory authorities, financial markets, and governments pay a great deal of attention to the results of these simulations (*Source*: "What Is a Bank Stress Test?" *IMF Survey Online*, July 29, 2010, http://www.imf.org/external/pubs/ft/survey/so/2010/pol072910a.htm, accessed February 8, 2012).

Du Pont Believes That Decision and Risk Analysis Contributes to Achieving Outstanding Financial Results

> Decision and Risk Analysis enables Du Pont's business teams to develop creative strategic alternatives, evaluate them rigorously, and select those with the greatest expected shareholder value.
>
> K. J. Engemann & H. F. Miller,
> "Operations Risk Management at a Major Bank," *Interfaces*, *22*, 6.

In the mid-1980s, Du Pont began acquiring major medical, agricultural, chemical, and automotive finishing businesses. At the same time, the company was reducing its staff. Consequently, many difficult decisions needed to be made by a smaller management group. Further complications included the facts that these decisions involved vastly different markets from all over the globe and, in many cases, time was short and the environment uncertain. Du Pont chose to move responsibility for these decisions to the business units by empowering local management to make important decisions.

Du Pont developed Decision and Risk Analysis (D&RA) tools to help these managers with these decisions. A core group of Decision and Risk Consultants (DRC) was established. DRC organized training programs, consulted with Du Pont businesses, and produced a D&RA newsletter and annual forum. DRC became the focal point of a network of D&RA champions deployed throughout the organization who promoted the value of D&RA through education and networking, consulted with businesses having more complex problems, and integrated D&RA with strategic thinking and planning activities throughout Du Pont.

Business Z

One example of D&RA at work occurred in mid-1990. Business Z, an actual Du Pont business based in the United States with sales and facilities worldwide, found its financial performance declining as a result of eroding prices and market share. Business Z's products had fallen behind some competitors and its production facilities were unable to produce the customized products now being demanding. Moreover, the industry's rate of growth was slowing, although still outpacing the general economy.

The Du Pont director responsible for Business Z formed a decision board consisting of himself and senior management. The Board's purpose was to select from the strategic options developed by the D&RA project team, which consisted of ten Business Z managers as well as a full-time DRC consultant. The D&RA plan was conducted in several segments:

- **Framing the problem.** The team developed and shared with the decision board a wide-ranging set of alternative strategies.

- **Assessing and analyzing the options** (analysis). At this stage, uncertainties (such as competitors' market shares, and prices) were assessed separately by region using small groups of experts. A spreadsheet model was used to construct net present values (NPV) of each strategy and *Supertree* (software that evaluated decision trees) was used to construct the probability distributions of these NPVs. This analysis stage took four months.

- **Making decisions.** The decision board arrived at a new strategy which was expected to increase Business Z's value by $175 million.

- **Planning implementation** (connection with the real world). Steps were identified to connect the recommendations to an implementation plan. Major activities, actions to minimize risk, contingency plans, measures of progress, and required changes to the organizational culture were identified.

Other Results

By the end of 1992, more than ten Du Pont businesses had used D&RA to develop, select, and implement business strategies. Each of these businesses was competing globally, had annual sales in excess of $150 million, and possessed multiple production facilities.

Management has stressed the intangible results of D&RA even more than the tangible ones. For example, because so many employees take part and contribute to the decision making, a sense of personal commitment is fostered. The process enhances team building, and increases effective communication among participants through the common purpose outlined within D&RA. Moreover, as greater attention is paid to strategy development, innovative new hybrid strategies often emerge.

D&RA has been particularly useful in allowing decision makers to focus on shareholder value as the primary decision criterion, and it has been an extremely useful framework for involving critical uncertainties such as customer behavior, competitive response, and the impact of society on the business operation.

Michael T. Sharples, Vice-President Finance, Du Pont, writes:

> [W]e consider D&RA a best practice at Du Pont. The value of D&RA became even more vivid to me . . . as I sat on the decision board of another major Du Pont business.

D&RA was used to structure and evaluate an opportunity which we believe will improve its NPV by a minimum of $200 million. The D&RA process improved communication within the business team as well as between the team and . . . management, resulting in rapid approval and execution. As a decision maker, I highly value such a clear and logical approach to making choices under uncertainty. (*Source*: F. V. Krumm & C. F. Rolle, "Management and Application of Decision and Risk Analysis in Du Pont," *Interfaces 22*, 6)

Operations Risk Management at a Major Bank

When the operations of a business are disrupted, losses usually result. When that business is a financial institution, the losses can be considerable. Some sources of potential disruption include fire or earthquake, employee accidents or illness, and criminal activities. Historically, banks protected their financial assets from major theft using vaults and security guards, but the advent of electronic funds transfer has produced new security problems for financial institutions. Today, the fact that the value of electronic "paperless" transactions far exceed the value of the banks' physical assets justifies devoting considerable resources to risk management.

What Is Risk Management?

Risk Management is the management of the uncertainties surrounding unlikely events that, potentially, have an adverse impact upon the operation of a business. The objective of risk management is to limit the impact of major disruptions to an acceptable level.

There are generally three options available to manage an identified risk:

- Management may take action to reduce the probability that the event occurs.
- Management may prepare and implement a contingency plan to minimize the effect of the event if it occurs.
- Management may choose to do nothing.

In the case of electronic funds transfer, management would wish to take steps to minimize the probability that theft occurs, and to put controls in place so that if theft does occur, it is speedily identified and the amount lost by the bank is minimized. This set of controls might include purchasing insurance so that if large losses occur, the bank is repaid for some or all of these losses.

Decision makers must determine whether to act and how to proceed. To do this, they must assess the severity of the risk and estimate the cost of controlling the risk. Good decisions must balance the probability of a risk occurring with the extent of the possible losses, and must be effective in limiting the losses to manageable levels.

Risk Management Methodology at the Bank

The first step taken by the bank was to develop a risk management methodology. This methodology was a step-by-step process, based upon decision analysis, to determine the appropriate response to an identified risk. Terms that would be used during planning were defined:

- A **threat** was a potential disaster that would lead to a loss of resources;
- An **event** was an actual loss of resources which disrupted service delivery and affected earnings;
- **Losses** were economic reductions in the company's wealth.

Next, the bank identified services where contingency plans were necessary, and reviewed the resources needed to deliver those services. Management at the bank also had to predict what threats the bank's operations faced, and come up with a list that included power outages, fire, acts of nature, sabotage, and strikes. Once these threats were identified, management determined what resources and services would be affected if any of the various threats materialized.

The losses that would result from the various events were then estimated. Losses could be direct, indirect, or simply a loss of assets. For example, a fire would result in a loss of assets if a building were destroyed, but direct losses would also occur as a result of not being able to carry out contracted services, while indirect losses would result from a loss of future customers. In making these predictions and estimates, management reviewed historical data and discussed event likelihoods with experts. Computer simulation was used to blend historical data and subjective opinions to arrive at occurrence rates.

The next step was to develop alternatives to deal with the possible events, either by reducing the probability of an event, or by reducing losses. Checklists were developed to assess similar risks and alternatives in different areas of operation. Management calculated the annualized cost of each alternative, and compared it to the expected annual risk exposure, and also considered existing insurance coverage and the positive effect on premiums that a comprehensive risk management plan could have. At this point, a decision tree was constructed to evaluate each alternative. One branch of the tree denoted that the alternative was adopted and a second that it was not. Probabilities of various events were attached, along with the estimated conditional losses that would result. In some situations, the numbers made decision making very easy, while in others the outcomes were so close that a more-detailed analysis was necessary.

In order to understand the level at which decisions would be considered material, the project team interviewed senior management in order to assess their attitude to risk. Risks were found to be significant only at very large monetary values, with the result that only risks with a large possible loss would be an issue; smaller losses would be "self-insured" (that is, the bank would take the risk and fund any losses that occurred). This final framework was not intended to replace a manager's judgment, but rather to support it; consequently, the results were compared to the operations manager's intuitive judgment, and any disagreements were closely examined and resolved.

Some Specific Projects

Several specific areas that were examined using this methodology, included:

- **Power generator**—Intuitively, management felt that a backup generator was necessary. Since other banks had acquired backup generators, there was not likely to be a holiday in the event of a regional blackout. The decision analysis indicated that a small backup generator was needed for the funds-transfer division only, since this division was the most deadline dependent.

- **Multi-location contingency strategy**—Dual data processing operations at geographically separate sites were proposed, with production computers at one site, and development computers at the other. There was a strategic influence on the decision to go ahead, as the bank wanted to see if it could use this decision to further strategic initiatives.

- **Transaction processing**—The bank considered various threats to a basement data center that handled a small portion of the bank's business. The decision was taken to move the center to the third floor.

- **Pricing risk into coin and currency**—Operational risks were identified for each coin or currency product (such as theft by employees or outsiders) and the controls inherent in the production process were also determined. The analysis methodology was used to ensure that the price charged for each product included the appropriate risk premium.

- **Authentication of funds transfers**—The risk that someone might intercept, modify, and retransmit electronic funds transfers was quantified and used by management to assess the need for internal authentication.

Success of the Project

Management completely accepted the institutionalization of a decision-analysis methodology to ensure uniform compliance with corporate policy with respect to risk: "Management proved to be surprisingly receptive to such concepts as events, probability, expected value, and utility, as long as they were presented in an intuitive rather than a mathematical framework." The project had the support of the president of the bank, and the bank was able to report yearly to its Board of Directors on a corporate-wide contingency planning program.

As a result of this work, the OR group became a department with worldwide responsibility for contingency planning and information security (*Source*: Engemann & Miller, "Operations Risk Management at a Major Bank").

Summary

In this chapter, we introduced a formal view of decision making that applies to sequential decisions made under uncertainty. The "decision tree" structuring process presented herein is a useful tool to help the manager understand complex decision situations with the associated risks and uncertainties. The framework presented is particularly useful in helping to identify the key factors or parameters that sway a decision one way or another, or when discussing a complex decision situation in a group setting.

What the Manager Must Know

- All decisions are made into the future and almost all involve uncertainty. It is important for every manager to develop methods to cope with, discuss, and manage uncertainty.

- The decision tree modeling process helps in understanding a sequence of decisions and events. Drawing the tree may yield insights about the problem structure that would not be identified through a less-rigorous analysis.

- The expected value is often a useful guide to the best decision: it represents the long-run average if a decision or event could be repeated a large number of times.

- The expected value might not correspond to any actual outcome, and it will often conceal the risk associated with adverse events.

- The probabilities of future outcomes are an important factor in most decisions. These can be derived from data or estimated by experts familiar with the situation. Many leading-edge companies make use of large databases to estimate probabilities that enable them to (for example) predict and explain customer behavior.

- Data and the probabilities derived from the firm's data can be a source of competitive advantage. A competitor can hire experts but cannot easily replicate a large historical database. A database of current accurate relevant data has often been shown to be the foundation to sustain a competitive advantage for many years.

Exercises

1. Chad operated an automobile sales business. A major dealer in town offered Chad a one-time opportunity to help them sell some "trade-ins." Under this deal (see table below), Chad could take one used car at a time from the dealer and try to sell

it. If he sold it, he could take another. There were three cars they wanted Chad to try to sell.

The Dealer concluded the offer as follows: "Chad, we have not dealt with you before so we plan to proceed cautiously: I'm sure you understand. If you accept this deal, you must take the compact first. If you sell the compact, then you can choose either of the other two, or you can end the deal. If you sell the second car, then you can take the third if you wish."

Car	Chad's Commission (On Sale)	Chad's Selling Costs	Chad's Estimate of Probability of Sale
Compact	$900	$600	3/4
Standard	$1,500	$200	2/3
Luxury	$3,000	$600	50/50

If he took a car, Chad would incur the selling costs in trying to sell the car, but risked not making the sale. What should he do?

2. Carlie needed a personal computer (PC) for school but her budget was tight, so she decided on a used machine. After some searching, she was down to two possibilities. One she had found in a national franchized computer store, where she could purchase the PC for $800 with a one-year guarantee. But she was intrigued by a second possibility: a local charity store was offering a used machine that had been donated (exactly the same model as in the store) for $500.

Carlie talked to a computer repair specialist, who said the principal problem with this model of PC was the hard drive, which was prone to failure: he estimated that half of the PCs of this model and age would require a new drive. He offered to test the computer and check the condition of the drive for $60. If the drive was no good, a new drive could be fitted for $300 and would be guaranteed for one year. He added a qualification that his testing was not perfect: about 25% of drives that passed his testing failed soon afterwards requiring a new drive ($300) plus a service charge of $100 for diagnosing the problem.

What should Carlie do?

Recommended Cases

Mike's Self Service (Ivey)

Freemark Abbey Winery (Harvard)

Listerine Lozenges (Ivey)

Gilbert and Gilbert (Ivey)

C. K. Coolidge (A) (Harvard)

BriLux: The FOT-320 Decision (Ivey)

Research and Development at ICI: Anthraquinone (Ivey)

Merck and Company: Product KL-798 (Darden)

Yangarra Resources (Ivey)

St. Swithin's Hospital (Ivey)

Seoul National Bank: The Chief Credit Officer's Dilemma (Ivey)

SIGA Technologies: Profiting From Uncertainty (Ivey)

Risk Analysis for Merck and Company: Product Kl-798 (Darden)

CHAPTER 4

DATA-DRIVEN DECISION MAKING

Barry Beracha, the former chief executive of the Sara Lee Bakery Group, has been quoted as emphasizing the importance of data as an input to management decisions:

"In God we trust. All others bring data."[1]

Data can provide a factual base for decisions: some firms say that they are "fact-based decision makers." Data, however, starts out as just numbers and it must be processed into information that is useful to the decision maker. One framework for extracting useful information from data is that provided by classical statistics. This framework provides a way of visualizing and interpreting data that raises many important questions about the data and the information derived from it.

In this chapter, we provide an introduction to several concepts from statistics that are used to visualize and interpret data. But first, we define statistics:

Statistics is concerned with making inferences about a *population* based on information contained in a *sample*.

Populations and Samples

The first important statistical concept is the distinction between a *population* and a *sample*. A manager will frequently wish to understand the activities or preferences of a certain group (the population), but, due to resource constraints, it is often not possible to gather information from all possible sources. Thus, a subset, known as a sample, is used. Large groups or *populations* may be *sampled* and the sample data summarized in a *statistic* and

---

[1]This quotation appears in Tom Davenport, *Competing on Analytics: The New Science of Winning* by Jeanne G. Harris, Harvard Business Press Books, 2007, but is more commonly attributed to W. Edwards Demming, the founder of modern quality control.

used to draw conclusions or inferences about the population. Patterns may be revealed and conclusions arrived at with confidence.

More formally, we say that:

- The *population* is the complete set of elements possessing measures of interest (i.e. parameters) to the decision maker.
- A *sample* is any subset selected from a population.

For example, when determining television-viewing habits, the population could be every person who watches television, and a sample would be a small group of people for whom detailed viewing statistics are gathered.

Numerical summaries and descriptive measures for a population are called *parameters*.

There is a risk in using sample data to estimate a population parameter. For example, if the sample is *biased*, then estimates derived from the sample may not provide a clear picture of the population. However, the discipline of statistics makes it possible to take this into account by being precise about the magnitude of the uncertainty in any estimated quantity.

Whenever an estimate of a parameter is made, the decision maker should be able to determine two things:

1. A best guess of the true measure of interest, the population parameter (this guess is a statistic).
2. The accuracy of the statistic as an estimate of the parameter.

Some examples of using sample data to draw inferences about a larger population include:

1. A market researcher is examining some of the responses to a question asked in a consumer survey of 4,000 shoppers at a mall. The shoppers were asked to rate a new product on a 10-point scale. The researcher has looked at 200 questionnaires picked randomly from the box of 4,000, and has found the sample mean (the mean rating on these 200 questionnaires) to be 6.6. The researcher can then make a best guess that the population mean (the mean rating of all 4,000 shoppers) will be 6.6, and will be able to make a statement as to how accurate this best guess is.

   In this example, the population of immediate interest is the 4,000 questionnaires in the box, and this population is identifiable and tangible—we could pick up the box and see the population. This is, however, rarely the case. The 4,000 questionnaires themselves represent a sample from a larger population of shoppers, and we would have to think quite hard about how we define *this* population. For example, do we mean male shoppers or female shoppers, or both? Do we include children or teenagers? Are we interested in shoppers in a single city, state, country? What about people buying for businesses?

With knowledge of the product, we could answer most of these questions. If the product were a new line of cosmetics for women, then our population of interest would be personal female shoppers, within an age range and geographic area determined by the designated target market for the product. With some research, we could estimate the size of our population, but we would have to work much harder to obtain any type of listing of this population; the latter task might be more effort than it would be worth.

2. A bank wants to determine consumer reaction to a new prepaid debit card. This is a plastic card that is "charged up" with money at an automatic banking machine and can then be used like a credit card. There is, however, no monthly bill to pay, and no interest charges, since money on the card is just like cash in the cardholder's pocket.

    The bank selects a typical town for its test and installs the necessary technology to read the card in a number of stores. A sample of selected consumers is then given the card and asked to try it out for a month. At the end of the trial period, customers fill in questionnaires, and attend interviews and focus groups. The data collected on customer reaction to the new card is used to infer how the population as a whole will view this new product. Here the population could be all potential users of the new debit card, and the sample is the group of customers given the card for testing purposes.

    This type of "test marketing" is carried out almost continuously somewhere in North America.

3. In some cases, the population of interest might not yet exist. Suppose that we are going to package a batch (or "lot") of potatoes into 10,000 bags of at least 20 pounds each. We want to know how many pounds of potatoes we are going to need—we'll need more than $10,000 \times 20 = 200,000$ pounds, because we have to overfill the bags to be sure that none contain less than the required weight (we are not going to cut up individual potatoes). We can calculate the total weight if we can estimate the mean weight of potatoes in each bag.

    One way to make this estimate would be to set up our packaging equipment and run off a sample of 20-pound bags. This would work well as long as the packaging equipment was capable of packing the entire lot without any change in the mean bag weight as packing progressed. In this situation, we can think of the packaging machine as being a process that is generating measures—in this instance, the weights of the bags of potatoes. Our sample of past measures from this process provides us with statistics that we can use to make inferences about future values of the process. Of course, if the process is fluctuating over time, a simple look at the statistics will give us an incorrect picture of the future.

Another case where it may be difficult to identify the population or sample would be new product introductions. This would apply to products such as BlackBerry® smartphones, iPads, e-book readers, and Facebook, none of which existed a short time ago.

Sampling and Bias

There is no guarantee that a statistic, even one carefully collected, will provide an accurate picture of a population. For this reason, it is important to know how the statistic was determined and what it represents. We have already pointed out that statistics have a built-in imprecision because they are based on partial data—the sample. However, this imprecision must be acknowledged, quantified, and differentiated from error caused by *bias*. Whether by design or carelessness, bias can occur.

A common cause of bias is selecting the "wrong" sample. Care should be taken to ensure that the sample is selected so that it has a good chance of providing a clear view of the population. In particular, this view should not be tainted by the personal preferences, opinions, or feelings of the individual selecting the sample. Otherwise, the sample will be biased, through collection of the data in a manner that will distort the analysis and conclusions.

Even samples chosen by neutral researchers can turn out to be biased. Consider the following example. A national supermarket chain wishes to discover how food shoppers perceive its prices. The company sends out five checkers from its Near-North Chicago store on a Monday with instructions to stand at a main intersection in the Chicago Loop from 8 a.m. to 9 a.m. and ask as many passersby as possible a series of questions about the chain's prices.

Clearly, there are several problems with this sample. A few are:

(a) Attitudes and perceptions of people from downtown Chicago are likely very different from those of people from other parts of the country, even from those of people from suburban Chicago.

(b) People passing by those intersections at that time are likely white-collar workers, and may not be representative of the community as a whole.

(c) People commuting at that time of day might not be the primary food shoppers in their household.

(d) People surveyed may have higher incomes than most American food shoppers, and may not be aware of, or be concerned with, food prices.

(e) Those who agree to answer the questions may have the willingness and the time to participate. These people may be more sensitive to prices than those who shop in a rush.

The design and selection of samples is a discipline and art in its own right. Often, samples are selected *randomly* from a population. Random selection avoids several potential biases in sample selection. Importantly, if the person selecting the sample can demonstrate that proper procedures were used to select a random sample, then it becomes more difficult to attack the sample taker for injecting personal bias into the data collection.

The importance of random sampling is widely recognized in medical and pharmaceutical research through the randomized clinical trial (RCT). In an RCT, patients first agree to participate in the trial, and are then assigned to either a trial group or a control group using a purely random process, such as a coin toss. Because patients have been assigned to their groups as a result of a random process, there is no systematic difference between them, and any observed differences can, therefore, be attributed to the new product.

Data that is collected through random sampling and is free from bias can be considered the "gold standard." If you are repeatedly gathering data, such as through customer opinion surveys, then it is worthwhile to spend some time and effort to design good collection methods. However, managers don't always have access to such high-quality data. There may be many reason for this: data has already been collected through a costly process; data might be collected from a company's accounting or ERP systems, which might have limitations; the sample may have been selected on the basis of convenience rather than on best statistical principles; and there may not be time or resources available to collect a perfect sample. Such samples can still be analyzed and described, but it is important to recognize the bias and other potential limitations in the sample when using the data to make decisions.

In the next sections, we present a number of concepts for summarizing data. This includes four important properties of data: *distribution*, *centralness*, *variation*, and *sequence*. When looking at data, a useful first step is to examine the data with respect to these four concepts.

Distribution

Frequency Tables and Histograms

Not all observations in a sample will be the same—if they were, there would be no need for statistics! The values and relative frequencies of observations is known as a *distribution*. Distributions are often summarized in tables or charts called histograms (a histogram is a plot of the frequency distribution of the data). Consider the distribution of household income in the United States.

The data in Table 4.1 can be represented visually using a *histogram* (Figure 4.1).

Table 4.1: US Household Incomes 2004

Income Level	Number of Households
Under $2,500	2,566
$2,500 to $4,999	1,389
$5,000 to $7,499	2,490
$7,500 to $9,999	3,360
$10,000 to $12,499	4,013
$12,500 to $14,999	3,543
$15,000 to $17,499	3,760
$17,500 to $19,999	3,438
$20,000 to $22,499	4,061
$22,500 to $24,999	3,375
$25,000 to $27,499	3,938
$27,500 to $29,999	2,889
$30,000 to $32,499	3,921
$32,500 to $34,999	2,727
$35,000 to $37,499	3,360
$37,500 to $39,999	2,633
$40,000 to $42,499	3,378
$42,500 to $44,999	2,294
$45,000 to $47,499	2,700
$47,500 to $49,999	2,371
$50,000 to $52,499	3,017
$52,500 to $54,999	2,006
$55,000 to $57,499	2,420
$57,500 to $59,999	1,786
$60,000 to $62,499	2,566
$62,500 to $64,999	1,774
$65,000 to $67,499	2,101
$67,500 to $69,999	1,637
$70,000 to $72,499	1,978
$72,500 to $74,999	1,413

(Continued)

$75,000 to $77,499	1,802
$77,500 to $79,999	1,264
$80,000 to $82,499	1,673
$82,500 to $84,999	1,219
$85,000 to $87,499	1,418
$87,500 to $89,999	984
$90,000 to $92,499	1,282
$92,500 to $94,999	917
$95,000 to $97,499	1,023
$97,500 to $99,999	846
$100,000 to $149,999	11,194
$150,000 to $199,999	3,595
$200,000 to $249,999	1,325
$250,000 and above	1,699
Total	113,145

Source: "Table HINC-06. Income Distribution to $250,000 or More for Households: 2004," U.S. Census Bureau, Current Population Survey, 2005 Annual Social and Economic Supplement, http://pubdb3.census.gov/macro/032005/hhinc/new06_000.htm, accessed March 2, 2008.

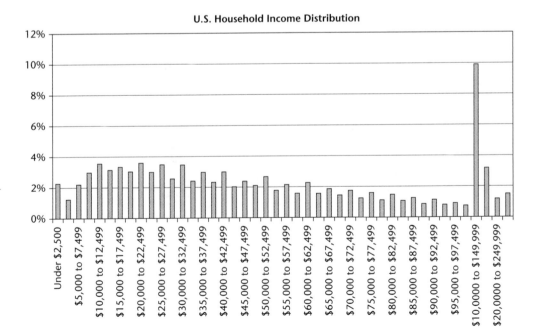

Figure 4.1 Histogram of U.S. Household Incomes 2004

The histogram or frequency-plot of a sample also allows us to describe the distribution of the sample and, hence, infer the distribution of the population. We use words such as *symmetrical*, *unimodal* (one peak), and *bimodal* (two peaks) to describe the distribution. The histogram shown in Figure 4.1 is easy to read and allows one to quickly make some observations:

1. The distribution is relatively flat for household incomes up to $100,000.

2. Approximately 10% of households have an income in the $100,000–$150,000 range.

3. Approximately 15% of households have an income in excess of $100,000.

There are at least three ways to create a histogram in Excel:

1. If the data is already sorted into a frequency table (as in Table 4.1), then you can use that table as the basis of a bar chart.

2. If the data is not pre-sorted (for instance, if you had the raw data on all 113,145,000 households instead of the summary data), then you would need to sort the data into *class intervals* or *bins* before creating the histogram. The first step would be to determine the range for each class interval, which determines the appropriate breakpoints for the bins. In the table above, the class interval is mostly $2,500, which leads to breakpoints at the income levels of $2,500, $5,000, $7,500, $10,000, etc. Once the list of bin values has been created in a column, the easiest way to make a histogram is with the Histogram tool in the Data Analysis add-in. Highlight the range of data as the Input Range, highlight the range of bins as the Bin Range, and check the checkbox for chart output. This will result in a summary table and a histogram on a new worksheet.

3. You can use the Excel functions = FREQUENCY() or = COUNTIF() to count the numbers of observations below each bin value, then draw the histogram by inserting a bar chart.

Probabilities and Distributions

Frequency tables are often used to estimate probabilities and conditional probabilities. Table 4.2 shows the distribution of employed individuals by gender and type of occupation in the United States.

We use this data to illustrate the estimation of probabilities and conditional probabilities with four examples.

1. Suppose a person is randomly selected from this group. What is the probability that the person is male? Answer: 77,487/145,363 = 53.3%.

Table 4.2: Employed Individuals by Gender and Occupation ('000) (U.S. 2008)

	Men	Women	Total
Management, professional, and related occupations	25,948	26,813	52,761
Service occupations	10,471	13,980	24,451
Sales and office occupations	13,067	22,477	35,544
Natural resources, construction, and maintenance	14,181	626	14,807
Production, transportation, and material moving	13,820	3,980	17,800
Total	77,487	67,876	145,363

Source: "Employed Persons by Occupation, Sex, and Age," Bureau of Labor Statistics, United States Department of Labor, ftp://ftp.bls.gov/pub/special.requests/lf/aat9.txt, accessed March 2, 2008.

2. Suppose a person is randomly selected from this group. What is the probability that the person works in "Service occupations" or "Sales and office occupations"? Answer: (24,451 + 35,544)/145,363 = 41.3%.

3. Suppose a woman is randomly selected from this group. What is the probability that she works in "Natural resources, construction and maintenance"? Answer: 626/67,876 = 0.9%.

4. Suppose that someone who works in "Natural resources, construction and maintenance" is randomly selected from this group. What is the probability that the person is a woman? Answer: 626/14,807 = 4.2%.

Examples 1 and 2 illustrate the estimation of probabilities from a frequency table, while examples 3 and 4 illustrate the estimation of conditional probabilities. Note that examples 3 and 4 illustrate an important but frequently misunderstood concept with conditional probabilities—namely, that $P(A$ given $B)$ is in general not equal to $P(B$ given $A)$. More specifically, in examples 3 and 4, P(woman given works in natural resources) $\neq P$(works in natural resources given woman). The examples given above provide examples of estimating probabilities using historical data, as discussed in Chapter 3.

Percentiles, Deciles, and Quartiles

The xth percentile of a distribution is the value, such that x% of the observations lie below that value and (100-x)% lie above that value. For example, in the household income data, $100,000 is approximately the 84th percentile of the distribution because 95,332/113,146 = 84.3% of all households have an income level below $100,000 / year and 17,813/113,146 = 15.7% have an income above this level.

Two related concepts are deciles and quartiles. For *deciles*, a distribution is divided into 10 ranges, such that each range contains 10% of the observations. Thus, the first decile contains all data up to the 10th percentile; the second decile contains all data between the 10th and 20th percentiles, and so on. *Quartiles* are formed in the same way, with ranges each holding 25% of the data.

The Normal Distribution

The normal distribution is ubiquitous in data analysis, often being described as the "bell-shaped curve." Many (but not all) naturally occurring phenomena are approximately normally distributed. Statisticians may try to approximate their sample observations by a normal distribution in order to take advantage of the convenient statistical properties of data that are normally distributed.

> **Example:** A Vox write-up of new research in 2010 notes that the world income distribution used to be bi-modal—the haves and the have-nots. Now it approximates a normal distribution, and it is unlikely that the world will ever have 1 billion people in poverty. (*Source*: http://www.economist.com/blogs/freeexchange/2010/01/good_news_out_there, June 25, 2010)

What is the normal distribution? Normal does not imply usual; it is the name of a particular family of distributions that are defined by a specific mathematical function called the *normal probability density function*. This family has several properties.

1. The distributions in the family differ according to the values of two parameters—the mean (μ) and the standard deviation (σ).

2. Each normal distribution is symmetrical about the mean, and unimodal (i.e., it has a single, unique mode).

3. The shape of the normal distribution is independent of the value of the mean, but does depend on the value of the standard deviation. As the standard deviation increases, the distribution becomes flatter, with a lower peak and elongated tails (Figure 4.2).

4. For any set of data, you can transform the data to their "scores" (or "z-scores"). The score for a data value x is calculated as

   $$score = (x - \bar{x})/s$$

   where $\bar{x}$ is the sample mean and s is the sample standard deviation. When the observations that form a normal distribution are standardized (i.e., when replaced by their scores), the result is also a normal distribution, but with mean 0 and

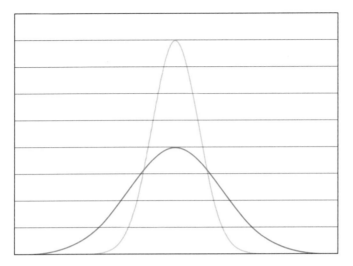

Figure 4.2 Examples of Two Normal Distributions with the Same Mean But Different Value of the Standard Deviation

standard deviation 1 (called the *standard normal distribution*). This result is independent of the mean and standard deviation of the original distribution (i.e., it is true for any normal distribution).

Three "rules of thumb" apply for the normal distribution (see Figure 4.3):

1. Approximately two-thirds of the observations should be within one standard deviation of the mean (the exact proportion is 0.6827),

2. Approximately 95% of the observations should be within two standard deviations of the mean (the exact proportion is 0.9545), and

3. Almost all the observations should be within three standard deviations of the mean (the exact proportion is 0.9973).

Excel includes functions that provide normal distribution statistics directly. The function = NORMDIST(x, μ, σ, 1) gives the cell the value of the cumulative left-tail area of the normal distribution, with mean μ and standard deviation σ. That is the proportion of the area under the normal curve that is less than x. For example, the following figure shows the area to the left of −1.15 in a normal distribution, with mean 0 and standard deviation 1. The shaded area is the value that would be obtained from = NORMDIST(−1.15,0,1,1) (Figure 4.4). Many textbooks also contain tables of normal distribution cumulative values.

The methods above can be extended to estimating any probabilities from a normal distribution. If x is normally distributed with mean μ and standard deviation σ, and A and B are

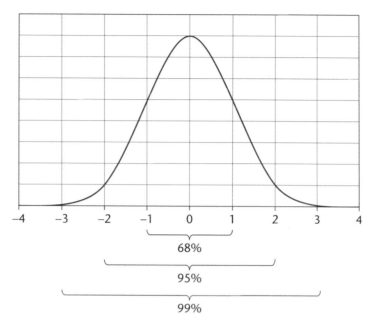

Figure 4.3 The Rules of Thumb and the Normal Distribution. Excel includes functions that provide normal distribution statistics directly. The function = NORMDIST(x, m, s, 1) gives the cell the value of the cumulative left-tail area of the normal distribution with mean m and standard deviation s. That is the proportion of the area under the normal curve that is less than x. For example, the following figure shows the area to the left of -2 in a normal distribution with mean 0 and standard deviation 1. The shaded area is the value that would be obtained from = NORMDIST(-2,0,1,1) (Figure 4.4). Many textbooks also contain tables of normal distribution cumulative values.

two specific numbers, then the probability that a randomly selected number x has a value less than A is given by:

$$P(x < A) = \text{NORMDIST}(A, \mu, \sigma, 1).$$

The probability that a randomly selected number x has a value greater than A is given by:

$$P(x > A) = 1—\text{NORMDIST}(A, \mu, \sigma, 1).$$

This follows from the fact that the total probability must sum to 1 and the event "$x > A$" is the complement to the event "$x < A$." (See the "Axioms of Probabilities" in Chapter 3.)

The probability that a randomly selected number x has a value greater than A and less than B is given by:

$$P(A < x < B) = P(x < B) - P(x < A) = \text{NORMDIST}(B, \mu, \sigma, 1) - \text{NORMDIST}(A, \mu, \sigma, 1).$$

It may be helpful to draw a sketch to verify why the last statement is true.

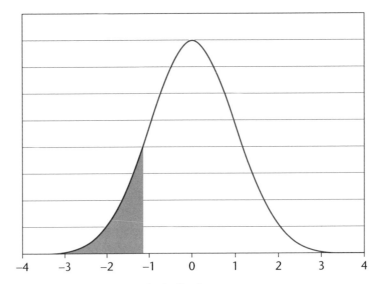

Figure 4.4 The Left-Tail Area of the Normal Distribution

Verifying the Properties of the Normal Distribution Using the NORMDIST Function

To become familiar with the = NORMDIST() function, we will check that the exact proportions within one, two, and three standard deviations of the mean of the normal distribution are 0.6827, 0.9545, and 0.9973, respectively.

We use = NORMDIST() to calculate areas for the standard normal distribution (i.e., $\mu = 0$ and $\sigma = 1$) that are to the left of –1, –2, and –3. Since the standard deviation is 1, these values correspond to the areas 1, 2, and 3 standard deviations below the mean. Note that the last argument of the NORMDIST function is always the number 1 when NORMDIST is used to generate probabilities.

= NORMDIST(–1,0,1,1) gives the value 0.158655

= NORMDIST(–2,0,1,1) gives the value 0.02275

= NORMDIST(–3,0,1,1) gives the value 0.00135

Recall that these are the proportions less than the given value; therefore, 0.158655 of the normal distribution is below the mean-minus-one standard deviation. Since the normal distribution is symmetrical, 0.158655 of the distribution is above the mean-plus-one standard deviation. We conclude that 2×0.158655 or 0.317310 of the distribution is outside the range from the mean-minus-one standard deviation to the mean-plus-one standard deviation, or $(1 - 0.317310) = 0.682690$ is inside this range.

Applying the same reasoning, NORMDIST() gives 0.9545 as the fraction within two standard deviations of the mean ($= 1 - 2 \times 0.02275$), and 0.9973 as the fraction within three standard deviations of the mean ($= 1 - 2 \times 0.00135$).

There are many situations where it is useful to be able to show that the distribution of a sample is well approximated by a normal distribution. There are other situations where a correct statistical analysis requires that a sample be normally distributed. It is, therefore, useful to be able to check whether a sample is well approximated by a normal distribution. For many purposes, this can be done by inspecting the histogram. More formal tests for normality exist, but they are beyond the scope of this book.

Not all samples are distributed symmetrically: many are *skewed*. The *skewness* of the distribution indicates the extent to which it is not symmetrical. If the skewness is 0, then the distribution is symmetrical. If the skewness is positive, then the distribution is positively skewed (also called right-skewed), indicating a small number of very large observations. If the skewness is negative, then the distribution is negatively skewed (also called left-skewed), indicating a small number of very small observations. Household incomes and house prices are two examples of right-skewed distributions.

Examples of skewed distributions are shown in Figure 4.5. In many instances, it is possible to determine whether a distribution is skewed by comparing the mean and the median: if

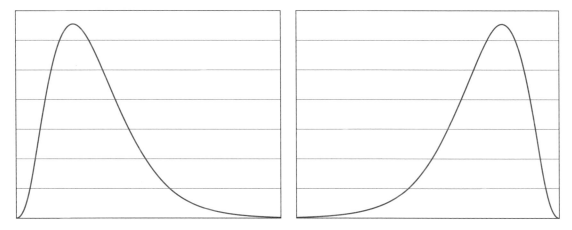

Figure 4.5 Skewed Distributions

the mean is greater than the median, then the distribution is right-skewed, and if the mean is less than the median, then the distribution is left-skewed. This can also often be determined by looking at a histogram and comparing it to the graphs in Figure 4.5. If a distribution is highly skewed, it might not be appropriate to approximate with a normal distribution.

The words *skew*, *skewed*, *skews*, and other related terms are among the most misused statistical terms. They have a precise technical meaning, as defined above, but are frequently used incorrectly as a catchphrase for any potential problems with the data or sampling methods.

Measures of Centralness

Managers frequently want a single summary measure of a set of data. Such measures are referred to as measures of centralness or central tendency. Three common statistics that are useful are the *mean*, *median*, and *mode*.

The *sample mean* (also known as the *average*) and denoted by $\bar{x}$, is calculated by adding the observations, then dividing by the number of observations in the sample:

$$\bar{x} = (x_1 + x_2 + x_3 + \ldots + x_n)/n$$

where $\bar{x}$ is the *sample mean*, x_i is the ith observation, and n is the number of data points or the sample size. The mean is a number that sits somewhere in the middle of the data, and is (in a sense) typical of the data.

Let μ denote the population mean, or the average of *all* the observations in the *population*. The population mean is an example of a *parameter*. We do not know the value of μ, but the sample mean can be used to estimate the value of the population mean. In fact, it can be shown that, as the sample size n gets larger, the sample mean converges to the population mean.

- The median for an odd number of observations is the middle observation, once the data have been sorted in order of magnitude. If x_1 denotes the smallest number, and if x_n is the largest, then the middle observation (of an odd number of observations) is $x_{(n+1)/2}$.

and

- The *median* for an even number of observations is the mean of the two middle observations, once the data have been sorted in order of magnitude. The two middle observations are $x_{n/2}$ and $x_{(n/2)+1}$.

The median is commonly used as a measure of centralness for skewed data (i.e., when there are a small number of very large or very small observations). A few large values will lift the mean and result in the mean providing a distorted view of the magnitude of the data. Some examples where medians are commonly used as summary statistics are income statistics, house price statistics, and hospital lengths of stay.

- The mode is the value (or class interval) that occurs most frequently in the data, or the interval in the histogram that has the highest bar.

A glance at the U.S. Household Income distribution (Figure 4.1) suggests that the modal U.S. household income is $100,000 to $149,999, but it would be a mistake to use this range as a measure of the centralness of this data. This is because the class interval for this bin is $50,000, while for lower bins the interval is $2,500. The mode will also likely change as the class interval changes: a class interval of $1,000 will likely lead to a different mode from a class interval of $5,000.

Variation

In addition to the magnitude of the data, it is often useful to know about the variability in the values: are all the values close together or are they distributed over a wide range?

There are a number of summary measures of the variation in sample data, including the range, the variance, and the standard deviation of the data:

- The *range* is a simple measure of variation: the largest value in the data minus the smallest value. This is a broad-brush statistic, since it says nothing about the variation of the other (*n-2*) data points in the sample. We, therefore, generally need more complex measures of variation.
- The *variance, s^2*, approximates the average of the sum of the squared distance from each point to the mean.
- The *standard deviation, s*, is the square root of the variance:

$$\text{standard deviation} = \sqrt{\text{variance}} = s$$

In Excel, the variance and standard deviation are calculated using the formulas = VAR() and = STDEV().

Clearly, when the variance is large, the standard deviation will also be large, and vice versa. Then why are there two similar concepts? The standard deviation is in the same units as the mean, which gives it some practical significance. However, in some applications (such as linear regression—to be discussed in Chapter 5), the variance is needed.

When is it important to know about variation? Consider the following two sets of data, which both have a sample mean of 5:

(1)   4, 5, 6

(2)   −100,000, −50,000, 25, 50,000, 100,000

Simply stating that the mean of both of these groups of numbers is 5 is clearly an incomplete statement: the two sets are vastly different. More than one statistic may be needed to reasonably describe data.

It is, therefore, quite common to summarize and report a sample result by reducing the n values in the sample to a mean and a standard deviation. There is an additional benefit to using means and standard deviations to summarize data: if the distribution is approximately "mound shaped," then the data may follow the three rules of thumb similar to those of the normal distribution (see Figure 4.6). Recall, the three rules of thumb for the normal distribution:

1. About two-thirds of the observations will be within *one* standard deviation of the mean.

2. About 95 percent of the observations will be within *two* standard deviations of the mean.

3. Virtually all observations will be within *three* standard deviations of the mean.

Note that these rules apply quite broadly, often even when the data are not perfectly mound shaped. For example, they apply to the household income data presented in Figure 4.1, even though this data appears quite flat.

These rules allow us to draw important inferences from the summary statistics. For example, if we are told that a sample of commercial drivers were found to work 50 hours/week with a standard deviation of 10 hours, we can infer that:

About 2/3 of drivers work between 40 and 60 hours/week,

about 95% of drivers work between 30 and 70 hours/week, and

almost all drivers work between 20 and 80 hours/week.

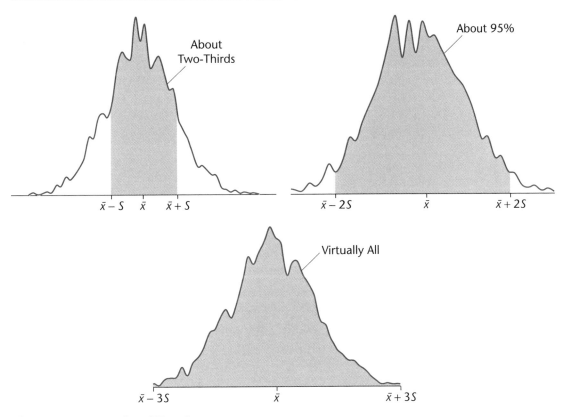

Figure 4.6 Three Rules of Thumb

Variance and standard deviation provide a measure of the possible spread of the observations and are frequently used as measures of *risk*, especially in finance.

Example of the Use of Standard Deviation in Finance

> Standard deviation is the widely accepted method of measuring investment risk. The standard deviation of the month-to-month ups and downs of a fund's return relative to the average, or mean, monthly return for the fund over the period allows one to compare the riskiness of funds with similar investment objectives over a particular time frame. Standard deviations can also be used as an indication of how much more risk a fund in one category has than a fund in another category.
>
> For example: The monthly annualized standard deviation of the UK's FTSE All Share Index was 19.2% during the three years to April 2010. Yet the average actively managed fund in the UK's All Companies sector had a standard deviation of 20.9%; that is, it was more volatile or riskier, according to calculations based on Morningstar data. (*Source*: www.ft.com/cms/s/0/242fecf0–6a83–11df-b282–00144feab49a.html; June 25, 2010)

Sequence

A sample that is collected or measured over time is called a *time series*. Identifying changes over time or "sequence effects" so that future values of a time series can be *forecast* is an essential skill for both corporations and for governments. The table below examples of questions about time series:

BUSINESS	GOVERNMENT
What will next month's sales be?	When will the recession end?
What about next year's sales?	Is unemployment increasing?
How should we budget costs next year?	Will the cost of living be low or high?

When we describe sample data, we often want to differentiate between random series and series that contain "patterns" over time. The time component of a time series may be *explicit*, as would be the case for annual sales data, but is often *implicit*. An implicit time series is one where the data are collected over a period of time, but where the time value is not explicitly recorded.

For example, if we conduct a survey outside a supermarket, the interviews have a time sequence whether we record the time of the interview or not. This may be an important dimension: for example, respondent's answers to a question such as: "Do you ever shop for ice cream?" may change as the daytime temperature warms up.

Stationary and Random Behavior of a Time Series

Managers routinely make decisions as if there were patterns in key time series—in this case, it is important to be sure that there is strong statistical evidence of non-random behavior. The sample statistics, such as mean and standard deviation, are useful in predicting future values of a time series *only if* the value of the series is not changing over time. In this case, variation around the (stationary) mean would be caused by uncontrollable and *random* factors whose effects are summarized by the standard deviation.

We should take a moment to discuss the meaning of *random*. The term *random* has been used conversationally to indicate haphazard behavior of observations or an even-handed way of collecting data (i.e., random sampling). In this context, by stating that the values are randomly distributed about a given value, we mean that there is no sequence or pattern to the values over time that gives us *more* information than these statistics provide.

Observations collected over time are said to be *stationary* if the parameters of the population being sampled are the same at each point in time.

Observations collected over time are said to be *random* if there is no discernible pattern in the sequence of the observations.

If there is a non-random or non-stationary sequence in a time series, the latest observations might help us to predict the next few observations with more precision than would the mean and standard deviation.

Components of Time Series

Time series are often usefully thought of as consisting of three components: *Trend*, *Cycles*, and *Random variation*.

Trend. Trend identifies long-term growth or decline. Trends can be linear or non-linear, increasing or declining (Figure 4.7). *Linear trends* change by a constant value over time (e.g., increasing at a rate of 1,000 units/year). Trends in economic data are often *non-linear* and often multiplicative—that is, change occurs by a constant percentage (e.g., firm sales or national saving may grow at 10% annually).

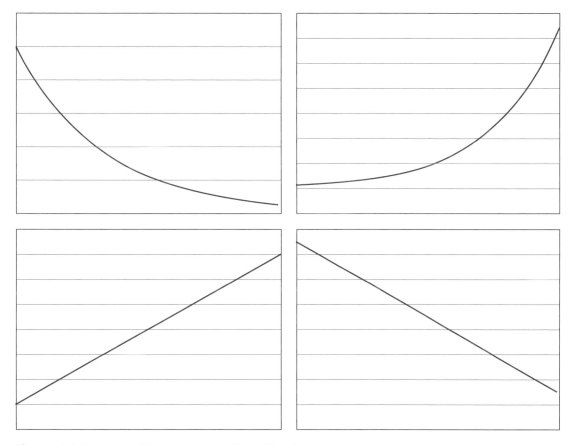

Figure 4.7 Examples of Linear and Non-Linear Trends

Cycles. Cycles produce a wavelike pattern that can be long term (years), or short term (months/weeks/days). Governments are interested in predicting long-term cycles (e.g., economic cycles), while business are usually concerned with shorter cycles, often called *seasonal variation* (Figure 4.8).

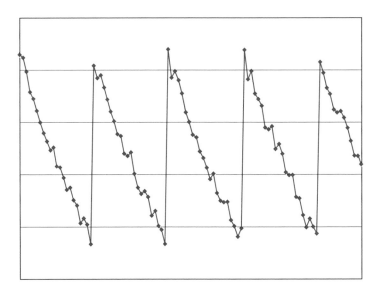

Figure 4.8 An Example of Cycles

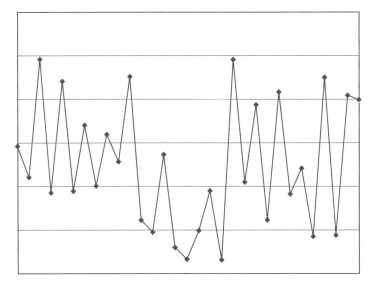

Figure 4.9 Example of Random Variation

Random Variation. Random variations are unpredictable changes in time series not caused by any other component. If random variation is strong compared to underlying cycles or trends, it may hide their existence (Figure 4.9).

Combining (and Separating) Trend, Cycles, and Random Variation

Time series are often made up of a combination of linear trend, cyclical, and random components. Consider the series in Figure 4.10A.

This series was constructed by adding a linear trend, seasonal variation, and random variation. The components of the series are illustrated in Figure 4.10AB:

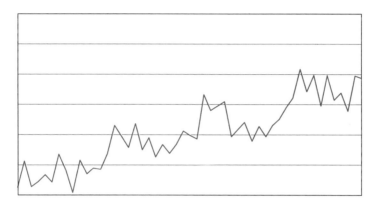

Figure 4.10 A A Composite Time Series

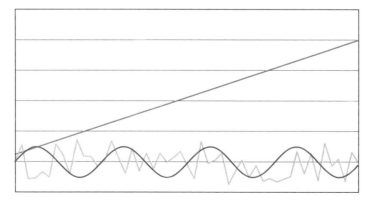

Figure 4.10 B Components of the Time Series in Figure 4.9

Understanding the components of a time series is important if we are to forecast or predict future values for the series. For example, if Figure 4.9 looks like our firm's sales over time, we will need to break out the components of the series in order to develop reasonable forecasts of future values. We can greatly reduce the variability in our forecasts by detecting trend and/or seasonal variation, or other non-random behavior, in a time series. Often, visual inspection of a graph of a time series is sufficient to detect non-random behavior, and there are also formal statistical methods of detecting non-random behavior.

An Example of a Cyclical Time Series

The U.S. unemployment rate followed a cyclical pattern from 1990 to April 2010 (www.bls.gov/bls/unemployment.htm; June 20, 2010) (Figure 4.11).

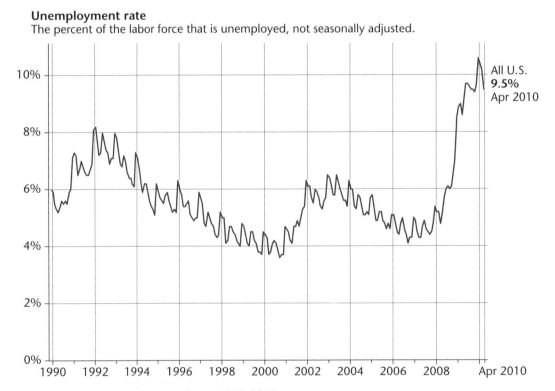

Figure 4.11 U.S. Unemployment Data, 1990–2010
Source: US Bureau of Labor Statistics - last updated May 2010

Estimation and Prediction

Statistical inference is an important task performed by statisticians. Many of the cases and examples considered thus far require you to make statistical inferences, although we have not formally described it in this way.

More formally:

- *Statistical Inference* is the process of drawing conclusions about populations using data from samples.

If we take repeated samples of the same size from the same population, the *distribution of the means* of these samples is called the *sampling distribution*.

- A *sampling distribution* is a distribution of the means (or other measures) of samples of equal size selected from the same population.

Managers encounter estimation and prediction problems every day. They work continually with numbers that are estimates, and must estimate important items in most decision situations. Often, managers use their experience and situational knowledge, plus whatever data is available, to make a best guess of some number of interest. This process of subjective estimation is most appropriate when only rough estimates are needed, or where data collection is expensive.

In everyday use, the words *estimation* and *prediction* are used interchangeably, but when used statistically, there are important differences between these two processes:

- **Estimation** is the process of making statistical inferences about population parameters from sample data.
- **Prediction** is the process of making statistical inferences about the value of new observations from sample data.
- A **point estimate** is a single number that is our best guess as to the value of a population parameter.
- A **point prediction** is a single number that is our best guess as to the value of a new observation drawn from the same population as the sample.

Both estimation and prediction begin with data gathering. Often, we must make use of existing data, perhaps of uncertain origin or quality. In this case, our estimates must be modified to reflect our suspicions about the data. In other situations, statistical estimation procedures begin with a random sample chosen from the population of interest. Note that in most business applications, the sample will be substantially smaller than the population—for example, using the results of a survey or a focus group to make inferences about the preferences of an entire country. In the discussion that follows, we assume that the sample is only a small fraction of the population. If the sample is a high percentage of the population, we must use a different approach (these techniques are beyond the scope of this book).

The Difference Between Estimation and Prediction

A population has parameters, such as a mean μ and standard deviation σ. These values are typically not known, unless it is possible to survey or measure all members of a population. *Estimation* is the process of using a random sample to estimate the values of population parameters (i.e., calculating sample statistics and s and using them to estimate the population parameters μ and σ.) The goal of *prediction* is to forecast a future value of the observation. For example, a typical problem would be to provide probabilities of observing future values from a distribution having mean and standard deviation s.

The objective of the statistical procedures is to develop a distribution (summarized by the mean and standard deviation), which summarizes our understanding of the possible estimates or predictions. The result is likely to be quite complex, and so we often report the result through a *point* or an *interval*.

A point estimate or point prediction is a single number representing our best guess of the uncertain quantity based on information obtained from a sample. We shall consider it to be the mean of the distribution of the estimate or prediction. Different samples may lead to different parameter estimates. To formally capture this possibility, estimates and predictions are often expressed with intervals.

- An **interval estimate** is our best guess of the range that should contain the population parameter.
- A **prediction interval** is our best guess of the range that should contain the next observation drawn from the same population as the sample.

The interval is much more informative if we include the probability that the actual outcome will be in the specified interval, which requires that we know something about the shape of the distribution. The Central Limit Theorem is very useful when we are making estimates of parameters.

The Central Limit Theorem

The Central Limit Theorem (CLT) is important for much of the theory surrounding estimation. The CLT is stated as follows:

> The distribution of the means of a group of large samples of equal size, drawn from the same population, is approximately a normal distribution with mean equal to the population mean and standard deviation equal to the population standard deviation divided by the square root of the sample size. This result is independent of the distribution of the population being sampled.

What is a *distribution of means*? Suppose that you wanted to calculate the mean of some population (the mean income in Canada). To estimate the mean, you gathered a random sample (100 individuals), calculated the mean income in the sample, and used that as an estimate of the mean of the population. If you repeated this process several times—that is, gathered several random samples of the same size—and recorded the means, you would have a list of sample means. Because there is variation throughout the population, the people included in each sample would be different, and hence the means would also be different. Thus, the list of means would form a distribution: a *distribution of means*. The CLT says that, regardless of the underlying distribution of the data, the *distribution of means is a normal distribution* with mean μ and standard deviation $s/\sqrt{n}$, where n is the sample size.

The CLT is often misinterpreted as saying that all distributions are approximately normal or that all naturally occurring phenomena would be approximately normally distributed if large enough sample sizes were observed. This is clearly not true. Rolling a die is an obvious example—the outcomes are uniformly distributed across the 6 sides, *not* normally distributed. As you roll the die more and more times, you would continue to expect roughly 1/6th of the rolls to show each number. While many naturally occurring processes are well approximated by a normal distribution, there are many which are not.

The CLT provides the theoretical justification for two important types of statistical inference: estimation and hypothesis testing.

The Distribution of an Estimate

The *distribution of the estimate* of the population mean is called the *sampling distribution*. The CLT tells us that for large samples, this is a normal distribution. For the normal distribution, the general formula for an $\alpha\%$ confidence interval for the mean is

$$\bar{x} \pm Z_{\alpha/2} \times \frac{s}{\sqrt{n}}$$

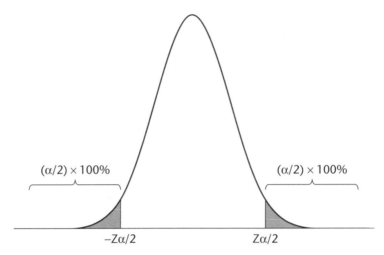

Figure 4.12 Percentage Points of the Normal Distribution

The term $Z_{\alpha/2}$ is a percentage point from the standard normal (i.e., the normal with mean 0 and standard deviation of 1) distribution. It is interpreted as the point where $\alpha/2 \times 100\%$ of thedistribution lies to the right of $Z_{\alpha/2}$. For example, if $\alpha = 5\%$, then $Z_{\alpha/2} = Z_{.025} = 1.96$ (Figure 4.12).

Hypothesis Testing

Often, managers must look at data from two or more samples and make judgments about the underlying populations. Many types of hypothesis tests are possible. The presentation here shall focus on differences between means. Here are some examples:

1. When designing new packaging for a product, management may test-market the product in several different packages and use this test information to decide which package will sell best.
2. It is common to test whether parts produced from a certain machine are "within specs."
3. Several court cases have centered on the hypothesis that occupational or environmental exposure to certain chemicals has led to adverse health outcomes.

Formulating a testable hypothesis requires a precise statement. The following are testable hypotheses:

Will the promotion cost more than the budget of $60,000?

Will the promotion cost between $30,000 and $50,000?

Compare these with some non-testable statements:

What will the promotion cost? (this is an estimation or prediction problem)

Will the promotion do us any good? (not testable without further information).

An article in the *New York Times* (Kenneth Chang, "Enlisting Science's Lessons to Entice More Shoppers to Spend More," September 19, 2006) provides many examples of the results of using hypothesis testing in the retail business:

- Stores use point-of-sales data to address questions about product groupings: For example, shelving two products side-by-side is most effective when customers include both products in their purchase. Data on customers' baskets can show which products should be shelved together.

- Narrow aisles lead to "butt brushes": the data show that shoppers who brush against each other often quickly leave the store without completing their purchases.

- Shoppers tend to turn to the right on entering a store: the data shows that product placed on the left near the entrance does not sell well.

- There is a decompression zone near the store entrance: product placed within five feet of the entrance is most often ignored.

QualPro Inc. of Knoxville, Tennessee, has done extensive statistical testing of car dealers' ads. Through this testing, they can determine what combinations of factors make more effective newspaper ads. For example: is a full-page ad more effective than a half-page? Is color helpful? Is a map showing the dealer's location helpful? The results of the testing: a full-page ad was no more effective than was a half-page, and color alone did not generate extra sales.

The statistical procedures used to formally investigate problems of this type are a second form of statistical inference called *hypothesis tests*. More formally:

- A *hypothesis test* is a formal statistical procedure to judge evidence from a sample against evidence from one or more other sources (that may be other samples).

A hypothesis test is a formal procedure to determine if the difference between the means is *statistically significant*. If you select two random samples, even if the two samples came from the same population, the sample means are likely to be different because the populations were sampled randomly. In other words, a hypothesis tells you if the difference is "big enough."

A hypothesis test has four essential elements:

1.   **The null hypothesis.**

The null hypothesis, usually referred to as H_0, is that there is no difference between the population means from which the samples were drawn.

2.   **The test hypothesis.**

The test hypothesis sometimes referred to as H_A, H_1, or the alternate hypothesis, is usually that the means of the populations sampled are different.

3.   **The P-value.**

The P-value is the probability of the observed data occurring given that the null hypothesis is true (in this case the "observed data" is the observed difference between means). The calculation of the P-value depends on the precise statistical properties of the specific test.

4.   **The rejection region.**

The rejection region is a formal answer to the question, "What level of evidence (or probability) is needed to reject the null hypothesis (that there is no difference between the means) and in so doing accept the alternative hypothesis (that the difference between the means is statistically significant)." An almost universally accepted rule of thumb is that a P-value of 5% or lower provides strong statistical evidence that the null hypothesis is false and, therefore, the test hypothesis is accepted as true. In a two-sample difference of means test, a P-value less than 0.05 leads to the conclusion that the difference between the population means is statistically significant.

The table below examples of both test and null hypotheses:

Test Hypothesis	Null Hypothesis
Will promotion cost exceed $60,000?	Promotion cost $\leq$ $60,000
$30,000 < promotion cost < $50,000	Promotion cost outside this range.

The t-Test

Formal hypothesis tests are often conducted using the t-test. The Central Limit Theorem states that the distribution of the sample means is a normal distribution for large sample sizes, but in many practical applications, the sample size is too small for the Central Limit Theorem to apply. In these situations, a *t-distribution* is used, giving rise to a *t-test*. In Excel, the functions TTEST and TDIST give P-values from t-tests. (In Excel 2010, these functions have been replaced by T.TEST and T.DIST. However, the old functions described here still work.)

We illustrate with t-tests for two situations.

1. Testing whether the means of two samples (whose data is in two arrays in an Excel spreadsheet) are different. In this case, the null hypothesis (H_0) is that the difference in the observed means is zero and the alternative hypothesis (H_A) is that the difference in the observed means is not zero. The formal hypothesis test tells us whether the observed means are far enough apart to conclude that they are different. In Excel, we use the TTEST function, and write = TTEST(array1, array2, 2, 2). The result will be the P-value associated with this test. We would compare this P-value with the rejection region to determine whether to reject the null hypothesis. For example, a P-value of 0.03 would lead us to reject the null hypothesis and conclude that the difference between the observed means is not zero.

2. Testing whether an observed mean is not zero. In this case, the null hypothesis (H_0) is that the observed mean is zero and the alternative hypothesis (H_A) is that the observed mean is not zero. Note that because of sampling error, even if the true mean is zero, the mean in our sample will almost certainly not be zero. The formal hypothesis test tells us whether the observed value is far enough away from zero to conclude that the mean is not zero. (We will see applications of this test in the next chapter when we discuss regression coefficients.) In Excel, we will use the TDIST function, and write = TDIST($\bar{x} \times \sqrt{n}/s$, n, 2), where $\bar{x}$ and s are the sample mean and standard deviation and n is the sample size. As in the previous case, the result is a P-value which we would compare versus the rejection region to determine whether to accept or reject the null hypothesis.

In the examples above, the third argument in both functions was the number 2, which indicates a "2-tailed" test. One-tailed tests are also possible. In the TTEST function, the fourth argument was the number 2, which indicates "Two sample, equal variance." The fourth argument can also be a 1 or 3, corresponding to different assumptions.

Errors in Hypothesis Testing

Because the samples are chosen randomly, drawing conclusion in hypothesis testing always involves some risk of being wrong (some have said that statistics means never having to say you're certain!). These errors are called *Type 1 Errors* and *Type 2 Errors*.

> A **Type 1 Error** is rejection of the *null hypothesis* (and hence a determination that the *test hypothesis* is true) when the *null hypothesis* is really true.

> A **Type 2 Error** is not rejecting the *null hypothesis* (implying that the *test hypothesis* is false) when the *null hypothesis* is really false.

For a given statistical test, the probability of making a Type 1 Error, given the truth of the *null hypothesis*, is the P-value.

In general, statisticians bend over backwards to avoid making Type 1 Errors. Convincing statistical evidence is required before rejecting the null hypothesis, and hence accepting the test hypothesis as true. The common rule for what constitutes "convincing statistical evidence" is that the probability of a Type 1 Error (the P-value) be less than 5% (or 0.05) implies that there be only one chance in 20 that the sample result would reject the null hypothesis by chance alone when it was, in fact, true.

The Distribution of a Prediction

The *distribution of a prediction* is the same as the distribution of the sample. Since we are predicting a new value drawn from the same population as our sample, we expect that the new value will reflect the probabilities contained in the sample. We need to check whether the distribution of the sample is well approximated by a normal distribution. If we can convince ourselves that this is the case, then the general formula for an α% prediction interval is

$$\bar{x} \pm Z_{\alpha/2} \times s$$

where $\bar{x} \pm Z \times s$ is a percentage point from a normal distribution.

Making Predictions

We have seen in earlier chapters that decision making into the future requires that probabilities of future events. Often, sample data and the distribution of a prediction can provide such probabilities. Since the distribution of the sample data is also the distribution of the prediction, we can use the sample data directly and count probabilities of various outcomes.

In small samples, we can improve our probability assessment by fitting the sample data to a theoretical curve and then reading the probabilities off the theoretical curve. Often, we find that sample data can be well approximated by a normal distribution, in which case the Excel function = NORMDIST($x, \bar{x}, s, 1$) provides assessments of probabilities for any value of x.

Example:

The last 6 properties in a subdivision have sold for 95.0%, 104.6%, 101.7%, 98.3%, 101.0% and 101.5%, of the listed price. We have $\bar{x} = 100.35$, $s = 3.30$.

Then = NORMDIST(99,100.35,3.3,1) = 0.34

= NORMDIST(100,100.35,3.3,1) = 0.46

= NORMDIST(101,100.35,3.3,1) = 0.58

Provide estimates of the probabilities that the next property will sell at less than 99% (0.34), less than 100% (0.46), or less than 101% (0.58) of the listed price.

An Example to Illustrate the Difference Between Estimation and Prediction

Example: Detailed recordkeeping over a 10-day period at a fast food restaurant found that the number of customers during the busy lunch rush on business days had an average of 120 customers, with a standard deviation of 20.

- Note that the sample size, $n = 10$ in this case because observations were collected on 10 different days.
- The *point estimate* is the sample mean: 120 in this case.
- The *95% interval estimate* or the *95% confidence interval* for the mean is the range centered on the mean that includes 95% of the sampling distribution. As stated earlier, the standard deviation of the sampling distribution is $s/\sqrt{n}$ (from the Central Limit Theorem). Thus, the *95% confidence interval* for the mean is $\bar{x} \pm 1.96 \times s/\sqrt{n} = 120 \pm 1.96 \times 20/\sqrt{10} = (107.6, 132.4)$.
- The *point prediction* is the sample mean, 120 in this case.
- The *95% prediction interval* is the range centered on the mean that includes 95% of the sample distribution. If we can convince ourselves that the sample distribution is approximately normal, we can use $\bar{x} \pm 1.96 \times s$ as the prediction interval or (80.8, 159.2).

Note that the point estimate and the point prediction are the same (and equal to the sample mean), but the intervals are very different. Why? With estimation, the goal is to guess the value of a population parameter. As you gather more data, you become more confident in your guess, so your range of uncertainty about the value of the population parameter (represented by the confidence interval) shrinks. With prediction, the goal is to guess the value of a future observation. As you gather more data, you become more confident in your estimates of the underlying population parameters. However, having more confidence in the values of the parameters does not shrink the range of uncertainty in your guesses of future values.

Data-Driven Decision Making in Action

Descriptive Statistics Pay a Key Role in Investment Decision Making

Many organizations (for example, Morningstar, Dow Jones, Reuters) publish reports assessing the investment potential of the wide variety of financial products that can be purchased by individual or institutional investors. For example, investors looking to buy (or sell) Mutual Funds and/or Exchange Traded Funds will often study such reports to help guide their decision making. These reports are full of descriptive statistics that summarize the historical performance of the assets. It is common to include average returns of an investment in the fund for the last year, the last two years, the last five years, and the last ten years, together with standard deviations of returns for these same time periods. There are usually also histograms of (monthly) returns, sequence graphs of prices, and a great many specialized statistics (for example, Sharpe Ratios) that have meaning to people working in the financial services industry.

To take a look at a typical report, go to www.morningstar.com and choose your favorite stock or fund (you have to register, but it is free).

Hypothesis Tests Drive the Development of New Medical Treatments

Once a promising new drug, pharmaceutical, or treatment has been developed, it must be tested to demonstrate that it is effective. These *clinical trials* often follow a set pattern. Two samples of patients are chosen, usually using some form of random selection. Patients in one sample (the *treatment* sample) are given the new drug, while patients in the second sample (the *control* sample) are given a placebo (that is a pill or injection that appears equivalent to the new drug but is actually sugar or water). Measures that show the effectiveness of the new treatment are taken for both groups, and hypothesis tests are used to try to prove statistically that the new treatment is more effective than the placebo. To avoid the biases introduced by those conducting the test, clinical trials are usually *double-blind*: that is neither the patient nor the physicians administering the drugs or collecting the data know whether the patient belongs to the control group or the treatment group.

Moneyball

The Oakland Athletics baseball organization faced the problem of having to compete with other much richer teams, requiring the manager Billy Beane to try to find players who were undervalued by his competitors. With the assistance of Paul DePodesta, who had a background in baseball statistics (also called *sabermetrics*), Beane assembled a team that successfully competed against teams with much larger salary budgets. Beane came to believe that the collective wisdom of many baseball insiders was not supported by the data, and used refined measures of player's on-field performance to use his scarce salary dollars to buy high-performing players that the other teams had ignored or did not value so highly. Beane's Athletics won the divisional title in 2000, 2002, and 2003.

The story of Billy Beane and the Oakland A's is told in the book: Michael Lewis, *Moneyball: The Art of Winning an Unfair Game*, W.W. Norton, 2004, and the movie *Moneyball*, starring Brad Pitt (2011).

Summary

In this chapter, we introduced some important ideas from statistics that help managers cope with data. These concepts provide many good questions to ask. For example: How was the sample chosen? What statistics were calculated?

These statistical ideas also provide a basic framework that the manager can use in working with data, and extracting useful information from data to help with decision making. Data extraction often includes:

- Using sample data to estimate probabilities or predictions of future values.

- Estimating population parameters using data from a sample.

- Testing hypotheses about population parameters, either single populations or multiple populations, using data from samples.

What the Manager Must Know

- When presented with a large volume of data, a useful first step is to ask whether the data is a sample, a population, or something else.

- It the data is a sample, it is important to know how the sample was selected. Was the sample selected using a process that is likely to provide a clear (and unbiased) picture of the population being sampled?

- Poor sample selection techniques may result in biased samples. A number of techniques exist to analyze data. However, if there is bias, then the results may not yield good information.

- It is often helpful to summarize data using the four basic properties of a sample: centralness, variation, distribution, and sequence.

- It is also useful to draw a histogram to see the shape of the entire distribution and a line plot to look for obvious sequence effects (such as trends and seasonality in time series data).

- Descriptive statistics (for example: mean, median, variance) and descriptors of distribution (symmetrical, normal-like, skewed) are a common part of management vocabulary when discussing data. It is important to be thoroughly familiar with these terms.

- Hypothesis testing provides a set of formal tools that establish statistical "proof" (called "statistical significance") of questions of interest. While statistical proof is rarely absolute, a P-value < 0.05 in a hypothesis test is almost universally accepted as providing strong statistical evidence in support of the test hypothesis.

Appendix 1 Statistics in Excel

Many of the statistics tools needed in Excel can be accessed as spreadsheet functions, or they are available through the Data Analysis ToolPak. Many spreadsheet functions have intuitive descriptive names (such as *average, median, min, max*). Other statistical functions can be found in the "Statistical" listing in the "Insert Function" dialog box.

It may be necessary to install the Data Analysis ToolPak the first time you use it. To do this in Excel 2007, click on the Office button, then select Excel Options, Add-Ins, and at the bottom of the dialog box select Manage Excel Add-Ins (see below). Then check the box for the Data Analysis ToolPak. A similar process is used to install the Solver Add-In, which is used later in this book. In Excel 2010, select Options from the File Menu, and then follow the same steps as in Excel 2007.

To install the Analysis tool pack in Excel 2003, select Tools–Add-ins, and then check the appropriate check box.

The Data Analysis add-in is accessed on the far right of the Data tab. When you click the Data Analysis button, the Data Analysis dialog box appears. From here, you select a data analysis function (e.g., histogram, regression analysis), and another dialog box will appear.

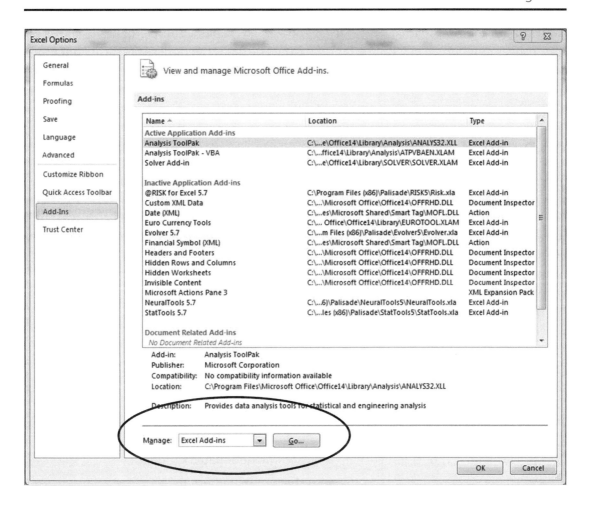

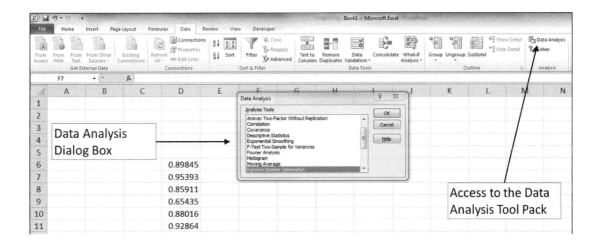

Note that, in addition to the Data Analysis ToolPak, Excel has a number of useful statistical spreadsheet functions. They can be found on the Formulas tab under Statistical Functions. Many have names that give a good description of their function (e.g., AVERAGE(), MEDIAN(), etc.).

Appendix 2 Technical Details

Binomial Sampling

In a binomial sample, each observation takes on one of two values only. These values can be described in various ways:

> Yes or No
>
> 0 or 1
>
> Good or Bad
>
> Heads or Tails
>
> Belonging or Not Belonging to some group.

Two statistics describe a binomial sampling result.

- The count (x) or number that belong to the designated group, or
- The proportion (p) of the sample in the designated group.

In a sample of n observations, where the count (x) of observations belong to the designated group, the value of p is given by:

$$p = x / n$$

If a fraction p belongs to the designated group, then a fraction $(1-p)$ does not belong.

If 4 out of 5 dentists recommend Brand X toothpaste, then 1 out of 5 does not.

Note the difference between the following two statements:

1. In a sample of 5 dentists, 4 recommended Brand X toothpaste, and
2. 80% of dentists recommend Brand X toothpaste.

The first of these reports a sample result, while the second makes a statistical inference about a population.

The variation of a proportion is also of interest. Two variations can be useful:

1. The variation of the count (x), and
2. The variation of the proportion (p).

If repeated samples of size n are selected from a population in which a proportion (p) of the observations belong to a designated group:

1. The variance of the count of "1s" $= n\,p\,(1\text{-}p)$
2. The variance of the proportion of "1s" $= p\,(1\text{-}p)/n$

Variation

For a data set $x_1, x_2, x_3, \ldots x_n$, with sample mean $\bar{x}$, the *variance* is calculated as

$$\text{variance} = s^2 = \frac{(x_1 - \bar{x})^2 + (x_2 - \bar{x})^2 + (x_3 - \bar{x})^2 + \ldots + (x_n - \bar{x})^2}{n - 1}$$

The *standard deviation, s*, is the square root of the variance:

$$\text{standard deviation} = \sqrt{\text{variance}} = s$$

In Excel, the variance of a sample can be calculated with the formula = VAR.S() (or = VAR() in Excel 2007 or earlier). The standard deviation of a sample can be calculated with the formula = STDEV.S() (or = STDEV() in Excel 2007 or earlier).

Skewness

Suppose there are n data observations, $x_1, x_2, x_3, \ldots x_n$. Let $\bar{x}$ be the sample mean and s be the sample standard deviation. Then the skewness is calculated as

$$\text{skewness} = \frac{(x_1 - \bar{x})^3 + (x_2 - \bar{x})^3 + (x_3 - \bar{x})^3 + \ldots + (x_n - \bar{x})^3}{(n - 1)s^3}$$

In Excel, skewness is calculated with the formula = SKEW().

Appendix 3 Graphing and Visualizing Data

Graphs can be very powerful tools to help summarize statistical information. However, they can also be used poorly. Excel and other statistical programs have several options that support the creation of very sophisticated graphs. However, complicated graphs are not always the best, and in many cases a simple graph does a better job at illustrating data than does a complicated one. In this appendix, we present a number of examples of good and bad practice in graphing data.

Creating Informative Graphs

Before presenting some insights about creating informative graphs, we present some poor graphs. These examples of less-than-informative graphs are all based on real situations and have been taken from the news (although the examples have been disguised). These examples can be viewed from the perspective of either the writer or the reader. The writer presumably wants to present data in a way that supports a particular point-of-view, while the reader is probably interested in seeing through the presentation to find the real facts.

For the purposes of this presentation, we divide graphs into three categories: Graphs that, although statistically correct, provide a distorted impression of the numbers; graphs that achieve their distortion of the data by taking liberties with statistical accuracy; and graphs that raise unnecessary questions.

Graphs That, Although Statistically Correct, Provide a Distorted Impression of the Numbers

The first example is one that shows a very common method of distorting the change in data. Figure 4.A3.1 illustrates a private sector version.

This type of chart is particularly effective if the vertical scale is "forgotten," as in this example. This technique achieves its distortion through the fact that the viewer of these charts tends to assess the relative height of the bars: We infer that business is down more than 100% (the 2008 bar is more than twice the height of the 2009 bar). A chart plotted with a zero vertical baseline (and appropriately labeled) may give a very different impression.

Here is a public sector version: Figure 4.A3.2 could be easily interpreted as a reduction of more than 50%.

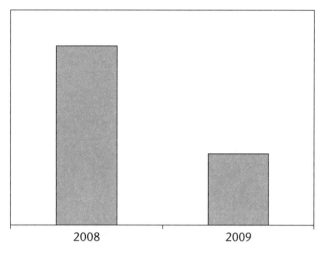

Figure 4.A3.1 Business Is Crashing?

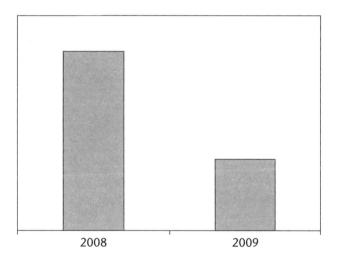

Figure 4.A3.2 Public Sector Data: The Budget Has Been "Slashed"?

Without a vertical scale and indication of zero on the vertical axis, the relative height of the bars is subject to misinterpretation. Again, adding a vertical scale and a true zero might provide a very different impression.

A second type of distortion involves the use of *unorthodox or confusing scales*. Take a quick look at Figure 4.A3.3.

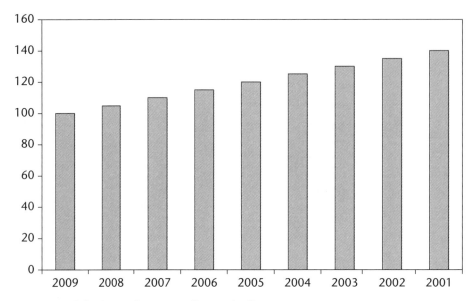

Figure 4.A3.3 Are Sales Increasing . . . or Decreasing?

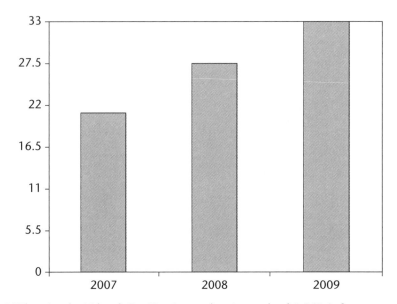

Figure 4.A3.4 What Are the Values? Can You Interpolate Intervals of 5.5 Units?

Most people looking at Figure 4.A3.3 initially see increasing sales. Only on more careful inspection do they recognize that the chart actually shows sales decreasing over time: we have a strong intuitive sense that time runs from left to right on a chart, and when this is violated, it may not be picked up immediately. Another example of creating confusion

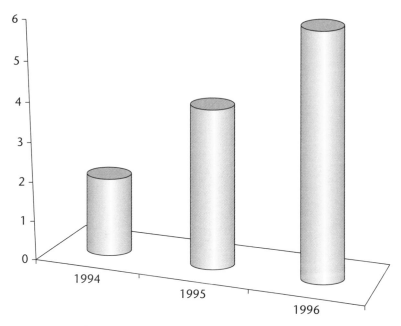

Figure 4.A3.5 Can You Read the Heights of the "Bars"?

through scales involves the use of unusual numbering schemes or interval labeling. How high are the bars in the bar chart in Figure 4.A3.4?

Most of us don't count in units of 5.5, so reading off the values from chart involves quite a bit of effort. A minor variant of this technique is to use undecipherable values on the horizontal axis. To really confound the viewer, do this for both axes. Such graphs appear quite often since, unfortunately, the automatic scaling feature in Excel makes their production very easy.

Another simple technique that often serves to disguise rather than clarify data values is the use of pictorial icons instead of bars, such as often happens when a graphic designer attempts to add visual appeal to a bar chart. When the icons are drawn in three dimensions, unraveling the chart to reveal the data can be particularly confusing. For example, can you read off the heights of the barrels on Figure 4.A3.5?

In Figure 4.A3.5, at least, the icons are the same width. If the width of the icons is changed, the viewer can be confused by the apparent volume change: a tall and wider icon has the visual effect of exaggerating the change, since the viewer sees a volume increase as well as the intended change in height. In Figure 4.A3.6, the volume change due to the changing "bar" width makes for additional confusion.

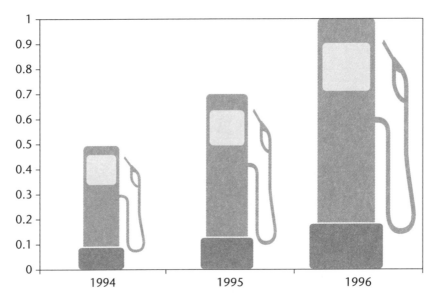

Figure 4.A3.6 Is Height or Volume Relative?

Graphical Techniques That Present a Distorted View of the Numbers by Violating Statistical Convention

By far the most common distortion is the use of truncation. Truncation of the bars in a bar chart is a common way of "tidying up" a graph, but statistical convention requires that the heights of the bars remain proportional to the data values. Figure 4.A3.7 is one graphic designer's illustration where it is almost impossible to find the true message in the data.

Another obvious graphical distortion is to somehow pretend that one can plot negative numbers differently than positive numbers (particularly if these are profits and losses). Figure 4.A3.8 shows a type of graph that is common in corporate annual reports.

If the hidden negative values were plotted the same way as the positives, the visual impression would be quite different!

Another common distortion is to ignore the numbers when plotting the graph. Try to figure out Figure 4.A3.9.

One would like to conclude that this kind of statistical effort would never pass the proof-readers, but the existence of such graphs in the business literature suggests that it is wise to check. This kind of distortion is much more difficult to spot if the numbers are not included with or on the graph!

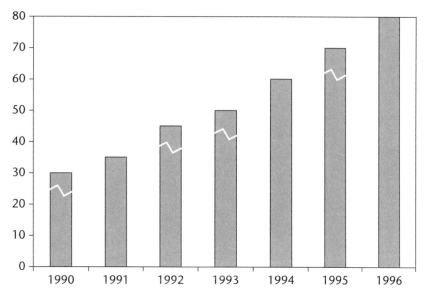

Figure 4.A3.7 Arbitrary Truncation May Conceal the True Message of the Data

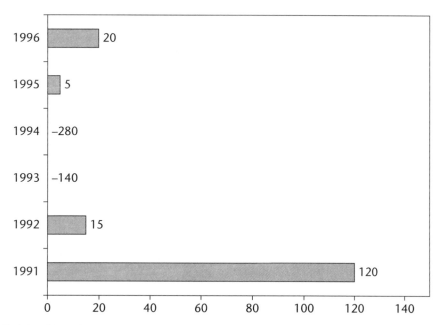

Figure 4.A3.8 No Negative News

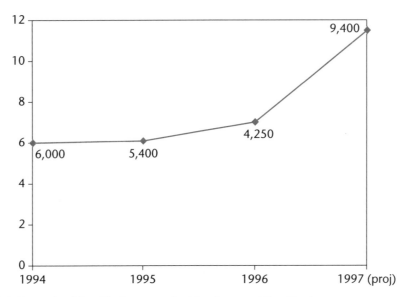

Figure 4.A3.9 Unresolved Conflict between the Numbers and the Chart

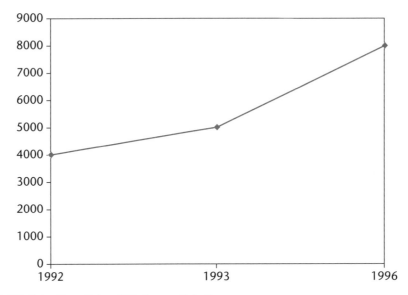

Figure 4.A3.10 Sales Have Taken Off: True or False?

Figure 4.A3.10 illustrates another example of sleight-of-hand that can be used make political points.

Finally, in the next section there are some examples of charts that, for one reason or other, ask more questions than they answer.

Graphs Where the Message Is Unnecessarily Confusing

The choice of words to use to label charts may well have an impact on the message sent or received. Poor labels can add confusion. It takes some effort to find the problem with the labeling of Figure 4.A3.11.

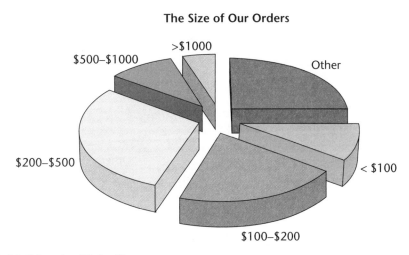

Figure 4.A3.11 What Are "Other"?

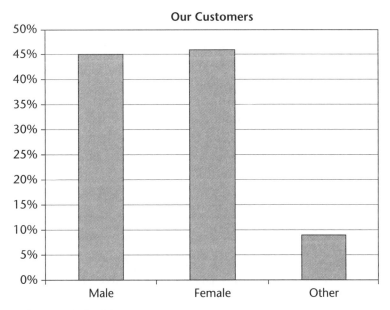

Figure 4.A3.12 Who Are "Other"?

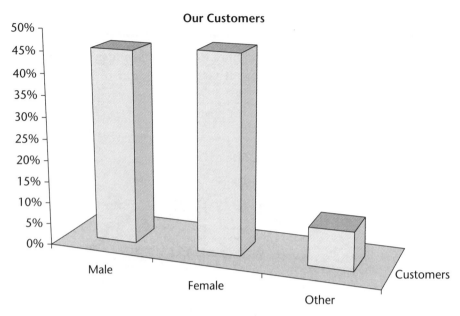

Figure 4.A3.13 3-D May Be Decorative But Is Often Difficult to Read

Sometimes, labels can be unintentionally humorous. In Figure 4.A3.12, the issue raised (by accident?) is more obvious:

If "Other" were labeled as "We Don't Know," or "Businesses," or "Unclassified," then the many obvious questions would be preempted.

Three-dimensional graphs can be particularly difficult to interpret. Figure 4.A3.13 shows the same data graphed using Excel in three dimensions.

Note how difficult it is to read the heights of the bars, because of the displacement of the bars away from the vertical zero. In order to read the heights, one has to take a piece of paper and mark the height of the bar, then transfer this distance to the vertical scale and read off the value. This seems like too much work when the purpose of the graphical presentation is to help the viewer understand the data.

So, What Makes an Effective Graph?

An effective graph can add significantly to the viewer's understanding and interpretation of data. An ineffective graph can display the wrong message or can confuse the message carried by the data. When constructing graphs, it is worth the effort to ensure that the image is clear, understandable, follows established conventions, and is statistically correct.

When viewing a graph produced by someone else, it is a good idea to do some basic checking to ensure that the visual message conveyed by the graphical elements is consistent with the message of the data.

Here is a list of good principles when drawing graphs:

- A good graph is accurate and as simple as possible.
- A good graph includes an informative title.
- A good graph has labeled axes and includes units.
- A good graph avoids use of 3-dimensional images.
- A good graph avoids use of bars when lines will do.
- A good graph avoids unnecessary zeros in the units.
- A good graph avoids grid lines when not needed.
- A good graph uses (0,0) as the origin whenever possible.

And a warning—when using Excel, be wary of the difference between scatterplots and line graphs. In a line graph, the values on the horizontal axis are treated as categories and will be evenly spaced, even if they are not supposed to be.

Exercises

1. A potato chip manufacturer was having problems with the Weights and Measures inspectors after the inspectors found some bags containing less than the required 42.5 grams (formerly 1.5 ounces) of chips. In response, the manufacturer had increased the weight setting on the bagging machines to 50 grams, but were now over-packing the bags and, consequently, giving away chips.

   A random sample of bags were taken off the line and the chips in the bags were carefully weighed, as shown below:

   1. What is the average weight of chips in a bag?
   2. What is the standard deviation of the chip weights?
   3. According to the three rules of thumb, how many bags per 1,000 are expected to be below the required minimum weight of 42.5 grams?
   4. Plot a histogram of the chip weights. Does the data appear to be well approximated by a normal distribution?

Sample of Chip Weights (grams)				
44.32	55.06	43.39	43.64	55.33
48.42	47.87	51.95	48.79	48.05
47.86	45.80	47.86	54.42	52.67
54.24	49.22	44.85	54.66	48.55
47.67	51.09	53.83	57.57	51.98
49.26	49.97	48.24	48.94	48.86

5. Using the normal distribution approximation, how many bags per 1,000 are expected to be below the required minimum weight of 42.5 grams?

6. What setting (mean chip weight) should be used to ensure that "almost all" the bags contain at least 42.5 grams of chips while minimizing the excess chips in the bags?

2. The chief cashier of a bank must manage the cash holding so as to gain interest by investing excess cash where possible, but at the same time keep sufficient cash on hand to meet the bank's needs. A major issue for the chief cashier is the uncertainty that results from the Federal Reserve Board's (the Fed's) clearing balance. The clearing balance is the difference between the dollar value of checks written by the bank's customers and cleared through the Fed, and the dollar value of checks received but written on other banks and clear through the Fed.

The chief cashier has recorded the last eight weeks of clearing balances (a longer period is available, but we will use just eight weeks here). The 40 observations of daily check clearings are shown below:

$21,697,208	−$10,243,791	$37,844,391	−$3,648,650	$3,894,647
−$32,977,193	$30,056,844	$81,001,561	$73,625,609	$5,027,402
$60,311,999	$117,896,711	$57,425,429	$34,537,810	$21,449,620
$29,981,227	−$1,672,896	$28,157,292	$5,757,982	$31,467,912
$28,030,404	$24,650,044	$10,019,384	$40,873,515	$31,238,163
−$8,448,464	$61,116,423	$21,886,686	$59,296,515	$23,307,164
$53,479,593	−$4,794,679	$27,584,465	$29,387,165	$93,434,414
$38,561,233	$24,066,627	$8,059,567	−$31,816,724	$65,555,653

1. Provide point and interval estimates of the mean daily clearing balance.

2. Provide point and interval predictions (or forecasts) of tomorrow's clearing balance.

3. A package goods supplier designed a new package ("white") that it thought was more appealing than its old package ("blue"). It conducted a 10-week trial of the two packages in selected "matched" stores with the results shown below (sales in thousands of dollars).

   1. Is there any statistical evidence that one or other package leads to higher sales?

Container Color		
Week	Blue	White
1	8.4	9.2
2	4.9	5.3
3	3.3	3.1
4	6.9	7.6
5	9.3	9.2
6	8.7	9.2
7	5.3	5.7
8	3.4	4.4
9	6.9	7.8
10	7.9	8.5

Recommended Cases

Firestone: Pay no dough if it doesn't snow (Ivey)

Ani Jewelers (Ivey)

Domglas (Ivey)

Ian Steele (Ivey)

Elite Rental Car Company (Ivey)

Bamberger's Department Store (Ivey)

Lanco Catalogue Sales (Ivey)

Lake Erie Paper (Ivey)

Visteon Inc. (Ivey)

Big East Bank (Harvard)

The Morrice Collection (Ivey)

SouthWest Hospital Corporation (A) and (B) (Ivey)

Pilgrim Bank (A), (B) and (C) (Harvard)

Dollar Thrifty Automotive Group: Online Discounting (Ivey)

Online Auctions—Dell Financial Services (A) (Ivey)

CHAPTER 5

PREDICTIVE MODELING

Two common management problems are forecasting and prediction. For example, managers must often forecast sales in future periods based on historical data, or they must predict the financial performance of a new product or a franchise opened at a new location.

Prediction is the more general term that refers to any attempt to assess the value of something unknown: we can predict someone's weight, the warranty claim rate of a product, or the cost-of-goods-sold. *Forecasting* is a more specific term that refers to prediction applied to time series data: we forecast future sales, or the growth rate of the economy. This chapter covers a set of techniques, called *predictive modeling* or *statistical regression*, that enable us to use data we have to predict or forecast something we do not know.

Regression with One Independent Variable

Predictive modeling exploits correlation between two variables—one of which we wish to predict, the other we know already.

Two variables, which we will call x and y, are positively correlated if they tend to move together—that is, when x is large, y tends to be large; or when x is small, y tends to be small. For example, sales of cars and steel are positively correlated—when automobile production is booming, so is the steel industry (in part because automobile manufacturing is a major consumer of steel). Figure 5.1 is a scatterplot that shows positive correlation.

Negative correlation exists when two variables tend to move in opposite directions—when x is large, y tends to be small; or when x is small, y tends to be large. The price of a shirt and the sales of that shirt may be negatively correlated—the higher the price, the fewer shirts sold (Figure 5.2).

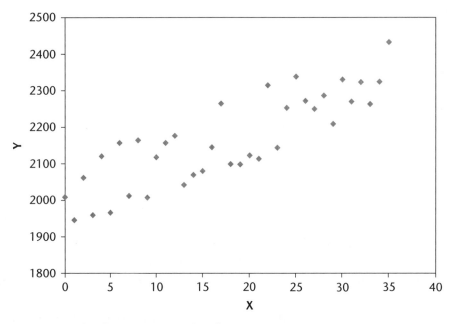

Figure 5.1 A Scatterplot Showing Positive Correlation

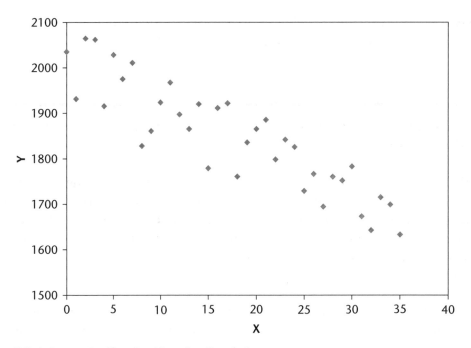

Figure 5.2 A Scatterplot Showing Negative Correlation

Conventions and Terminology

In order to discuss regression and correlation, we will make use of straight-line graphs and the formulae that summarize them. There are conventions to plotting or graphing variables. We call x the *independent variable* and always plot x values on the horizontal axis. We will call y the *dependent variable* and always plot y on the vertical axis. We speak of the value of variable y *depending on* the value of variable x. Our objective is to predict future values of the dependent variable y by taking into account known values of x.

Causality

We will be using x to predict y. However, a general statement about statistical dependence should not be confused with the stronger statement that x causes y. To prove causality from x to y usually requires careful observation and experimentation. For example, in the pharmaceutical industry, dependence can be ascertained by observing how patients respond in clinical trials, whereas causality would require an understanding of the underlying biological mechanisms that led to the observed trial results.

Although causality is an important research issue, it is frequently not important in the managerial use of correlation. Often we are looking for an exploitable relationship between two variables. If the known value of some variable, x, helps us to predict the unknown value of some variable, y, which is an important factor in our decision-making, then whether x causes y or y causes x is irrelevant to our use of the relationship. Provided x and y are correlated, we can use x to predict y without resolving the causality issue.

For example, it is fairly well established that the number of housing starts is a leading indicator of economic activity. When housing starts increase, the level of business activity picks up. For a firm in the roofing business, this link has a plausible, causal interpretation: more new houses mean more new roofs. For an automobile dealership, the dependence of new car sales on housing starts is less obvious. However, a dealer who finds that housing starts are a useful indicator of future car sales should still go ahead and exploit the observed relationship.

Linear Regression

Linear regression is a tool to fit a model between a dependent variable (y) and an independent variable (x). We shall present linear regression in the context of the Paradec example.

Paradec Inc.—Bank Service Charges

Ed Sutton, treasurer of Paradec Corporation, had just been notified that Paradec's bank had charged the corporation $8,400 for banking services for March 2009. Sutton's first reaction was that a corporation of Paradec's size ought to be able to negotiate a better banking deal, and he wondered whether he should call the bank and arrange an appointment.

Paradec was a medium-sized manufacturer of plastic molded products, with annual sales of $435 million in 2008. They operated a major manufacturing facility in the Midwest, and distributed in 12 neighboring states.

Paradec had dealt with a single bank for many years. Their demands for banking services had expanded considerably since that time, as had the service charges paid to the bank. These service charges included check processing fees, deposit and wire service charges, standby credit charges, and fees for various other services using by the corporation (account consolidations, statements, etc.).

Sutton's problem in reviewing these charges was that he had no real basis for comparison. It occurred to him that bank charges of $8,400 per month might indicate that Paradec's cash management group was not doing a very good job of managing the corporation's bank accounts.

Still concerned about bank charges, Sutton attended a meeting of the local cash management association later that week. Over lunch, he asked several members about their banks' service charges and found his colleagues to be very interested in exchanging information on the topic. In an hour, he was able to write down the names of 20 corporations and their monthly bank charges, as estimated by their cash managers. When he returned to the office, he listed the figures shown below:

Bank Charges (in $/month)

13,750	4,000	1,150	15,000
2,500	15,000	9,000	6,000
3,000	6,000	4,500	3,500
5,000	7,000	1,000	1,500
5,000	8,000	2,500	2,000

The mean charges for these 20 corporations worked out to $5,770 per month. Compared with this mean, Paradec's charged seemed high, but Sutton recognized that there were many reasons for differences in bank charges across corporations. In particular, larger firms would be expected to pay higher charges than would smaller firms, since the larger firm would likely process more checks and use more extensive bank services. Sutton therefore gave his assistant the task of finding out the 2008 annual sales for the 20 corporations for which he had data. Sutton loaded both 2008 sales (in $million) and bank charges (in $/month) into a new Excel workbook (columns A and B, Table 5.1).

(Note that Sutton has not included Paradec's data. He is interested in investigating how Paradec compares to other corporations: if he included his own data, he would, to some extent, be comparing Paradec with itself).

Table 5.1: Paradec Data

	A	B
1	Paradec Corporation	
2	Sales	Charges
3	850	13750
4	491	2500
5	202	3000
6	493	5000
7	294	5000
8	277	1150
9	600	9000
10	150	4500
11	462	1000
12	250	2500
13	332	4000
14	570	15000
15	468	6000
16	400	7000
17	309	8000
18	864	15000
19	188	6000
20	368	3500
21	34.2	1500
22	220	2000

Paradec Analysis

Examination of these observations seems to confirm Sutton's view that larger corporations pay higher bank charges than do smaller corporations. That is, corporation sizes, as measured by 2008 annual sales, and bank charges are positively correlated. In particular, the largest corporation has the highest bank charges (row 18, Table 5.1) and the smallest corporation has almost the smallest charges (row 21), but there are several observations that do not seem to fit the simple relationship (for example, row 14).

We can see the correlation between sales and bank charges more clearly if we plot the data (Figure 5.3). Below is a plot of sales as the independent variable (plotted on the horizontal or x-axis) and bank charges as the dependent variable (plotted on the vertical or y-axis). This choice of dependent and independent variables is based on the reasoning that bank charges should depend on firm size.

The mean charges for these 20 corporations worked out to $5,770 per month. Without further information, we can estimate the banking charges for Paradec (not in the above sample) or any other firm to be about $5,770 per month. In statistical terms, this is a prediction problem, and the distribution of the sample provides our distribution of the prediction. For example, there is 0.1 probability (based on 2 occurrences in 20) that a company will pay more than $15,000 monthly in bank charges.

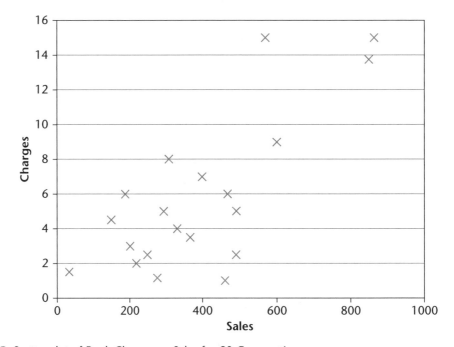

Figure 5.3 Scatterplot of Bank Charges vs Sales for 20 Corporations

However, the scatterplot in Figure 5.3 illustrates a strong correlation between bank charges and firm sales: the charges a firm pays for banking services *depends on* the size of the firm, as measured by its 2008 annual sales. If we know the size of the firm, we ought to be able to more accurately predict bank charges. This seems sensible—a larger company with more sales is likely to make greater use of bank services.

Figure 5.3 shows a positive correlation between the two variables. The bank charges cluster in a pattern that has higher values at higher levels of sales. To reflect this, we have drawn a line on the graph that seems to summarize the relationship (Figure 5.4). We could imagine drawing this line by moving a straight edge around on the graph, trying to find a spot where the line seemed to be as close to as many points as possible. A line drawn in such a way would be determined by judgment; there would be no "correct" line—different individuals would arrive at different lines.

To summarize the graph, we use the equation for a line. In a scatterplot with one dependent variable and one independent variable, the general form of the equation for a line is:

$$\hat{y} = a + bx$$

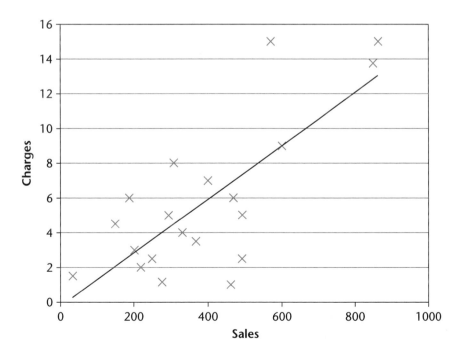

Figure 5.4 Scatterplot of Bank Charges vs Sales for 20 Corporations with a Line of Best Fit

where $\hat{y}$ is the predicted value of the dependent variable (called *Fitted-y*), x is the observed value of the independent variable, a is called the *intercept*, and b is the *slope*. For the specific application of Paradec Corporation, we could rewrite the equation for the line as:

Fitted bank charges (\$/month) = $a + b \times$ Annual sales (\$ million)

This equation is a representation or model of the relationship between two variables. When developing this model or equation, is it convenient to be able to calculate the values of the slope and intercept (so we don't have to plot the data and fit a line by eye every time.) The most widely used method to calculate the slope and intercept is called the *least-squares method* and the resulting line is called the *regression line*. This line can be used to estimate, or predict, the value of the dependent variable (bank charges) at any given value of the independent variable (annual sales), and is also called the *prediction equation* or the *regression equation*. How do we use the regression equation to make predictions? If we know the values of a, b, and x (annual sales), we can then solve for *Fitted-y* (the predicted bank charges) by using the regression equation. In the next section, we will discuss how to use Excel linear regression to find a and b.

Using a Scatter Plot

Inspection of a scatter plot can provide useful information. Here are three things to look for:

1. Does the plot show correlation between the variables? Try fitting a line to the data by eye—does this line slope up or down? If there is no obvious slope to this line, or no clear place to draw the line, then the relationship between the two variables is probably too weak to be exploitable.

2. Is the relationship between the variables linear? Often a curve fits the shape of the data points better than does a straight line—try fitting differently shaped curves by eye. Nonlinear relationships are very common in data where the dependent variable is time (for example, think about the value of a savings account growing with compound interest). In some cases, nonlinearity results from seasonality; in others, from the fact that variables may change at a percentage (i.e., proportional) rate over time, rather than at a linear rate. If visual inspection reveals a nonlinear relation, then it would be inappropriate to fit a model that assumes a linear relationship. We will discuss some techniques to handle nonlinear models later.

3. If we fit a line or curve to the data, are the data points uniformly scattered around the line or curve? "Uniformly scattered" means that the observations show the same degree of dispersion from the fitted line for all values of y'. This property is called *homoscedasticity*. Homoscedasticity is an underlying assumption of

regression models, so if this property does not hold, then it may be inappropriate to use a linear regression model.

Linear Regression Using Excel

The values of the regression coefficients (*a* and *b*) are easily calculated by adding a trend line to the graph or by using the Excel Data Analysis Tool Pack. To add a trend line to the graph, right-click on any point in the series. Choose "Add trendline" from the pop-up menu. The default is a linear trendline. Select "Display equation" and "Display R-squared value" in the dialog box (Figures 5.4A and 5.4B).

Reading from the graph, we have the following regression equation:

Fitted bank charges (in $/month) = −244.63 + 15.378 × Annual sales (in $million)

The slope (*b* = 15.378) suggests that, on average, corporations pay $15.378 extra in monthly bank charges for each additional $1 million of sales revenue.

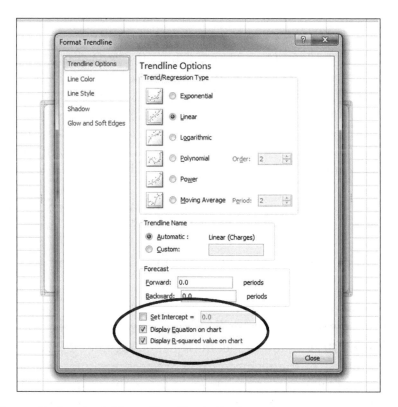

Figure 5.4a Screen Capture for Adding a Trendline in Excel

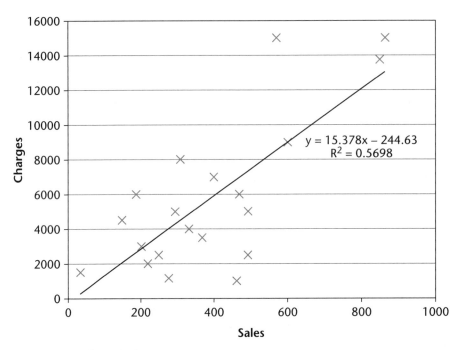

Figure 5.4b Excel Trendline Display

The constant or intercept term ($a = -244.63$) defines the vertical position of the line and has no meaning in this context. It suggests that a corporation with $0 sales revenue would receive $244.63 monthly from the bank. This number may seem nonsensical; however, we would not use this model to predict bank charges for a corporation with $0 sales revenue since we have insufficient data points near $0 to use to fit the model. The constant term is needed to make predictions within the approximate range represented by our sample, but may have no meaning when the independent variable is zero.

The model can be used to estimate an average level of bank charges for a corporation with any level of sales. For example, for Paradec with sales of $435 million:

Estimated bank charges = $-244.63 + 15.378 \times 435 = \$6,444$/month

R^2—The Goodness of Fit Measure

The graph in Figure 5.4b also shows under the equation the line "$R^2 = 0.5698$." In assessing the potential usefulness of the regression line, we seek measures of how well the line fits the sample data. One index of "goodness of fit" is the R^2. The unadjusted *R-squared* (or R^2) is formally defined as the proportion of the total sum-of-the-squares that is explained by the regression line. It is also described as the proportion of total variability in the dependent variable y that is *explained by* the regression model.

We conclude: Bank charges vary across the 20 corporations in our sample (some are high, some are low, etc.). Our regression model, which indicates that companies with low sales have low bank charges, and companies with high sales have high bank charges, explains 56.9% of the variability in bank charges.

R^2 is a useful measure of goodness of fit and can provide guidance on choosing a model when comparing alternate models. However, there are limitations: R^2 is a descriptor only, and, on its own, it does not indicate whether there is statistical evidence of correlation (that is, the regression is *statistically significant*.) There will always be a non-zero slope, even when x and y are unrelated, and thus R^2 will always be greater than zero.

How good does R^2 need to be? This depends entirely on the application. In the physical sciences, where it is possible to run perfectly controlled experiments, it may be necessary to have R^2 values in excess of 0.9. On the other hand, with models that attempt to predict human behavior (for example, understanding what makes people respond to an advertisement), an R^2 value of 0.05 might be considered good.

How Is the Regression Line Determined?

The regression line equation can be used to calculate a predicted value of y for each value of the independent variable x. In general, these predicted values will differ from the actual observed values. This difference is called the *residual*, which is the vertical distance from each observation to the regression line:

$$\text{RESIDUAL} = \text{ACTUAL VALUE} - \text{FITTED VALUE.}$$

Or, for the ith observation in the data set:

$$\text{Residual}_i = y_i - \hat{y}_i$$

A positive residual indicates that the observation lies above the regression line; a negative residual indicates that the observation lies below the line (Figure 5.5). A residual can be calculated for each data point (x_i, y_i). The regression equation is the equation for the line that minimizes the sum of the squared residuals (or the squared vertical distances between the points and the line). In other words, among all possible lines that could be drawn through the cluster of data, the least-squares regression equation is the one that results is the smallest possible value for the sum of the squared residual values.

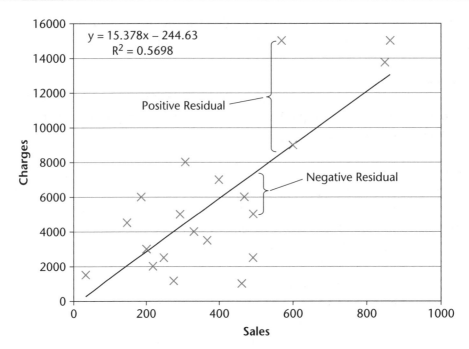

Figure 5.5 Residuals for the Paradec Regression

Regression Details and Diagnostics

The trend line gives two useful pieces of information, but we are often interested in more than that. We can gain additional information by using the Excel Data Analysis Tool Pack. In Excel 2007 and 2010, the tool pack is found under the "Analysis" section of the "Data" tab. In earlier versions, it is a menu item in the "Tools" menu. In all versions of Excel, it may be necessary to install the add-in first.

A regression line can be created by entering the data in the regression tool of the analysis tool pack, as shown in Figure 5.6 for the Paradec data.

It is useful to check the options for "Residuals and "Residual Plots." Clicking "OK" results in the output shown in Figure 5.7.

Some of the information on this screen, such as the R^2, and the intercept and slope, which appear under the *coefficient* values, is familiar from the trend line plot shown earlier. The other information is new and will be discussed in more detail.

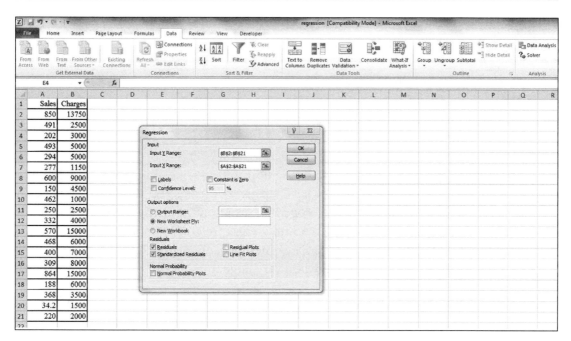

Figure 5.6 The Regression Menu in Excel Data Analysis Tool Pack

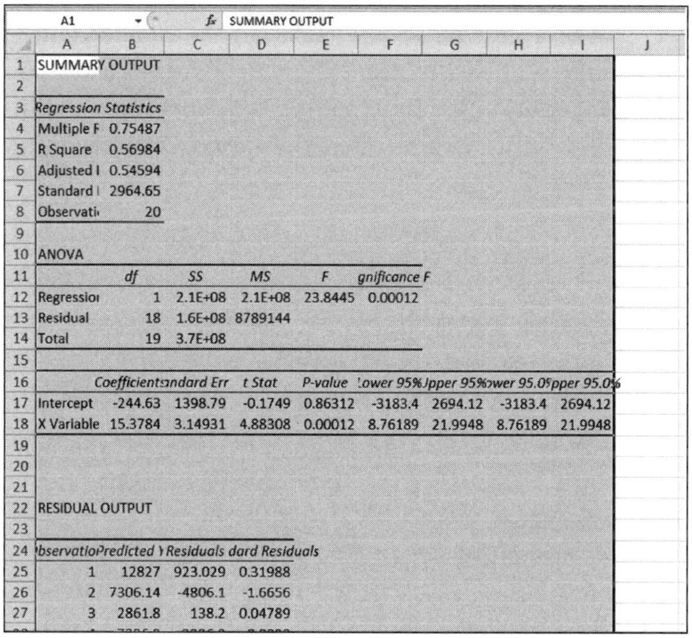

Figure 5.7 Regression Output from Excel Data Analysis Tool Pack

Is There Statistical Evidence of Correlation, or Are the Regression Coefficients Significant?

The observations being used to estimate the regression coefficients are a sample drawn from a much larger population, or from an ongoing process. We can compute a slope and an intercept for *any* sample, but the larger question is: what inference can we make about the population from the data in the sample?

If *x* and *y* were independent and unrelated, the slope of the regression line should be close to zero. Knowing the value of *x* would *not* help us to predict the value of *y*. Note that we say "close to zero." Only in highly contrived examples will the computed value of the slope (*b*) be exactly zero. Even when *x* and *y* are unrelated, sampling error will cause the regression line to have a non-zero slope. When we are dealing with large numbers, a slope that is statistically close to zero may be a very large number indeed, in absolute terms.

How do we know when a slope is close to zero *in statistical terms?* Are *x* and *y* related? To answer the question, we perform a formal hypothesis test on the regression slope (see Appendix 1 in this chapter for full details).

For our example, the *P-value* is 0.00012, which is less than the commonly accepted standard of 0.05, so we can conclude that there is *strong statistical evidence* that larger corporations do, in fact, pay more for bank services than do smaller corporations. A common verbal statement of this result is that the slope of the regression line is *statistically significant at the 0.05 level*. Of course, this statement makes no allowance for non-sampling error from poor sample selection. It assumes that the sample has been randomly chosen from the population.

Regression Diagnostics—Is the Model Valid?

An underlying assumption about the regression model is that the residuals are independent and identically distributed around the regression line. We can always fit a regression line to a set of data. However, if this condition is not met, the regression line is not useful.

One tool to investigate the validity of the model is the residual plot. The residual plot is a graph with fitted values ($\hat{y}_i$) along the horizontal axis and residual values ($y_i - \hat{y}_i$) along the vertical axis. This graph is easily produced using the "Residual Output" section of the model output. A residual plot for Paradec is shown in Figure 5.8.

What are you looking for in the residual plot? The underlying assumptions of regression analysis are that the residuals are homoscedastic and identically distributed. Violations of

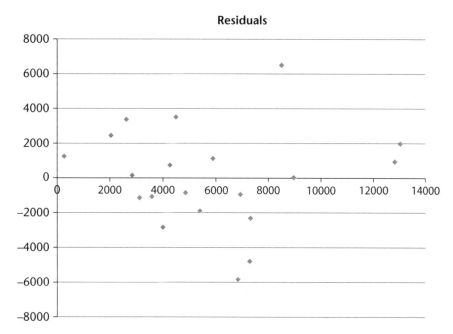

Figure 5.8 Residual Plot from Excel Data Analysis Tool Pack

these assumptions would show up as patterns in the residual plot. Unacceptable patterns in the residual plot include any signs of a trend, or waves ("seasonality" is common in data collected over time) or residual values that appear to increase as x increases.

Using the Model Predictively

If the regression is valid, then we can use it to make a prediction. *Fitted-y* provides the mean value of y at any value of x, or the *point estimate* of y:

Point estimate of y given x = Mean value for y given x
$$= a + bx$$

The uncertainty in the estimate of y takes into account that we do not expect the points to be exactly on the line, but rather normally distributed about the line according to the same distribution as the residuals. If we can convince ourselves that the residuals are well approximated by a normal distribution, then we can use a normal distribution with mean *Fitted-y* and standard deviation given by the *standard deviation of the residuals* to make our predictions.

Note that Excel Data Analysis Tool Pack uses the term "standard error" to denote the *standard deviation of the residuals* although this is not the usual use of the term "standard error."

The *approximate 95% prediction interval* is given by the range from *Fitted-y* minus two *Standard Deviations of the Residuals* to *Fitted-y* plus two *Standard deviations of the Residuals*. 95% of the time, *y* is expected to be in this range (approximately). Note that this is an approximation to the interval because there is also uncertainty on the values of *a* and *b*, but this range does not account for this uncertainty.

Returning to the Paradec example, an approximate 95% prediction interval for bank charges is given by

Approximate Interval = 6,444 +/− 2 × 2964.6 = (516, 12,374)

Based on the residuals being normally distributed around the regression line, we can also find the probability that the bank charges would be above or below any given level using the normal distribution function:

The Excel function = NORMDIST(Y, *Fitted-y, standard deviation of residuals*, 1) will give the probability of bank charges less than any value Y.

Has the Regression Line Reduced Uncertainty?

As we saw in Chapter 4, the usual measure of uncertainty in statistics is the standard deviation. Before computing the regression line, the standard deviation of the dependent variable is the sample standard deviation (*s*). After fitting a regression line, the uncertainty of any prediction is approximated by the standard deviation of the residuals, which is always smaller than the sample standard deviation. Why?—because the regression line itself always explains some of the variation in *y*. If the regression explains a large part of the variation in *y* (that is, the R^2 is close to 1), then the standard deviation of the residuals will be much less than the standard deviation of *y*: predictions made using the regression model (and taking into account specific values of *x*) will be much sharper than those based on *y* values alone.

This is illustrated in the Paradec example: The standard deviation of the sample is 4399.6, whereas the standard deviation of the residuals is much lower at 2964.6. Taking into account annual sales using a regression model has improved our accuracy in predicting bank charges.

The Regression Model with More Than One Independent Variable

Until now, we have worked with regression models of the form $\hat{y} = a + bx$. In many instances a manager will have several piece of information that can be used in making a prediction. For example, a model predicting the total demand for some product might include information on the price of the product, the price of competitors' products, the amount spent on advertising, quantitative measures of the performance of the product (such as the number of megapixels for a digital camera), and other factors. These can all be incorporated into the regression model by extending the single variable linear model to a multi-variable model of the form:

$$\hat{y} = a + b_1 x_1 + b_2 x_2 + b_3 x_3 + \cdots + b_n x_n$$

where n is the number of independent variables included in the model, and $x_1, \ldots, x_n$ are the values of the independent variables.

A useful concept is the indicator or "dummy" variable. A variable x is an indicator variable if it takes only the values 0 and 1. Such variables are often used in regression models if you suspect that an independent variable, which is binary, might influence the dependent variable. Common examples are male or female, smoker or non-smoker, high income or low income. In general, this concept should not be extended to more than two categories. For example, in a study of people who drive American-made cars, it would not be appropriate to define a variable x taking on the value 1 if Chrysler, 2 if Ford, and 3 if General Motors. Why? The regression equation contains a term bx, which requires a linear relationship among the groups, not three different categories.

If there are multiple categories, you must use multiple indicator variables. For example, suppose "level of education" is used in a model, and the levels of education are "high school," "university," and "graduate school." Then you could define x_1 which is 1 if high school and 0 otherwise, and x_2 which is 1 if university and 0 otherwise. Note that you do *not* need to define variable x_3 for graduate school in this example. Why? Because if x_1 and x_2 are both 0 (not high school and not university), then the person must have a graduate school education. This can be further generalized—if there are n categories, you need to define *n-1* indicator variables.

To illustrate these concepts we continue with the Paradec Corporation

The Paradec Corporation (B)

The regression results presented earlier had convinced Ed Sutton, treasurer of the Paradec Corporation, that the $8,400 monthly bank charges for March 1994 were on the high side, but not outrageously so. He decided to discuss the situation with Jane Holland, Paradec's cash management supervisor, before approaching the bank to try to negotiate a better deal. Sutton found Holland unimpressed with his regression model and with the conclusion he had reached:

Most of our banking costs are determined by the number of transactions we put through our bank accounts," she informed him. "For example, last month we averaged 2,100 checks mailed each business day, and a further 600 deposits to our accounts each day. With these high activity levels, I'm not at all surprised that our bank charges are a bit on the high side.

This seemed entirely reasonable to Sutton, and he returned to his office satisfied that Paradec's bank charges were not unusually high.

Additional Information

A month later, Sutton attended another meeting of the local cash management association. Halfway through lunch, Sutton was asked what he had done with the bank charges data that he had collected at the last meeting. Sutton spoke of his regression experiments, and his conclusion that Paradec's bank charges were in line with those of other corporations of their size and activity level. Brian Hoebel, who, Sutton knew, had an M.B.A. from one of the better business schools, raised an issue that jarred Sutton's confidence. Brian asked Sutton what he knew about the disbursement and deposit activity levels of the 20 corporations in his sample. Sutton didn't know very much. Brian then pointed out:

Your conclusion that Paradec's high activity levels account for the somewhat high bank charges in the regression model depends crucially on your assumption that your activity levels are above average for a firm of your size. I'm not sure this is the case—I know many corporations that write more than 2,100 checks a day. In fact, our firm averages more than 7,000 checks/day. Similarly, I know of many outfits that receive more than 600 deposits/day—the utility where my wife works handles 30,000 incoming payments each day. If Paradec's activity levels were in fact *lower* than those of the other firms in the sample, then Paradec's bank charges could be even further out of line than your simple regression model indicates.

Sutton was convinced that his regression result was valid, but he was also convinced that disbursement and payment activity levels were important factors. In particular, he recalled that he paid a bank service fee of 50 cents for each personal check that he wrote.

At the office, Sutton set his assistant the task of calling the cash managers of the 20 corporations in the sample to obtain estimates of the number of daily disbursements (*Disbs*) and deposits (*Rcpts*). A couple of days later this new information was available and loaded into Excel.

Sutton carefully examined the latest data and noted the fact that corporation numbers 2, 6, and 9 all have lower-than-expected bank charges. From his knowledge of local business,

Sutton recognized that these three corporations all bank with First City Bank, a relatively new bank noted for its aggressive pursuit of corporate customers. As far as Sutton was aware, no other corporations in his sample bank with First City Bank. Sutton wondered, first, whether these customers of First City Bank were getting a better deal from their banker than were the other corporations from their banks, and second, whether recognizing the possibility of this better deal would help him to evaluate Paradec's bank charges.

In order to address these issues, we add the *indicator variable (Banker)* in range E2 . . . E21. This indicator variable has value one (1) for corporations which bank with First City Bank and zero (0) for all others (see Table 5.2):

Table 5.2: Paradec data with multiple variables

PARADEC CORPORATION				
Sales	Charges	Disbs	Rcpts	Banker
850	13750	1000	400	0
491	2500	15	75	1
202	3000	75	175	0
493	5000	560	40	0
294	5000	100	150	0
277	1150	100	50	1
600	9000	1000	75	0
150	4500	850	722	0
462	1000	110	5	1
250	2500	350	350	0
332	4000	1200	50	0
570	15000	7550	20	0
468	6000	300	50	0
400	7000	200	700	0
309	8000	380	3500	0
864	15000	2100	600	0
188	6000	1700	450	0
368	3500	100	350	0
34.2	1500	75	200	0
220	2000	100	25	0

	A	B	C	D	E	F	G	H	I
	I30		ƒx						
1	SUMMARY OUTPUT								
2									
3	*Regression Statistics*								
4	Multiple R	0.878222							
5	R Square	0.771274							
6	Adjusted R Square	0.744365							
7	Standard Error	2224.466							
8	Observations	20							
9									
10	ANOVA								
11		df	SS	MS	F	gnificance F			
12	Regression	2	2.84E+08	1.42E+08	28.66234	3.58E-06			
13	Residual	17	84120235	4948249					
14	Total	19	3.68E+08						
15									
16		Coefficients	andard Err	t Stat	P-value	Lower 95%	Upper 95%	ower 95.0%	pper 95.0%
17	Intercept	-81.2395	1050.403	-0.07734	0.939255	-2297.4	2134.917	-2297.4	2134.917
18	Sales	12.09959	2.510363	4.819858	0.00016	6.80319	17.396	6.80319	17.396
19	Disbs	1.252692	0.323748	3.869345	0.001231	0.569644	1.935741	0.569644	1.935741

Figure 5.9 Summary of Paradec Regression Output

Sutton now wanted to keep the results from his simple regression model, but add extra independent variables to try to account for the considerable differences in disbursement levels across corporations (Figure 5.9).

Apart from some differences in the numbers, this output looks similar to the earlier simple regression examples. The major difference is the addition of a new row, labeled with the name of the second independent variable (*Disbs*). To understand the output, we need to understand the regression equation with multiple variables.

Understanding of the multiple regression model begins with the regression equation and the regression coefficients. The new regression equation is:

Charges = –81.2395 + 12.09959 Sales + 1.252692 *Disbs*

or, in more familiar notation:

Bank Charges (in $/month) = –81.24 + 12.100 × Sales (in $2003)
+ 1.2527 × Disbursements (daily average)

Each regression coefficient has a *P-value*. These correspond to formal hypothesis tests, as described for single variable models.

In this case the *P-value* shows the outcome of this hypothesis test: for statistical significance, we require the *P-value* for the regression coefficient for each independent variable (the slopes) to be < 0.05. Since this is the case here, we can state that there is *strong statistical evidence* that firms with higher sales and greater disbursements pay higher bank charges.

The output also shows a *P-value* for the y-intercept that can be used to test whether the y-intercept is significantly different from zero. In this example, the *P-value* for the y-intercept is 0.94, which does not pass this test—a fact which may add plausibility to our model, since the y-intercept (–81.24) suggests that a corporation with no sales and no transactions *collects* $81.24/month from its bank. The *P-value* of –0.94 for the y-intercept tells us that $81.24 is, in statistical terms, very close to zero.

The significance test for the *y*-intercept is frequently ignored since the origin is often far removed from the bulk of the observations. Consequently, the test result may not affect the usefulness of the model since the origin is outside the relevant range of experience being modeled.

Another feature that adds managerial plausibility to our model is the regression coefficient for *Disbs*. This coefficient is the bank service charge per disbursement per day, and so the fact that it is positive is reassuring. Assuming 20 working days per month, then $1.25 per month translates to 1.25/20 = 6.25 cents per disbursement—a number in accord with our expectations of banking costs.

Further useful information on the fit of our model is provided by the R^2 and the standard deviation of the residuals. When comparing this output with that from the Paradec simple regression model, certain differences stand out. First, the unadjusted R^2 has increased from 57.0% to 77.1%. A larger R^2, for the same sample of *y* values, denotes a better fit, and so this increase is a sign that the fit of our model has improved. Along with the R^2, the adjusted R^2 has also increased from 54.6% to 74.4%. This improvement is also reflected in the standard deviation of the residuals (*Standard Error* in Excel), which has *decreased* from 2,965 to 2,224, indicating that the observations are fitted by the two-variable regression more closely than they were fitted by the initial regression line.

Care is necessary in interpreting these changes. The unadjusted R^2 generally increases (it can never decrease) when a second variable is added to a regression model, and this increase is often accompanied by a decrease in the standard deviation of the residuals These changes are, in part, the result of the mathematics behind regression models—more independent variables always allow for a better fit.

How do we know when the addition of the second variable represents a *real* improvement to our model? The most important statistic is the *P-value* for the incoming variable—if the *P-value* is low (generally this means *P-value* < 0.05), then the added variable has improved our model. A second test is whether the adjusted R^2 has increased. If the new variable results in an increase in the R^2 but a decrease in the adjusted R^2, then the new variable has probably not improved the model.

The remaining statistics for a multiple regression model have the same interpretation as for simple regression, with the exception that the square root of the unadjusted R^2 is no longer the absolute value of the simple correlation between y and x. In multiple regression, this is called the *coefficient of multiple correlation* and is a measure of the correlation between $\hat{y}$ and y.

Finally, in order to use our multiple regression model predictively, we must check the residuals for evidence of outliers, nonlinearity, homoscedasticity, or distributional problems. The diagnostic tests used are identical to those for the simple regression model, since, even though with multiple regression we have several independent variables, we have only a single and only a single relationship between $\hat{y}$ and y.

Once we are satisfied with the regression model, we can make our prediction or estimate. In the case of a two-independent variable model, we must use values for two independent variables, in the example sales of $435 million with 2,100 disbursements/day, in the regression equation:

$$\text{Bank Charges} = -81.24 + 12.1 \times \text{Sales} + 1{,}2527 \times \text{Disbursements}$$
$$= -81.24 + 12.1 \times 435 + 1.2527 \times 2{,}100$$
$$= 7{,}813$$

Prediction Intervals

As with the single variable regression model, we can use the standard deviation of the residuals to provide an approximate prediction interval, if we can convince ourselves that the residuals are well approximated by a normal distribution. Thus, a 95% prediction interval is approximately $\hat{y} \pm 2 \times$ (*standard deviation of the residuals*) or, in Paradec's case, from 7,813 ± 2,224 or from 3,365 to 12,261. Paradec's charges are well within this range.

The Multiple Regression Model with Three or More Independent Variables

The extension of the multiple regression model to include a third, a fourth, and further independent variables is straightforward, although the geometry of these models is complex and difficult to picture.

The table below shows the Data Analysis Tool Pack Summary regression output when all four independent variables are included in the regression model.

SUMMARY OUTPUT	
Regression Statistics	
Multiple R	0.968447
R Square	0.937889
Adjusted R Square	0.921326
Standard Error	1234.046
Observations	20

	Coefficients	P-value
Intercept	−290.191	0.650016
Sales	13.09703	1.22E-07
Disbs	1.09082	3.14E-05
Rcpts	1.285848	0.004141
Banker	−3667.12	0.000429

We now have four slopes (one for each independent variable) and one y-intercept. The new regression equation is:

Bank charges = −290.191 + 13.09703 *Sales* + 1.09082 *Disbs*
                + 1.285848 *Rcpts* − 3667.12 *Banker*

The *P-values* are all < 0.05, suggesting that all four independent variables are statistically significant.

Further evidence that the fit has improved is provided by the R^2 and the standard deviation of the residuals. The R^2 has increased (from 0.77 to 0.97), indicating that this model explains a greater proportion of the variance of y than does the two-independent variable model. This is confirmed by the reduction in the standard deviation of the residuals (from 2,224 to 1,234) and the accompanying increase in the adjusted R^2 (from 0.74 to 0.92).

Finally, we would test for model validity as in all previous cases.

To estimate bank charges for corporations that do not bank with First City Bank, we set indicator variable *Banker* equal to zero. For corporations which bank with First City Bank, we add the value of the indicator variable, *Banker* (equal to one) multiplied by its regression coefficient. Since the regression coefficient, in this case, is negative, this means we subtract 1 × (−3,667.1) for corporations banking with First City Bank.

For example, the company in Row 1 (Table 5.2) does not bank at First City Bank:

$$Charges = -290.190 + 13.09703(850) + 1.090820(1000) + 1.28547(400) + (-3667.124)(0)$$
$$= 12447.44 + (-3667.124)(0)$$
$$= 12447.44$$

And for the company in Row 2, which *does* bank at First City Bank:

$$Charges = -290.190 + 13.09703(491) + 1.090820(15) + 1.28547(75) + (-3667.124)(1)$$
$$= 6253.253 + (-3667.124)(1)$$
$$= 2586.129$$

The *P-value* for the regression coefficient of the indicator variable is less than 0.05, and so we draw the conclusion that corporations banking with First City pay *significantly* less in bank charges than do others. Our estimate of the difference in charges, adjusted for differences in sales and activity levels, is $3,667.1/month less in charges for First City customers.

While this result is statistically significant, we must be cautious in drawing inferences about *causation*—the result tells us that three corporations have significantly lower bank charges than do the remainder of the sample, but we identified these three corporations, in part, because Sutton observed that this was the case. We need further evidence to decide whether the link to First City Bank or other characteristics of the corporations *cause* the observed difference in charges.

In evaluating this regression model, we note that the *P-values* for the regression coefficients all indicate significance except that for the y-intercept, which suggests that the y-intercept is not significantly different from zero. The unadjusted R^2 has increased from the two-independent variable model, and the standard deviation of the residuals is considerably reduced. A quick check of the residuals suggests no major problems.

The point estimate from this model ($8,469) is slightly higher than are Paradec's bank charges of $8,400/month. The standard deviation of the predicted y-value is only $1,285, the smallest of all the models considered, but is still large enough that the difference between actual and estimate (8,469 − 8,400 = 69) is only a small fraction of a standard deviation (69/1,285 = 0.054). The 95% prediction interval is the range from $5,730 to $11,209.

A conclusion? The data that Sutton has collected provide no statistical evidence that Paradec pays unusually high (or unusually low) bank charges. Based on the data we have, there is no exact mapping from the number of disbursements/month, receipts/month, annual sales, or banker to a corporation's bank charges. Either there are other factors that go into the bank's monthly fee calculation (perhaps the corporation's credit worthiness?), or else the banks' terms are flexible and vary by customer.

Developing a Multiple Regression Model

In the development of a multiple regression model, we often have only limited ideas as to which independent variables will prove useful. At the same time, we may have access to data on a large number of potential independent variables. Our task is then to use the available data (and perhaps add some additional variables) to develop a useful multiple regression model. Here are some rules of good practice.

Rule One: *It is important that the independent variables that are examined for inclusion in a regression model are sensible.*

Before starting model development, we must have some basis for a belief that the value of our dependent variable is influenced by the values of the chosen independent variables. We want to avoid regressing y against everything in sight (often called "fishing"). We will, of course, be surprised quite often—relationships that we thought sensible will not prove to be significant and will not add to the usefulness of our model. You may be required to explain to your client or supervisor why your model is a reasonable one. An inability to do so can hurt your credibility.

Rule Two: *Keep the number of independent variables quite a bit smaller than the number of observations.*

The unadjusted R^2 usually increases when a new variable is added to a regression model. As the number of variables in the model approaches the sample size, the R^2 will approach one (1). This is a phenomenon of the geometry of regression, and has no statistical importance. How do we know when we are creating a problem? One clue is the *Adjusted R^2*. If the *Adjusted R^2* fails to increase when a new variable is added, or if, when we examine our model, we find that the *Adjusted R^2* is very much smaller than the unadjusted R^2, then we may be running out of degrees of freedom—we have too many independent variables for our sample size.

Rule Three: *Try to choose uncorrelated independent variables.*

In practice, most independent variables show a degree of correlation with other independent variables. If, however, the independent variables are excessively correlated, then the problem of *multicollinearity* emerges. The principal symptom of this problem is a very unstable regression model. This instability shows up in the *P-values,* which become very unstable. In extreme cases, a regression coefficient that is significantly different from 0 can lose its significance when an independent variable with which it is correlated is entered in to the model.

A rule-of-thumb? If two independent variables show a simple correlation of 0.4 or greater, use one or the other, but not both, in the same regression model. If both are used, interpret the resulting *P-values* cautiously.

A *correlation matrix* is a common way of displaying the simple correlation coefficients among a group of variables. A correlation matrix can be produced using the Excel Data analysis add-in.

Rule Four: *Whenever possible, rerun the final model with a second sample, or alternatively, divide the initial sample into two sub-samples, develop the model using one sub-sample and then test the model on the other sub-sample.*

This procedure addresses two issues—*shrinkage* and *selection errors*. We use the term *shrinkage* to describe the decline in the predictive power of a regression model when the model is taken out of the sample in which it was developed. This shrinkage occurs because the model is fitted to a specific sample that incorporates sampling variation. When moved to a second sample where different sampling variation is present, the fit of the model will not be as good. The magnitude of the shrinkage depends on how substantial is the sampling variation compared to the modeled relationships. A useful regression model will be stable when moved from sample to sample, as long as the samples are drawn from the same population.

Selection errors occur because of the rules we use to add independent variables to our model. If there are 100 potential variables, and we use a *P-value* < 0.05 as our acceptance criterion, then, by chance, we expect to include five independent variables; even if all 100 variables are independent of *y*. Using a second sample to validate our model will identify these chance correlations and enable us to drop those variables.

Rule Five: *Keep the purpose of the model in mind when choosing the criterion for including independent variables in the model.*

The straightforward case occurs when the *P-value* for the incoming variable indicates significance, that is, it is less than 0.05. *When a significant new variable is added*, the unadjusted R^2 will increase, as will the adjusted R^2, and the *standard deviation of the residuals* will decrease. If we are trying to *explain* the behavior of the dependent variable, then we should include only those independent variables that enter at a *P-value* less than 0.05.

However, if we are building a predictive model, we are interested in having the smallest possible *standard deviation of the residuals,* since this will give us the sharpest prediction interval. In this case, we may have useful information from outside the sample data. While we want be confident that our predictive model is not based on spurious correlations (so we would like significant *P-values*), we may want to include a new variable with a *P-value* slightly greater than 0.05 if this improves the predictive power of the model, especially if we, or a decision maker, have some other evidence to substantiate the observed dependence. This other evidence might be a strongly held opinion, or arise from some other data not included in the model.

Summary

Linear regression models can be a powerful tool to assist managers in understanding correlation, forecasting, and prediction. They can help managers to understand relationships between variables and reduce the uncertainty associated with predictions by using something we know to predict something we do not know.

Regression model building is part art and part science. The artistic part is to identify useful independent variables and to choose a good combination of these variables for modeling. The scientific part is to ensure that the final model is valid: this usually means that the *P-values* associated with the independent variables are all less than 0.05, and that the residuals plot show no evidence of nonlinearity or other patterns. In many instances, a linear model with the given variables does not provide a good fit and new variables, such as indicator variables, must be added or some form of data transformation (such as logging the y-variable) undertaken.

The Paradec Corporation regression models included different combinations of independent variables, and demonstrated that the addition of additional independent variables having *P-values* < 0.05 will increase the accuracy of the prediction, as shown by increasing the R^2 and reducing the Standard Deviation of the Residuals, and consequently narrowing the prediction interval.

What the Manager Must Know

A manager is very likely to be involved in discussions which center on the output of regression models.

- Regression is a powerful tool to help explain, forecast, and predict.
- A first step in constructing a regression model should always be to draw the scatterplot to see if it looks like correlation exists.
- The regression line is constructed to achieve a best fit between the data and the summary line providing a balance between overestimates and underestimates.

- The *P-value* for the slope in the regression model < 0.05 provides universally accepted strong statistical evidence of correlation between two variables.

- A number of statistical tests provide guidance on whether a regression model is valid.

- An important feature of regression models is their ability to reduce the uncertainty in predictions.

Predictive Modeling In Action

MBA Program Admissions Decisions

MBA programs face the challenge of selecting students to fill each entering class. It is in the interest of the school or university to select the students who will perform the best in the program. Most schools have used regression models to try to predict student performance in their MBA program to try to help the admissions committee make good admission decisions. Typically, they regress the grade point average (GPA) for graduated students (the dependent variable) against various measures (independent variables) that were available to the admissions committee at the time that the student was applying to the program (typically measures like high school GPA, years of work experience, current salary, and test scores). Many schools require students applying for admission to take standard tests (the Graduate Management Admission test [GMAT] or Graduate Record Examination [GRE]) because regression has shown that student performance is highly correlated with their scores on these tests.

Regression in the News

Newspapers frequently publish the results of statistical analysis of interesting, sensational, or controversial issues. Often, regression models form the basis for the statistical analysis and the reported results depend on the *P-values* in the regression models. Some examples:

"HORMONES MAY BOOST FUTURES TRADERS' PROFITS"

Futures traders with higher morning testosterone levels made higher profits, a provocative new study by a Canadian researcher has found. Those with lower levels of the hormone in their saliva at 11 a.m. made, on average, lower profits or lost money the rest of that day, says John Coates, a former Wall Street trader who is now a senior research fellow at the University of Cambridge in England.

For eight days, twice a day, he took saliva samples from 17 men working on a mid-size London trading floor.

"We found that a trader's morning testosterone level predicts his day's profitability," he and his colleague, Joe Herbert, conclude in a paper published yesterday in the online edition of the Proceedings of the National Academy of Sciences.

It is the first study to make a connection between hormones and trading, but forget about asking your broker for a spit sample. The experiment was a preliminary step, says Dr. Coates, towards understanding the role testosterone and other hormones play in financial risk-taking. (*Source*: Anne McIlroy, *Globe and Mail Update*, April 14, 2008)

"CLEVEREST WOMEN ARE THE HEAVIEST DRINKERS"

Women who went to university consume more alcohol than do their less-highly-educated counterparts. Cleverer women tend to drink more. Those with degrees are almost twice as likely to drink daily, and they are also more likely to admit to having a drinking problem. A similar link between educational attainment and alcohol consumption is seen among men, but the correlation is less strong. (*Source*: *Daily Telegraph* (UK), April 5, 2010)

"A STRANGE RELATIONSHIP: BANK MERGERS AND CRIME"

According to a study published in *The Journal of Finance*, there is a small relationship between bank mergers and criminal activity: neighborhoods where bank mergers occurred experience higher crime rates. (*Source*: *International Herald Tribune*, March 17, 2006)

Appendix 1

Formal Hypothesis Test for Regression Coefficients

In "plain English" terms, we are trying to decide whether there is statistical evidence of a relationship between x and y. Why? We can draw a line of best fit through *any* scatterplot and often this line will appear to have a clear non-zero slope; however, this does not mean that the variables are correlated and the results used in our decision making. We require a formal statistical test to determine whether there is enough statistical evidence to conclude that the relationship is significant. These tests are automatically part of the results when using the Excel Data Analysis Tool Pack to build a regression model.

The formal hypothesis test is defined below, and as shown in Figure 5A.1.

Null Hypothesis: Population slope = 0 (i.e., $b = 0$)

Test Hypothesis: Population slope is not equal to zero (i.e., $b \neq 0$)

Test Statistic: *P-value*

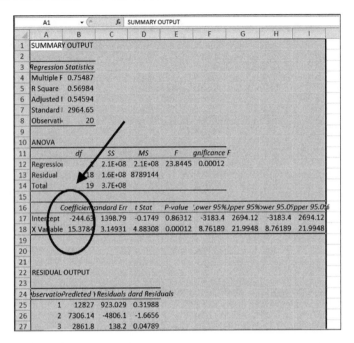

Figure 5A.1 *P-values* in Excel Regression Output

Rejection Region:	Reject the null hypothesis (and accept the alternate hypothesis) if the *P-value* < 0.05
Probability of Type 1 Error:	0.05 or 5%.

The *P-values* for this test are given in the *P-value* column of the coefficients table in the regression model output screen (Figure 5A.1).

The definition of the rejection region as "*P-value* < 0.05" is arbitrary. Values of 0.01 and 0.1 are also commonly used, although 0.05 is the very widely accepted standard.

Note that the description above related to hypothesis tests on slope values. The same test and interpretation can be done for the intercept term, although we are usually less interested in testing whether or not the intercept is statistically different from zero.

Nonlinear Models

Earlier, we mentioned the linear model does not always fit the data well. If we fit a linear model to nonlinear data, we often find high R^2 values and low standard deviations of the residuals, but when we examine a scatterplot and trend line, it is obvious that the line is a poor fit to the data (Figure 5.A.2). If our model was designed to predict future observations (periods 21 and beyond) this trend line would provide obviously poor predictions.

There are several techniques for dealing with nonlinearities in a regression model that involve a transformation of either the dependent or independent variable (or both), and then using the transformed variable(s) in a linear regression model.

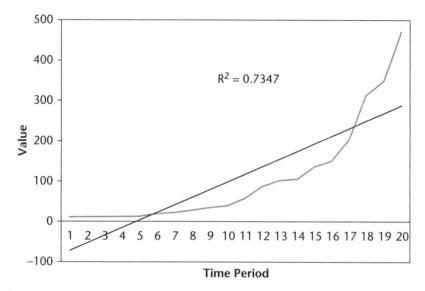

Figure 5A.2 A Linear Trendline When the Series Is Nonlinear

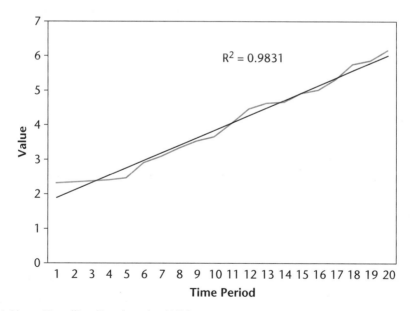

Figure 5A.3 A Linear Trendline Fitted to the *LN(y)*

The first transformation is the *logarithmic* transformation. If you are confronted with a situation where it appears that y increases over time or with x on a percentage basis: that is y increases at about 10% for every unit change in x, then replacing y with the logarithm of y will produce a linear relationship. Such relationships are very common in economic data; for example, economic growth and price changes are always expressed as annual percentage rates. In Figure 5A.3, we plot the same data as in Figure 5A.2, however with y replaced by the logarithm of y [= LN(y)].

In this transformation, we have replaces the inappropriate linear model:

$$\hat{y} = a + bx$$

With the model:

$$\hat{z} = a + bx$$

where $z = ln(y)$. Since the new model is linear, we can use linear regression to fit this model and make use of all the features of the linear regression model. Note however, that when making predictions we must remember that the model will give us predictions of z (equal to the log of y) and we must convert these back to y [using $y = EXP(z)$] to return to predictions of *Fitted-y*.

When a percentage increase in x leads to similar percentage change in y (for example, a 10% increase in sales might lead to a 10% increase in commissions paid to the salesforce), then it would be appropriate to log both y and x before attempting to fit a linear regression model.

A second useful transformation in time series data that is very common in the analysis of economic data is the difference model: instead of regressing y vs x, we regress the change in y against the change in x. Other common data transformations include using the quadratic ($z = y^2$) and square root ($z = \sqrt{y}$; in Excel " = SQRT(y)") functions to transform one or more of the variables.

How do you know if a transformation is needed? This should be obvious from the scatterplot. Hence, the first step in regression analysis should *always* be to examine a scatter plot of the data.

Exercises

1. The S&P Stock 500 Exchange index had the following values in January 2012.
    1. Is there statistical evidence of a trend over this time period?

Date	S&P 500 Index
04-Jan-12	1,277.30
05-Jan-12	1,281.06
06-Jan-12	1,277.81
09-Jan-12	1,280.70
10-Jan-12	1,292.08
11-Jan-12	1,292.48
12-Jan-12	1,295.50
13-Jan-12	1,289.09
17-Jan-12	1,293.67
18-Jan-12	1,308.04
19-Jan-12	1,314.50
20-Jan-12	1,315.38
23-Jan-12	1,316.00
24-Jan-12	1,314.65
25-Jan-12	1,326.06
26-Jan-12	1,318.43

2. What would be the predicted value for the index for the next business day after January 26?

3. What is the 95% prediction interval for the next business day?

2. The following table lists a number of properties in a location popular as a vacation spot that have sold at auction.

1. What factors affect the winning bid?

2. Build a model to predict the winning bid.

3. What is the point prediction for the winning bid for a residential property coming up for auction on July 20, 2011, with an estimated value of $1,500,000?

4. Does this prediction change if there is a lot of interest in the property (that is, many bids are expected)?

5. Does the prediction change if the buyer is expected to be a non-resident?

6. What is the 95% prediction interval for the same property auction?

Date of Sale	Winning Bid	Estimated Value	Number of Bids received	Type of Property	Buyer
22-May-10	1,028,885	1,176,800	6	Commercial	Nonresident
6-Jun-10	372,455	427,100	4	Residential	Resident
13-Jun-10	940,016	1,090,200	7	Residential	Resident
29-Jun-10	288,703	336,700	6	Residential	Resident
14-Jul-10	2,166,426	2,445,300	7	Residential	Nonresident
6-Aug-10	751,420	848,100	4	Commercial	Nonresident
13-Aug-10	1,305,550	1,553,500	6	Residential	Resident
28-Sep-10	211,412	278,300	9	Residential	Resident
5-Oct-10	331,677	385,900	5	Commercial	Resident
28-Oct-10	2,749,662	3,074,100	7	Commercial	Nonresident
12-Nov-10	1,156,443	1,284,900	5	Commercial	Nonresident
28-Nov-10	1,956,165	2,203,100	5	Commercial	Resident
5-Dec-10	348,470	431,300	7	Residential	Resident
20-Dec-10	1,530,358	1,735,600	7	Commercial	Nonresident
5-Jan-11	1,883,154	2,105,300	6	Residential	Nonresident
20-Jan-11	393,344	446,100	6	Commercial	Nonresident
12-Feb-11	609,573	695,400	6	Commercial	Resident
27-Feb-11	4,920,658	5,806,700	9	Residential	Resident
6-Mar-11	377,600	472,200	5	Commercial	Resident
13-Apr-11	466,776	593,000	5	Residential	Resident
29-Apr-11	892,531	1,032,900	3	Commercial	Resident
14-May-11	1,025,087	1,146,000	8	Commercial	Nonresident
22-May-11	517,964	629,500	7	Commercial	Resident

Recommended Cases

Alfonso's Department Store (Ivey)

Burnhamwood University (Ivey)

Brent-Harbridge Developments (Ivey)

Lansink Appraisals (Ivey)

Professor gets engaged (Ivey)

Springbank Drive (Ivey)

The Morrice Collection (A) and (B) (Ivey)

Edgecomb Metals—The Troy Plant (A) and (B) (Darden)

Northern Napa Valley Winery (Ivey)

Orion Bus Industries: Contract Bidding Strategy (Ivey)

Colonial Broadcasting (Harvard)

A-Rod: Signing the Best Player in Baseball (Harvard)

The Oakland A's (A) and (B) (Darden)

CHAPTER 6

SIMULATING THE FUTURE

At first, computers were seen as large, fast, calculating devices but a breakthrough occurred in the 1950s when it was realized that the arithmetic engine in the computer could be used to "mimic" the future by driving a simulation model. The use of computer simulation is now widespread in well-managed companies; major facilities or products constructed today are "run in the computer" to debug the design and to check out the host of decisions that must be made before construction can begin. Some examples:

- Simulation was used to evaluate the design of the terminals of the Channel Tunnel linking Britain and France.
- Simulation is routinely used to assist in the design of new airplanes, where a new plane makes thousands of simulated "flights" in the computer before a single piece is constructed.
- Automobile manufacturers make extensive use of simulation studies to try to identify design changes which would improve the efficiency of their existing manufacturing facilities, and also use simulation to design new facilities.
- Hospitals have used simulations to plan the layout and capacity of operating theaters, outpatient clinics, and guided vehicle systems.
- Pharmaceutical companies develop simulation models of disease progression so that they can evaluate the benefits of new drugs.
- Simulation models are used to assess emergency planning and response, such as response to a bioterror attack, and the list goes on and on.

Simulation is widely used as a tool to improve operations, but there are also many examples of simulations being used for tactical and strategic decisions. Simulation models can assist management at all decision-making levels: a firm that makes a strategic decision to be a low-cost producer may well use simulation models to study its entire operation, with a view to identifying cost savings or opportunities for efficiencies (see the reading on Vilpac Truck manufacturing at the end of this chapter).

An important strategic use of simulation is the strategic corporate simulation exercise. Here a simulation model of the strategic level of a firm is constructed, and the management of the firm gathers at a retreat, where they "play through" various possible strategic decisions using the simulation model to assess their impact and desirability. The organizations marketing these exercises claim that management emerges from these experiences with a much-improved understanding of their organization, as well as valuable insight into the impact of the chosen future strategy. Simulation models are also extensively used for lower-level management training purposes (for example, flight simulators for training pilots, and "war-game" simulators for training military officers).

Simulation is now its own industry. One estimate put the size of this industry in 2000 at $8 billion annually. The simulation industry includes hardware and software suppliers, consultants, trainers, and specialists. The manager facing a problem where simulation might be useful can tap into this industry in many different ways, such as by buying software that makes simulation easy to do, or hiring a consulting firm specializing in simulation. In order to be able to make an informed choice in a situation such as this, the manager must know some of the basic concepts of simulation.

We use two classification schemes for simulation models. The first classification scheme is based on the incorporation of randomness in models and divides simulation models into *deterministic models* and *stochastic models*. Deterministic simulation models do not involve randomness and were discussed in Chapter 2. Stochastic (or Monte Carlo) simulation models attempt to explicitly account for randomness and uncertainty and are the focus of this chapter. The second classification scheme is based on the logic used to construct the models and divides simulation models into *event models* and *process* or *discrete event models*.

Stochastic or Monte Carlo Simulation

Stochastic simulations differ from deterministic simulations in that they are driven by computer-generated *random numbers*. The outputs of a stochastic simulation are statements about probabilities of events or situations occurring.

Random numbers can be generated in almost any computer software. In Microsoft Excel, the function = RAND() in a cell assigns that cell a value between 0 and 0.9999999999999999, with all values in this range equally likely. We refer to these as uniformly distributed random numbers between 0 and 1. Each time the Excel spreadsheet is recalculated, the values assigned to cells that include = RAND() are recomputed using new values for = RAND(). A number of special simulation add-in packages, such as Crystal Ball and @Risk, can also be used to generate random numbers in Excel.

The 0–1 uniformly distributed random numbers are an essential driver for two important classes of stochastic simulation: *process simulation* and *event simulation*. Before discussing these types of simulation models, we give an example of using uniformly distributed random numbers to simulate coin tosses in Excel.

Example: Simulating a Coin Toss in Excel

Suppose we wish to determine how many "Heads" we would get if we flipped a coin 10 times. We could, of course, conduct this experiment directly without great effort, but we can also simulate the experiment in Excel.

First, we need a random number for the first coin flip, so we enter = RAND() in cell B1. Since the probability of the result "Heads" is 0.5 (or 50%), we call any value generated by the function RAND() that is less than 0.5 a "Heads." We now check if the first flip was a "Heads" or a "Tails" by checking the random number in cell B1 using:

= IF(B1 < 0.5,"Heads","Tails") in cell C1.

Since we wish to simulate 10 flips, we copy B1:C1 for 10 rows, giving the results shown in the table below

	Random Number	Result
1	0.531469595	Tails
2	0.619855829	Tails
3	0.802060377	Tails
4	0.672607578	Tails
5	0.481524841	Heads
6	0.759934666	Tails
7	0.262231407	Heads
8	0.012167391	Heads
9	0.154074838	Heads
10	0.172520765	Heads

The result: in 10 simulated coin flips, we observed five heads. Note that if you try this in your spreadsheet, you will generate different random numbers with, likely, different numbers of simulated "Heads" and "Tails."

Now recalculate the spreadsheet by hitting the function key F9. You have just repeated the experiment and observed a new result, shown in the following table:

	Random Number	Result
1	0.600149161	Tails
2	0.033025144	Heads
3	0.155916196	Heads
4	0.296754084	Heads
5	0.156104772	Heads
6	0.381698084	Heads
7	0.455109364	Heads
8	0.521707372	Tails
9	0.882119534	Tails
10	0.331103616	Heads

The new result shows 7 Heads (and, as before, your result will be different). Each time you hit F9, you will generate a new set of results showing a different number of Heads. In general, each time you hit F9, you will estimate a different number of Heads.

We could estimate the probability of tossing "Heads" (although we already know the answer!) by pressing F9 several times, recording the result each time, and then calculating the average.

Another method would be to copy the table for 10,000 rows, simulate once, and calculate the average number of "Heads" by doing this. This is illustrated in the table below:

	Random Number	Result
1	0.143676882	1
2	0.993753226	0
3	0.786978986	0
4	0.053195708	1
5	0.151885131	1
6	0.064306051	1

⋮		
9996	0.151099155	1
9997	0.198298732	1
9998	0.490522103	1
9999	0.430986007	1
10000	0.664654268	0
	Total	4997

When we recalculate the spreadsheet with 10,000 simulated coin flips, there may be a pause while recalculation occurs. This is a general occurrence: large-scale simulations can take quite a bit of computer time to work through. This example, however, clearly illustrates one advantage of using the computer to flip 10,000 simulated coins rather than conducting the same experiment "live." How long would it take to flip 10,000 coins and record the results?

Simulation Logic

Event Simulation

Event logic often follows a tree structure, where the tree is made up of uncertain events where branching occurs. Event logic uses random numbers to simulate the uncertain events and generate paths through the tree (or "scenarios").

As an example, consider the problem of estimating the cost of claims for a group of employees covered by a long-term disability insurance plan. Typically, such plans pay the covered employees a percentage of their salaries in the event that they suffer some kind of disability that keeps them from working for a period in excess of several months.

Actuaries, employed by the insurance companies, maintain records of past claims experience from which probabilities can be derived. Estimates of the probability of disability occurring, and of the disability lasting any number of months are available for various customer classes (professionals, blue collar workers, various industry groups, etc.).

Using these probabilities, and data on group members' salaries, characteristics, and a knowledge of the terms of the long-term disability policy, event simulation can be used to estimate the claims experience for the plan. The simulation would examine each individual in the group in turn, and use random numbers to generate a claims scenario for that individual over the lifetime of the plan. This claims scenario would be derived by using a random number each simulated time period to determine whether or not the individual became disabled. If disability occurred, a second random number (or set of random numbers) could be used to determine the duration of the disability (other random numbers could determine the type of disability, or the benefit level if this was important to the claim).

By examining each individual in turn, each time period, a typical claims scenario for the group can be derived. Examining multiple claims scenarios (if the model were in a spreadsheet, generating a new scenario simply requires hitting the F9 recalculation key) enables the average and variability of the group claims to be examined. Such a simulation would enable management at the insurance company to develop an understanding of the riskiness of the plan, and to adopt a sensible pricing (and perhaps re-insurance) policy.

Event simulations are frequently used to construct distributions of outcomes. For example:

> An event simulation was used to construct the distribution of the likely value of a star pitcher to a professional baseball team. The final distribution was dependent on the probabilities that the pitcher would start different numbers of games, the number of games that the pitcher might win, the distribution of the increase in attendance when the pitcher appeared, the probability of the team making the playoffs and World Series, etc.

> Event simulations are routinely used to construct payoff distributions for various group insurance plans. For example, an office workforce consists of a certain distribution of females and males of known ages, and the probabilities of various disabilities by age/sex classes are known to the insurance companies from experience with long-term disability plans. An insurance company quoting on a new long-term disability plan can simulate the claims distribution for any office workforce.

Process or Discrete Event Simulation

In a process simulation, events are simulated in the order in which they take place, and the order is important. One reason that the order is important is that events in the current time period have an impact on future time periods. Thus, at each point in time, it may be important to know the entire history of the simulation. This is common in many queuing systems. For example, if a bank, fast food restaurant, or airport check-in line gets busy now, then a line will form and it will take some time for the line to clear out. Customers who arrive while the line is clearing out will have to wait longer than usual. This sequence dependence cannot be easily capture using event models.

Process simulation has become an important tool for improving existing processes and designing more effective new processes. Process simulation attempts to model a real-world process "in the computer" so that the process can be studied with the view to making process improvements.

Some of the many successes of process simulation include:

- A process simulation model of a steel works has been used to streamline materials flow in the works.
- Process simulations are routinely used in business process re-engineering projects.
- A process simulation of a bank branch has been used to improve customer flow and service in the branch.
- A process simulation of a hospital has been used to improve the floor plan of an outpatient clinic.

Process models are often used for operational and process problems, whereas many high-level strategic problems are better addressed with event models.

Developing a Simulation Model

There are six general steps in developing a simulation model:

1. Gathering and analyzing data.
2. Generating a stream of events.
3. Building the logic of the model.
4. Validating the model.
5. Running the model and collecting results.
6. Analyzing the model output.

Before describing these steps in detail we present the Tennessee Tour Bus Company example.

The Tennessee Tour Bus Company

The Tennessee Tour Bus Company makes tour buses, the kind used for concert tours or other traveling shows. The basic bus is purchased from the manufacturer and is customized in a two-stage production process.

At the bodywork stage (the "body shop"), the interior of the bus is customized, including the fitting of sleeping rooms, lounge areas, and a kitchen, and modifying the window arrangement. Each bus receives about the same bodywork and this takes 10 working days. The bus is then moved to a painting area (the "paint shop"), where it is painted. The paint-work on these tour buses is usually quite spectacular, including individual artwork, as well as a high-quality overall finish. In some cases, the name of the touring performer is painted on the outside of the bus, or the paintwork may include images or motifs chosen by the performer. The time taken to paint a bus averages 10 days, but is highly variable: sometimes the paint "wrinkles" and has to be redone. In a few cases, painting can be accomplished in two days, but there have been instances when a bus took 18 days to paint satisfactorily.

"Raw" buses can be stored in a large lot outside, so there is always a bus for the body shop to work on, and painted buses are weatherproof and can be stored outside, and so the paint shop can always unload a finished bus. However, buses that are ready for painting must be kept inside, and the only place available is the body shop. If bodywork finishes a bus, but painting is busy, then the body shop is "blocked"; work must stop until painting finishes and the bus can be moved into the paint shop. If "painting" finishes a bus, it can begin work on the next bus only if fitting has a finished bus ready: otherwise painting is "starved" and must wait for bodywork to finish a bus before it can start work again.

Management has noticed that the body shop is often blocked and the paint shop is often idle with no bus to paint. The suggestion has been made that a floor space large enough to park one complete fitted, but unpainted, bus be created between the two processes. Bodywork would then be able to "unload" a complete fitted bus into this space even though painting was still busy. Similarly, painting would sometimes be able to start a new bus if one was available in storage, even though fitting was still working.

How much extra throughput will the additional storage space allow?

Step 1: Gathering and Analyzing Data

Development of a stochastic simulation model generally begins with observation of an existing system and data collection (although if we are modeling a new plant, we may have to make some assumptions about the new plant based on our understanding of existing equipment).

Even when modeling the future, some things may not change. For example, changing the layout of a bank or outpatient department at a hospital may not have much of an effect on the stream of customers or patients arriving.

In general, it is important to understand both the frequency and timing of events. When "customers" are arriving for service, we would like to know when they arrive, not just how many arrive. In general, we will not be able (nor will it be economical) to collect sufficient data to run our simulation model on real data alone. For example, if a customer arrives about every ten minutes, we could sit for half a day with a clipboard and a watch and record about 24 arrivals. This would generally be too few to run a simulation of a reasonable length; it would not be unreasonable to run 10,000 simulated "customers" through a process simulation (more about run lengths later).

Step 2: Generating Streams of Events

How can we produce a long stream of simulated events that matches the characteristics of a much smaller sample? We use 0–1 uniformly distributed random numbers to generate a simulated stream of events. This can be done in two ways: either through the use of the empirical distribution, or by fitting a theoretical distribution.

In order to illustrate the two approaches, we consider the example of generating a simulated stream of customers arriving at some facility. Suppose that we gathered the following arrival times for the first 20 customers who arrived. For simplicity, we have expressed all times in minutes from the time we started collecting observations. For each arriving customer, we have also computed the time (in minutes) since the last customer arrived (Table 6.1).

Table 6.1: Customer Arrival Times

Customer Number	Arrival Time	Minutes Since Last Arrival
1	17.4	17.4
2	20.2	2.8
3	27.1	6.9
4	37.9	10.8
5	52.8	14.9
6	67.4	14.6
7	103.7	36.3
8	106.5	2.8
9	108.4	1.9
10	120.6	12.2
11	120.8	0.2
12	156.7	35.9
13	157.4	0.7
14	162.2	4.8
15	167.2	5.0
16	184.6	17.4
17	188.7	4.1
18	202.3	13.6
19	208.0	5.7
20	226.9	18.9

Method 1: Using Empirical Data

We could simulate a stream of random arrivals using the following procedure. First, we randomly choose a value from the "Minutes since last arrival" column (these values are often called "inter-arrival times"). This is done by generating a uniformly distributed integer between 1 and 20. The random integer is then used to pick a row from the table, and a database function is used to retrieve the inter-arrival time corresponding to that row.

If the table above was in cells A3:C22, then the formula for doing this is

= VLOOKUP(RANDBETWEEN(1,20),A3:C22, 3,1).

If you are using a version of Excel that does not have the RANDBETWEEN formula, then an equivalent formula is = VLOOKUP(INT(RAND()*20)+1,A3:C22, 3,1).

Each time the sheet is re-calculated, a new inter-arrival time is chosen. Because each of the integers from 1 to 20 is equally likely to be generated, each of the observed inter-arrival times is equally likely to be selected. This process is sometimes referred to as "sampling with replacement."

To generate a sequence of arrival times, the following procedure would be used. The first arrival time would go in the first row and be generated using the formula above. The second arrival time would go in the second row and be equal to the sum of the first arrival time and a newly generated inter-arrival time using a new value of = RAND(). Subsequent arrival times would go in subsequent rows and be a cumulative total of the last arrival time and a new inter-arrival time (hence the term "inter-arrival time).

Method 2: From a Theoretical Curve or a Known Distribution

The inter-arrival times in Table 6.1 could be approximated by a curve. In this instance, an *exponential distribution* with a mean of 11.3 fits the observed inter-arrival times reasonably well. We can, therefore, use this theoretical curve to generate inter-arrival times. We generate 0–1 uniformly distributed random numbers and then "invert" according to a theoretical function. For an exponential distribution, the inversion is done using the following formula (for more details, see the Appendix):

= –11.3 * LN(RAND())

This generates the inter-arrival times. A sequence of arrival times is generated as a cumulative total, just as when values are drawn from a table of empirical data.

Step 3: Building the Logic of a Simulation Model

We illustrate this step by showing how to construct a process model for The Tennessee Tour Bus Company.

We begin the spreadsheet model by placing the key parameters in cells. Cell D5 contains the time taken at the "fitting" stage (10 days), and the minimum and maximum times to paint a bus are placed in cells B6 and C6.

We first model the existing system. To construct the logic of the model, we identify each bus passing through the shop as a row. Row 10 charts the flow of the first bus through the (empty) shop. This bus begins bodywork at time 0 and is finished at time 10 (= B10+$D$5). It then moves directly into painting (at time 10), and painting takes some time between 2 (= $B$6) and 18 (= $C$6) days. We generate the time to paint the bus as a random variable distributed uniformly between 2 and 18 days using = $B$6 + ($C$6 − $B$6) * RAND(). This means that the completion time for the first bus is given by = D10 + $B$6 + ($C$6 − $B$6) * RAND() in cell E10.

Row 11 charts bus number 2 (= 1+A10 in A11). This bus begins bodywork at the time when the previous bus enters painting, freeing up the body shop (= D10 in B11), and completes bodywork at = B11+$D$5 (in Cell C11). Bus 2 can only enter painting if it has finished bodywork and Bus 1 has finished painting, and the formula = MAX(C11,E10) in cell D11 captures this. In the example below, the delay between the end of bodywork (at time 20) and the entry into painting (at time 25.46) indicates that the body shop was blocked for 5.46 days and could not start the next bus. (Bus 3, therefore, begins bodywork at time 25.46 days). Bus 2 completes painting at a time generated by = D11+$B$6+($C$6-$B$6)*RAND() in cell E11.

Rows 12 and following chart as many buses as we wish to include (and we have memory space for) using the spreadsheet copy command from row 11. We copy A11:E11 to rows A12:E129, charting 120 buses through the simulated shop.

To obtain a performance measure for the shop, we note that since the shop always starts empty, the first few buses take less time to complete than do later buses, which may be held up by congestion. A simple way to remove this "start-up" effect is to ignore the first few buses when computing the performance measures. One performance measure is, therefore, the total time taken to complete buses numbers 21 thru 120, or = (E129 − B30) (in cell E3).

We now model the proposed system, with the one-bus inventory space, in columns G through K of the same spreadsheet. The logic is essentially the same, but we include an

	A	B	C	D	E
1		**Tennessee Tour Bus Company**			
2		Existing System			
3		Time to complete 100 buses			1,209.35
4	**Parameters**				
5	Bodywork			10	
6	Painting	2	18		
7					
8	Bus	Start	End	Into	Finished
9	Number	Bodywork	Bodywork	Painting	Painting
10	1	0.00	10.00	10.00	25.46
11	2	10.00	20.00	25.46	40.11
12	3	25.46	35.46	40.11	42.43
13	4	40.11	50.11	50.11	60.26
14	5	50.11	60.11	60.26	70.14
15	6	60.26	70.26	70.26	80.74
16	7	70.26	80.26	80.74	91.92
17	8	80.74	90.74	91.92	99.40
18	9	91.92	101.92	101.92	117.29
19	10	101.92	111.92	117.29	132.81
20	11	117.29	127.29	132.81	147.90
21	12	132.81	142.81	147.90	159.50
⋮					
129	120	1,416.69	1,426.69	1,434.10	1,441.77

extra column to record the time at which the bus enters the inventory space. For Bus 1, this is the same as the time of completion of bodywork, but for later buses it is the maximum of the time at which the bus completes bodywork (column H) and the time at which painting begins painting the previous bus (column J) (since beginning painting leads to removing the bus from inventory into the paint shop making the inventory space

Tennessee Tour Bus Company

	Existing System						Proposed System			
	Time to complete 100 buses			1,209.35			Time to complete 100 buses			1,089.00
Parameters										
Bodywork			10							
Painting	2	18								
Bus	Start	End	Into	Finished		Start	End	Into	Into	Finished
Number	Bodywork	Bodywork	Painting	Painting		Bodywork	Bodywork	Inventory	Painting	Painting
1	0.00	10.00	10.00	25.46		0.00	10.00	10.00	10.00	23.34
2	10.00	20.00	25.46	40.11		10.00	20.00	20.00	23.34	40.87
3	25.46	35.46	40.11	42.43		20.00	30.00	30.00	40.87	51.58
4	40.11	50.11	50.11	60.26		30.00	40.00	40.87	51.58	62.45
5	50.11	60.11	60.26	70.14		40.87	50.87	51.58	62.45	64.63
6	60.26	70.26	70.26	80.74		51.58	61.58	62.45	64.63	69.07
7	70.26	80.26	80.74	91.92		62.45	72.45	72.45	72.45	88.03
8	80.74	90.74	91.92	99.40		72.45	82.45	82.45	88.03	99.01
9	91.92	101.92	101.92	117.29		82.45	92.45	92.45	99.01	107.32
10	101.92	111.92	117.29	132.81		92.45	102.45	102.45	107.32	123.81
11	117.29	127.29	132.81	147.90		102.45	112.45	112.45	123.81	126.70
12	132.81	142.81	147.90	159.50		112.45	122.45	123.81	126.70	144.55
:										
120	1,416.69	1,426.69	1,434.10	1,441.77		1,263.96	1,273.96	1,276.57	1,286.00	1,295.32

available, if needed). The appropriate formula is = MAX(J10,H11) in cell I11. The time at which Bus 2 enters painting is the latest (maximum) of the time Bus 1 completed painting and Bus 2 entered inventory (= MAX(K10,I11) in Cell J11). The last change to make is to note that bodywork can start on Bus 2 as soon as Bus 1 enters inventory (= I10 in cell G11).

Copying the formulae in G11 through K11 to the range G12:K129 simulates 120 buses passing through the proposed system. The time taken to complete the last 100 of these buses (= K129 – G30 in cell K3) provides a performance measure for the proposed system. The spreadsheet containing both models appears as follows:

Step 4: Validating the Model

Before running the model and using model results, it is important to validate the model, that is, to make sure that the model is accurate and produces reasonable results. A first check on model validity is to ensure that the model has *face validity*. Face validity means that it looks correct to managers and other people with subject matter expertise. A second check on validity is to ensure that the model does not generate numerical errors, as may happen if the model encounters division by zero, or other mathematical operations that cannot be performed. A third check is on the calculations themselves. In event models, it may be possible to carefully examine the calculations involved in a single scenario to ensure that they are correct. In process models, it may be possible to trace one person or object as it moves through the system, again checking to ensure the correctness of the calculations. Finally, a powerful tool for model validation is to compare the results versus known historical data, if it exists.

Step 5: Running the Model and Collecting Results

The = RAND() function used in the model is recalculated each time the spreadsheet is recalculated (for example, by using the F9 recalculation key) and so there is not one set of result: some statistical analysis is required. Each use of F9 provides one snapshot of the operations of the two systems, each processing 100 buses. By repeatedly pressing F9, we can obtain a sample that provides a sense of the variability in our performance statistics. The table below shows the results from 20 recalculations of these statistics:

We see that this sample of 20 observations provides an estimate that the addition of the inventory space will reduce the time to complete 100 buses by an average of 129.28 days, representing a time saving of 1.29 days per bus. In terms of an average productivity gain, if we operated the system with the inventory space for the same time as the original system (1,206.93 days), we would average 100*1206.93/1077.65 = 112 buses instead of 100, for a productivity gain of 12%.

	Existing System	Proposed System	Difference
	1,209.35	1,089.00	120.35
	1,214.36	1,069.96	144.40
	1,169.96	1,095.11	74.85
	1,220.62	1,101.32	119.30
	1,261.45	1,089.12	172.33
	1,249.74	1,034.96	214.78
	1,170.50	1,084.57	85.93
	1,212.27	1,056.99	155.28
	1,204.29	1,110.79	93.50
	1,202.89	1,047.34	155.55
	1,216.04	1,082.45	133.59
	1,232.45	1,085.77	146.68
	1,195.25	1,032.77	162.48
	1,222.16	1,099.14	123.02
	1,203.54	1,110.26	93.28
	1,184.61	1,017.11	167.50
	1,203.11	1,068.50	134.61
	1,198.58	1,092.95	105.63
	1,192.60	1,063.85	128.75
	1,174.76	1,120.98	53.78
Mean	1,206.93	1,077.65	129.28
Std. Dev.	23.77	28.26	38.09

Step 6: Analyzing the Model Output

Generally, there are two types of analyses that people perform with simulation models. The first is to look at the descriptive statistics for the purpose of understanding the distribution. This involves plotting the histogram of model results to see the shape of the distribution and calculating relevant descriptive statistics (e.g., mean, median, standard deviation). A histogram of simulated output is often called a *risk profile*.

A second use of simulation data is making predictions. Our first analysis of the Tennessee Tour Bus model resulted in a sample of 20 runs of our model. If we ran the model a 21st time, what will be the time-savings for the new sample of 100 buses? The *prediction interval* addresses this issue. The *prediction interval* is the interval from the mean minus two standard deviations to the mean plus two standard deviations. Approximately 95% of the time (or 19 times out of 20), the next model run will produce a result within this interval. We conclude that an approximate 95% prediction interval for the estimated savings is manufacturing time is the interval from 53.1 to 205.5 days. Computing this interval on a *per bus* basis, we conclude that we expect the addition of the inventory space to save us between 0.53 days and 2.05 days per bus, 19 times out of 20.

The *prediction interval* provides an idea of the variability of the model result and in this case this wide interval suggests considerable variability. One method to narrow this interval is to increase our sample size from 100 buses to 1,000 buses. To do this, we copy row 129 down to row 1029, and recalculate the completion time for 1,000 buses by modifying the formulae in cells E3 and K3 to reflect the fact that row 1029 is now the final row of the model (that is change E129–B20 in E3 to E1029–B30). Twenty replications of the 1,000 bus simulator produced the results shown below.

Existing System	Proposed System	Difference	Difference per/bus
12,139.66	10,900.52	1,239.15	1.239
11,984.13	10,665.72	1,318.41	1.318
12,201.25	10,862.62	1,338.63	1.339
11,908.07	10,634.58	1,273.50	1.274
11,997.66	10,666.02	1,331.64	1.332
12,048.57	10,806.04	1,242.52	1.243
11,925.03	10,656.97	1,268.07	1.268
12,017.70	10,753.29	1,264.41	1.264
12,081.35	10,854.13	1,227.22	1.227
11,930.21	10,693.05	1,237.16	1.237
11,944.47	10,598.82	1,345.65	1.346

11,833.91	10,587.75	1,246.16	1.246
12,090.19	10,879.47	1,210.72	1.211
12,096.82	10,791.06	1,305.77	1.306
11,770.65	10,492.56	1,278.09	1.278
12,091.28	10,829.69	1,261.59	1.262
11,987.41	10,678.94	1,308.47	1.308
12,027.18	10,704.44	1,322.74	1.323
12,126.91	10,840.52	1,286.40	1.286
12,123.65	10,856.55	1,267.10	1.267
	Mean	**1,278.67**	**1.2787**
	Std. Dev.	**39.59**	**0.0396**

From these results, the *95% prediction interval* for the estimated time-savings for a new sample of 1,000 buses is 1278.67 ± 2*39.59 days, or on a per bus basis 1.2787 ± 2*0.0396 days. The prediction interval is between 1.199 days and 1.358 days per bus, 19 times out of 20; the increased sample size has narrowed this interval considerably.

Extending the sample size in this way imposes a cost: the model takes more memory and takes longer to run. Both of these are noticeable in the small simulator developed above, and become even more of a factor in larger and more complex simulation programs. We, therefore, look for ways to achieve more precision in our estimates without increasing the sample size. Since these methods reduce the variance in our model results, they are called *variance reduction methods*.

Variance Reduction Methods

One simple variance reduction technique enables the interval to be narrowed considerably. This technique is to simulate both the existing and the proposed system processing *the same buses*. Since the bodywork time for each bus is constant (at 10 days) in both systems, all buses are already the same in terms of bodywork. Painting times, however, are generated from separate random numbers in each system and are different: Bus 1 takes 25.46 – 10, or 15.46, days to paint in the existing system, but 23.34 – 10, or 13.34, days to paint in the proposed system. Changing the formula in cell K10 to = J10+E10-D10 and copying to K11:K129 sets the painting time for each bus in the proposed system at the same duration as that generated using = RAND() for the simulation of the existing system. We could accomplish the same effect by generating 120 simulated buses "off-line," each with its own processing times, and then feeding this data set of simulated buses through our simulators of the existing system and of the proposed system. Collecting real processing time for 120 buses and running this through both simulators would also have the same effect.

Twenty replications of the simulation now produced the results shown below:

Existing System	Proposed System	Difference
1,251.28	1,094.93	156.35
1,182.18	1,048.02	134.17
1,224.69	1,101.27	123.42
1,216.93	1,066.17	150.76
1,192.56	1,079.97	112.58
1,231.77	1,084.62	147.15
1,194.57	1,044.48	150.09
1,199.48	1,079.11	120.37
1,231.31	1,109.51	121.80
1,207.50	1,073.17	134.34
1,243.48	1,084.97	158.51
1,220.10	1,074.59	145.52
1,235.92	1,095.11	140.81
1,182.31	1,033.08	149.23
1,232.93	1,101.07	131.86
1,238.85	1,105.20	133.65
1,190.25	1,047.34	142.91
1,174.41	1,040.46	133.95
1,203.66	1,073.63	130.04
1,189.65	1,078.21	111.44
	Mean	136.45
	Std. Dev.	13.80

We note that the use of the same simulated buses has reduced the standard deviation of the mean processing time for 100 buses from 40.04 to 13.80 days, *with no additional computation requirements*. The prediction interval has slimmed from 0.53 to 2.05 days per bus to 1.08 to 1.64 days per bus.

A Second Look at Process Simulation Logic: The Flowchart

The flowchart provides another way of detailing the logic of a simulation. Flowcharts are particularly useful if a simulation model is to be coded into a computer language. We will examine three types of process logic: *discrete time* logic, *discrete event* logic, and *entity life-cycle* logic.

A flowcharting, illustrating *discrete time* logic for a simulation model of the Tennessee Tour Bus Company's existing operations is shown in Figure 6.1:

The following steps are involved:

- **Initialization.** We begin by setting the starting conditions for the model. We define a variable "CLOCK" that will keep track of the clock time and set its starting value to 0, set the state of the paint shop to "IDLE," and generate the time that the first bus will complete body work.

- **Main Loop.** Now that the starting conditions are set, we enter the main loop of the model. Each time around this loop, we advance the clock by one "tick" and check to see whether an event has occurred that has changed the state of the system. We first check to see if the body shop has finished working on its bus. If it has not, we check to see if the paint shop has finished its work. If neither has finished, we move the clock forward one "tick" and loop again.

If the bodywork has finished, we check to see if the paint shop is "BUSY." If it is busy, then there is nothing we can do but go round the loop again; the body shop is "blocked." If painting is "IDLE," we move the bus from the body shop to the paint shop; in the model this involves setting the paint shop to "BUSY," generating a new paint shop completion time, and also a new body shop completion time (since moving the bus into the paint shop coincides with beginning bodywork on a new bus). We now go round the loop again.

There are a number of important items to be considered that are not included in the flowchart (Figure 6.1).

Stopping Rule: Note that the flowchart (Figure 6.1) contains no way of terminating the simulation. This could be done by exiting the main loop when the clock reaches a certain

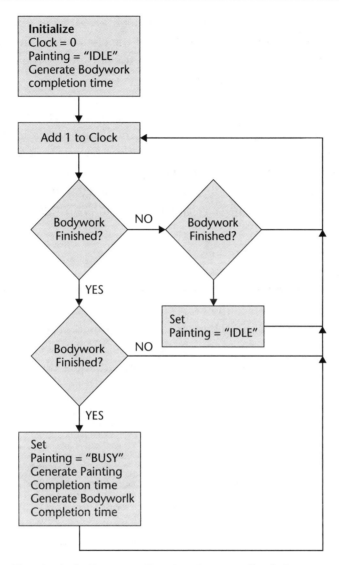

Figure 6.1 Discrete Time Logic for Tennessee Tour Bus Company Simulation

time, or exiting when a certain number of buses have been processed through the plant. The appropriate stopping method will depend on the statistical design of the experiments, and what data is being collected. To replicate the spreadsheet model (above), we would keep a count of the number of buses painted and terminate the simulation when this reached 120, printing out the value of "clock" when this occurred.

Statistics Collection: The flowchart (Figure 6.1) contains no statistics collection. We must determine what output we wish to collect, and then devise logic to collect the necessary statistics. For example, if we wish to know the percentage of time that the paint shop is idle, we set up a counter that counts each "tick" of the clock where the paint shop is idle. At the end of the simulation, dividing the value of the counter by the ending value of the CLOCK variable provides the required rate.

The Size of the "Tick": If we chose to "tick" the clock forward in very small time increments, than we spend a great deal of time spinning round the simulation loop with nothing happening. If we go to a larger time increment, we may not be able to recognize events when they actually occur; for example, if we compute processing time in minutes, but tick the clock forward in hours, then a bus could be sitting completed in the body shop for up to 59 minutes before we move it into a vacant paint shop. This difficulty leads directly to discrete event logic.

Discrete Event Logic

In discrete event logic, we replace the even "ticking" of the clock by variable time increments. This recognizes that nothing happens in the simulation model unless some event triggers changes in the state of the system. We illustrate the concept with The Tennessee Tour Bus Company. Figure 6.2 illustrates the flowchart for a discrete event simulation model.

For the discrete event simulation we define three variables:

- *Clock* is the clock time.
- *Bodytime* is the completion time of the bus occupying the Bodyshop.
- *Painttime* is the completion time of the bus occupying the Paintshop.

We will use *Painttime* = 99999 (a number larger than the maximum value of the clock variable) as a code to denote that the paint shop is empty.

Initialization requires that we set Clock to 0, set *Painttime* to 99999 (start with the paint shop empty), and generate the time of the first event, which is the completion of bodywork for the first bus.

The logic of the main loop (Figure 6.2) involves determining which event occurs first, body completion or painting completion, advancing the clock to the time of that event, and then processing that event.

If bodywork completes first, check to see if the paint shop is empty (or *Painttime* = 99999); if so, move the bus from the body shop to the paint shop and generate completion times

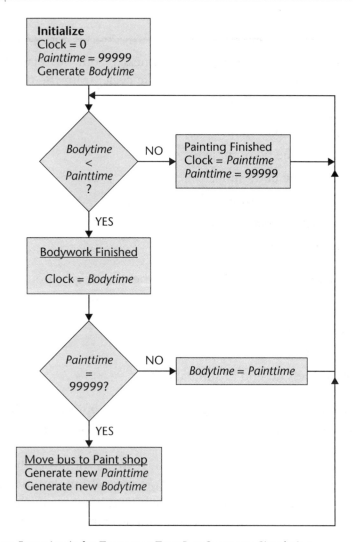

Figure 6.2 Discrete Event Logic for Tennessee Tour Bus Company Simulation

for both bodywork on the next bus, and painting of this bus. If the paint shop is not empty, set *Bodytime* equal to *Painttime* so that on the next loop, the end-of-painting event will be processed.

If painting completes first, set the clock to *Painttime*, empty the paint shop (*Painttime* = 99999), and loop again.

As a final example of the logic of simulation, we view the system from the perspective of the entities moving through the simulated process. This is known as *entity life-cycle logic*.

Entity Life-Cycle Logic

We can represent a bus moving through the Tennessee Tour Bus plant as an entity that goes through the following activities during its life-cycle: from the time of arrival at the plant to that of departure from the plant:

1. The bus seizes the body shop.
2. The bus occupies the body shop.
3. The bus releases the body shop.
4. The bus seizes the paint shop.
5. The bus occupies the paint shop.
6. The bus releases the paint shop.

The body shop and pain shop are also entities; these both go through the same simple life-cycle:

1. Open for business (at time 0).
2. Working.
3. Closed for business (at end of simulation).

[If we wished, we could schedule working hours each day, but since we have assumed that the state of the system is unaffected by the close-down and startup, this is unnecessary].

In the Tennessee Tour Bus example, there will be a stream of bus entities going through the same list of activities at different times. In more general simulation models, there may be many different types of entities, each with their own life-cycle description. These processes may interact as entities compete for the same resources, resulting in the formation of queues, bottlenecks, and so forth.

Graphics and Animation

Simulation modeling was once the world of the "black-box" simulation model into which data was entered, and from which numbers emerged. Simulation has now moved beyond this toward *graphical* and *visual interactive simulation*, where the model-user or decision maker can watch a dynamic, color graphic display of model output, and can interrupt the model, change data or decision rules, and continue.

The first visual interactive simulation models emerged from attempts to build interactive simulation models of car plants. Modelers ran into the problem of displaying the status of the model so that the user could see when to interact (and the effect of the interaction).

After experimenting with the display of intermediate numerical results, and transferring these results to physical models of the system, the modelers began producing dynamic computer-generated graphic displays. As technology has developed, the quality of these displays has improved enormously, and we now have simulation software that can produce multi-colored, three-dimensional dynamic graphics showing the operation of large systems—and all on a personal computer.

Animation can be used in two different ways: *post-processed* animation and *visual interactive* animation. In *post-processed animation*, the moving pictures are used to illustrate the results of running a non-graphic simulation model. The user can watch the moving pictures but cannot interact with the model, and cannot make changes. In *visual interactive animation*, the model is actually running while the pictures are being displayed: the user can stop the model, make changes, and continue, and can immediately see the results of the interaction visually. Simulation software that takes the visual interactive approach includes SEE-WHY (the first commercially available simulation software to include animation), SIMSCRIPT II.5, SIMAN/CINEMA, AUTOMOD, Simul8, Promodel, Medmodel, Arena, and many others.

The Benefits of Graphics and "Animation"

Simulation packages that include dynamic graphics or "animation" have been a huge market success: almost all commercial simulation software now includes this capability. This market success appears to be the result of several factors:

- The graphics output has wide appeal. Users enjoy seeing a visual display of their system in operation.

- The graphics displays and interaction help the user to understand the model, and to take an active part in using and experimenting with the simulation.

- Interaction with the model increases confidence in it and increases the probability of results being implemented. Users feel that they are participants in the problem-solving process rather than spectators.

- The visualization helps to obtain managerial commitment to the simulation study by helping the decision maker and modeler to validate the simulation model. This increases the probability that useful change will occur.

- The picture enables the user to shift attention between different parts of the simulation easily and quickly.

- The graphical output might reveal situations that the modeler or decision maker might never have envisaged. A moving picture can capture unusual "transient" states (or "crises") that would not be visible in long-run average results from a traditional simulation.

- The graphical displays provide a focal point that appears to be helpful for group decision making, particularly for investigating the causes of conflicting opinion in the group.

- Graphics appear to be useful when qualitative dimensions enter into the decision making, and where the decisions depend on the state of the system.

- Animation appears to be useful for decision making in very complex systems (where there may be multiple decision criteria).

Many of these points are captured in the following quotation from one of the pioneers of visual interactive simulation:

> If the model progresses as the manager expects, then credibility in its use is increased. If, however, the model diverges from the expectations of the manager then this leads to direct communications between the analyst and the manager. Either the model is correct, in which case the manager learns from the situation, or the model is logically incorrect. If the latter is true then the manager can usually state the logical inconsistency in the model, since he is watching the dynamic visual representation. At the next interactive session with the inconsistencies rectified, the model soon ceases to become the analyst's model and becomes the manager's own management model. This observation has occurred on all management visual simulations developed to date. (*Source*: R. D. Hurrion, *European Journal of Operational Research*, 5, 1980)

Large-Scale Simulation Models

The modeler building a large-scale simulation model has many software options available. First, the model can be coded in a third-generation language (such as C/C++, Java, or Visual BASIC). These languages are highly flexible, but require that the model, including all input and output statements, be coded from scratch. Special-purpose languages (such as GPSS, SIMSCRIPT, and SLAM) provide the modeler with a variety of skeletal simulation models: by filling in the "blanks," the modeler can access standard simulation model logic, which may significantly shorten the programming task. To take advantage of the existing input and output formats provided by the spreadsheet, a simulation model could be coded in a spreadsheet macro language (for example, using the VBA macro language included in Microsoft Excel).

Simulation in Action

Simulation at Kentucky Fried Chicken

The Kentucky Fried Chicken (KFC) Operations Group used simulation models to assist in evaluating operations within its restaurant system in an effort to remain a key player in a highly competitive industry.

KFC was a member of the PepsiCo, Inc. conglomerate, whose restaurant system was the largest in the world. KFC, headquartered in Louisville, Kentucky, operated more than 8,100 restaurant sites, with 5,000 in the United States and the remaining 3,100 distributed throughout 58 other countries. KFC was a competitor in the quick service restaurant (QSR) industry and, as such, faced intense competition, as new players and products were constantly entering the field. Customers demanded good food, good service, low prices, and, most of all, speedy delivery. Any resources wasted during production or delivery of the product, when multiplied by the number of sites in operation, represented a huge detriment to success.

In order to ensure continued financial returns and optimal productivity, KFC formed an operations research group to provide solutions for certain operational problems. Two examples of these operations were service systems for large volume restaurants and drive-through operations.

Information from large volume restaurants was developed into a representative customer order database. A simulation model was built that used this database to allow equipment configurations, queuing methods for producing menu items, order-taking and other service and packaging procedures to be analyzed. The model accepted alternative menu mixes and determined their impact on the restaurant. The results provided the optimal equipment configurations, minimum labor requirements, and alternate packing techniques required to increase restaurant volume substantially.

A similar simulation model was developed for KFC's drive-through operations. The analysis performed involved evaluating alternate drive-through layouts, varied numbers of pay/pick-up windows, and varied menu board locations. The results of the model provided the minimum capital expenditures required to increase drive-through capacity and profits.

Simulation models for other areas of operations are being developed in an effort to maintain KFC's competitive success (*Source*: L. Cook, "Simulation Applications at KFC," *Softletter*, 7, 1 (Spring 1991), published by Pritsker Corporation, Indianapolis, Indiana).

Keeping Ahead of the $2 Billion Canal

The Welland Canal is a major link in the St. Lawrence Seaway. This seaway was built jointly by the United States and Canada to enable ocean-going freighters to travel up the Great Lakes to the ports of Duluth, Chicago, Thunder Bay, etc. The Welland Canal enables these freighters to bypass Niagara Falls and was used in the 1960s and '70s primarily for transporting grain from Duluth to the Atlantic (then overseas), and for transporting steel and iron ore from Europe and eastern Canada to the heart of North America.

Efficiency was the primary reason why the canal was so essential as a mode of transportation. Shipping was three times more efficient than rail and 12 times more efficient than road transportation, because ships could carry large loads that exceeded the weight and capacity limitations of rail or road transport.

The Capacity Problem of the 1960s and 1970s

In 1964, an average of 20 vessels were waiting at each end of the canal for passage through the lock system, at an average cost of $12,000/day. At the same time, there was heavy political pressure to transport grain overseas, demanding that the canal perform more efficiently. The whole situation turned into a simple problem: demand must meet supply, and that was how the success of the canal was measured.

By 1967, with $26 million in improvements to the canal recently completed, capacity of the canal was again exceeded by demand, although it was generally believed that this was temporary, and that eventually a new canal would have to be built to satisfy the escalating demand from shipping. It was estimated that the cost of a new canal would exceed $2 billion. One official of the St. Lawrence Seaway Authority, the governing body in charge of the Welland Canal's day-to-day operations, stated:

> With increasing demand and growing ship sizes, how would the St. Lawrence Seaway Authority meet its mandate to maintaining an efficient level of service while delaying the inevitable $2 billion expenditure for building a new canal?

The Solution Using Simulation

In 1974, the Operational Systems Analysis Section (OSAS) was created to try to understand the fundamental problems of the canal, with the objective of keeping capacity ahead of demand. The OSAS realized that the canal system was quite complex. For example:

- There were eight locks in series, separated by bodies of water (known as "reaches") of varying lengths.
- There was one-way movement between some locks (some reaches were too narrow to allow passage of more than one ship at a time).
- Each lock had to provide service in two directions to raise or lower vessels.
- Several bridges between locks introduced delays because only one vessel could go under a bridge at a time.
- Arrivals of ships were random; there was no set schedule that ships followed.
- Vessel sizes and speeds varied considerably.

The OSAS team decided to build a simulation model to study activity in the canal. This would enable them to conduct what-if analyses with all the variables, including those listed above, that affected the performance of the canal. *Without such a model, it would be too expensive to test every proposed upgrading project, since thousands of suggestions for improvements had been put forward.*

The OSAS team, with help from outside experts, built a complex simulation model of the Welland Canal in just 14 months, at a cost of $116,400.

Use of the Simulation Model

The simulator could use historical data of ship arrivals or randomly generated data to make projections of the future. An early example of the use of the model to test ideas to improve canal throughput was the investigation of the "Lock 7 problem."

Lock 7 was thought to be the slowest area of the canal. Two options had been proposed. The first, a popular option of many experts, was to spend $10 million to reconstruct the approach wall above the lock to permit the exiting and entering vessels to pass much closer to the lock, reducing large vessel times above the lock by 10%. Following analysis using the simulator, it was found that this option would not increase the capacity of the entire canal; in fact, there was no benefit to be gained by speeding up this one lock.

The second, albeit less popular, option was to widen the channel above Lock 7 to accommodate more ships and to permit two-way traffic. After running this option through the simulator, it was quickly recognized as a successful option, increasing the capacity of the canal by about 5%, at a cost of $8 million.

The Impact of the Work

Over a period of several years, the simulation model was used to investigate many innovative decision rules and canal alterations designed to increase the capacity of the canal. By 1980, management at the Seaway Authority was confident that they would be able to modify existing canal operations to meet the expected demand on the canal until at least the year 2000. The $2 billion expenditure for the new canal was, therefore, delayed for at least 20 years.

This simulation model prevented many projects that were not cost-effective from being started, while enabling the St. Lawrence Seaway Authority to successfully keep ahead of demand, thus delaying construction of the new $2 billion canal. In recent years, demand at the Welland Canal has dropped off sharply, as grain exports have dropped dramatically. The canal is not as busy as it was in the '70s and early '80s, but the lessons learned from the simulation project remain valuable (*Source*: W. A. Dawson et al., "Keeping Ahead of a $2 Billion Canal," *Interfaces*, *11*, 6, 1981).

War Games with the U.S. Military

The U.S. military needed field training to improve the battlefield skills of military commanders and their staff, but federal budget cuts made real-life field exercises a rare and expensive luxury. As an alternative, the various branches of the U.S. military (Army, Navy, Air Force) developed computerized battlefield simulators.

The Result: A New Level of Training

The new simulation was given its first major test in the Ulchi Focus Lens 1992 (ULF 92) training exercise. The military set up a global network, with the Army's simulator run on hardware in Korea, and the Air Force and Navy simulators run in Germany. Players from Europe, the United States, and Korea played together without leaving their bases.

The distributed interactive simulation (DIS) was cheaper and faster to organize than a real exercise, and had several other benefits:

- It allowed people in different functional areas to train together and practice coordinating their efforts,
- It was possible to simulate environments that could not be used in real exercises.
- Military commanders could test what-if scenarios and assess their relative effectiveness.
- There was no damage to the environment from lead shells, depleted uranium shells, or heavy equipment.
- There was no risk of provoking adversaries as might be the case when staging a real exercise. (*Source*: D. S. Hartley III, "War Games," *OR/MS Today*, August 1993)

Vilpac Truck Manufacturing

The North American Free Trade Agreement (NAFTA) has provided a major new opportunity for North American manufacturers, including the Vilpac Truck Manufacturing Company of Mexicali, Mexico, which found itself positioned to take advantage of Mexico's increased competitiveness and prosperity. Vilpac was a joint venture between PACCAR Industries, a manufacturer of Kenworth trucks in Portland, Oregon, and the Vildosola family of Mexico, and was producing up to 22 units/day, with a workforce of 1,200 and annual sales of $415 million.

The tremendous increase in cross-border hauling as NAFTA took effect, together with Mexico's expanding highway system, promised a solid future for Vilpac, but trade liberalization also posed the threat of increased competition from major truck manufacturers, such as Volvo and General Motors. Vilpac, however, was not typical of many U.S./Mexico joint ventures under the *maquiladora* program, where Mexico was used mainly for high labor content production. Vilpac recognized that it had to change in order to become a world-class manufacturer, and the key to this transformation was investment in technology rather than labor.

World-Class Manufacturing

For the world-class manufacturer, manufacturing is seen as a competitive weapon and not simply as just another functional area. To achieve a level of manufacturing that is "world class," the firm must attain a high degree of understanding of its operations and processes. This understanding leads to control, where the controlled operations can be manipulated with the effects being known before the consequences are incurred. The knowledge a company has about its operations can then be used for advanced planning, making the company proactive rather than reactive in the marketplace. At Vilpac, planning involved anticipating customers' needs in the future, implementing new manufacturing methods for increasing quality, or reducing costs. The world-class manufacturer uses a process of continuous improvement to sustain its competitive advantage, never being content to maintain the status quo.

Re-engineering Vilpac

Before pursuing world-class manufacturing standards, Vilpac underwent extensive process re-engineering under the direction of C.E.O. Don Gustava Vildosola. This re-engineering process started with the development of a new understanding of the corporation and its strategic business objectives, and a complete analysis of current operations and systems. The business processes were then re-engineered to correct fundamental deficiencies in the existing system.

Process re-engineering was not limited to manufacturing operations, but also involved the mapping out of all existing processes, with ideal processes being identified by viewing all operations from the customer's perspective. An essential part of this methodology was the development of a comprehensive detailed simulation model of the manufacturing system, which was used to assess the performance of proposed manufacturing processes. Once identified, these ideal processes contained the correct amount of quality assurance, technology, employee involvement, and continually focused upon the customer. By following these steps, redundancies were eliminated and modifications were planned with a view to replicating the ideal process.

The existing plant and workforce had to be considered, so a migration plan was developed to implement the change from the status quo to the newly designed processes on a continuous improvement basis. Each step in the migration process was defined in terms of strategic objectives and activities, which included training, defining metrics, establishing alliances, and further analysis and modeling.

The Simulation Model

The simulation itself had to handle a great deal of randomness. Although the randomness made model construction more difficult, it enhanced its usefulness, as no production engineer could account for all the possibilities when designing or assessing the impact of modifying plant procedures. More than 95 different machines with varying yields, 1,900 parts, 1,177 setup times, 60 maintenance malfunctions, 30 critical tools, 26 material handling systems, five end products, and 11 production sequences were incorporated into the model. Clearly, the ability to balance and coordinate these processes through successive iterations with the aid of this model produced significant planning advantages.

The creation of the simulation program provided a great deal of impetus for managers to work together in both the strategy formulation sessions and the re-engineering workshops. Managers realized that if their views were not expressed in the simulation, then future decisions would not address their concerns. Management had to be (and were) convinced that this new technology would be used to determine future capital expenditures, such as introducing a new product line, expanding capacity, or purchasing new equipment. The integration of strategy throughout the company was an unexpected but valuable benefit.

Another benefit of the model was the ability to test changes in the plant without spending any money unless the modifications proved successful. The managers were interested in altering capacity, product mix, inventory controls, setup times, maintenance policies, and process flows. Only those improvements that could be seen to have a positive impact on the company were implemented. The simulation model enabled Vilpac to avoid common pitfalls—such as shifting bottlenecks, accumulating inventories, and rejecting new products for fear of congestion—while concentrating attention on important constraints, such as critical setup times and equipment capacities.

The simulation provided several management criteria for each configuration tested, including throughput time, cycle time, cost, inventory level, utilization rates, and most importantly, the value added in each process. Suggestions for change were evaluated and implemented based on their cost effectiveness and overall priority.

The Payoff

The computer simulation has dramatically increased the productivity and profitability of Vilpac Truck Manufacturing Company by focusing management attention on the aspects of the plant where improvements offered the largest rewards. The ability to assess the consequences of changing the plant before investing money has led to better decision making and a corresponding increase in company performance.

The results have been dramatic, with an increase in net profits of 70% and a corresponding decrease in fixed costs of 26%, despite a 260% increase in production. Other intangibles include improved quality and market share, as well as the ability to offer the highest wages in the Baja region of Mexico (*Source*: J. P. Nuño et al., "Mexico's Vilpac Truck Company Uses a CIM Implementation to Become a World Class Manufacturer," *Interfaces*, *23*, 1, 1993).

Summary

All companies face risk and uncertainty. In this chapter, we introduced stochastic or Monte Carlo simulation models, which are a powerful set of tools for aiding decisions in the face of risk and uncertainty. Stochastic simulation models are divided into two important types: event models and process (or discrete event) models.

We introduced six steps involved in building and using a simulation model, and we presented several examples of companies that have had great success in implementing simulation models.

A manager may well find opportunities to build and use small simulation models, likely in a spreadsheet or using user-friendly graphical interactive software. This will require that the manager be able to sketch out the logic of the model, enter the model into the software, and run the model and interpret the results.

What the Manager Must Know

Simulation can help the manager improve the firm's competitiveness in many important ways. Simulation models enable complex processes and situations too be "run" in the computer and experimented with at very low cost in order to improve understanding and decision-making.

Simulation models are often used in situations where the manager faces considerable *risk* or *uncertainty*. In order to make use of these valuable tools, the manager must be aware of the capabilities of simulation models, and of the existence of the "simulation industry," which includes both software vendors and consulting firms. The manager also needs to:

- Be able to recognize the kinds of problems where simulation can yield useful solutions.

- Understand the basic types of simulation model, and be able to give direction on how a simulation model is to be constructed.

- Understand the issue of simulation model validation, and the steps necessary to determine whether a model is a valid representation of the real system.

- Understand and be able to interpret simulation model output, and be able to participate intelligently in a discussion involving the results of a simulation study.

Appendix 1 An Example of Curve Fitting to Empirical Data

The 20 observed inter-arrival times (Table 6.1) are plotted as a cumulative frequency distribution in Figure 6.A.1.

That is, the height of the curve at x gives the fraction of observations with an inter-arrival time less than x. Also superimposed on Figure 6A.1 is the mathematical function:

$$P = 1 - e^{(-t/11.3)}$$

where P is the cumulative probability,
   t is the inter-arrival time, and
   11.3 is the *mean inter-arrival time* (calculated from the data).

This theoretical curve fits the observed points reasonably well. We can, therefore, use this theoretical curve to generate inter-arrival times. We note that P takes on a value between 0 and 1; by generating P values as 0–1 uniformly distributed random numbers and then "inverting" the theoretical function, we obtain the inter-arrival times. The "inversion" is accomplished as follows:

For: $P = 1 - e^{(-t/11.3)}$
then: $1 - P = e^{(-t/11.3)}$
and: $\ln(1 - P) = (-t/11.3)$
$t = -11.3 \ln(1 - P)$

Since $(1 - P)$ has the same distribution as P, we can generate an inter-arrival time that fits the empirical data using the statement:

$= -11.3 \times LN(RAND())$

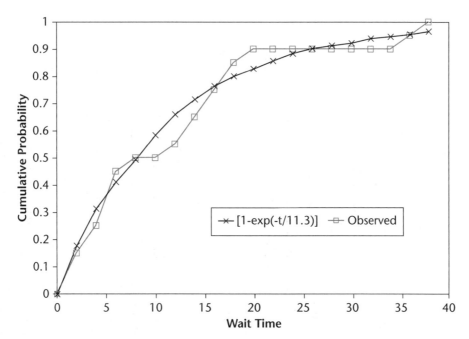

Figure 6.A.1 Fit between Empirical Data and Theoretical Curve. (Abstracted from *OR/MS Today*, Simulation Software Survey, October 2007. Online at http://www.lionhrtpub.com/orms/surveys/Simulation/Simulation1.html, accessed July 28, 2009.)

Appendix 2 Simulation in Excel Using = RAND()

Random numbers can be generated in almost any computer software. In Microsoft Excel, the function = RAND() in a cell assigns that cell a value between 0 and 1, with all values in this range equally likely. We call these 0–1 uniformly distributed random numbers. Each time the Excel spreadsheet is recalculated, the values assigned to cells that include RAND() are recomputed using new values for RAND().

Try the following exercise: In any cell in the spreadsheet, enter = RAND(). Now recalculate the spreadsheet (function key 9) and observe the changes in the value generated by RAND(): each time the spreadsheet is recalculated, the values of all RAND() functions are recomputed.

Figure 6.A.2 shows a histogram of the frequencies of 10,000 random numbers generated by the Excel RAND() function. All class intervals are expected to occur with the same frequency, although, in any sample that we collect, there will be observed variations from this expectation. Since frequencies accumulated in 20 class intervals are plotted, our expectation is to find 500 (= 10,000/20) values in each interval, and this is approximately the case. Theoretically, = RAND() can produce the value 0.0 exactly, but not the value 1.0 exactly: this is only a theoretical issue, since the probability of generating 0.0 "exactly" is

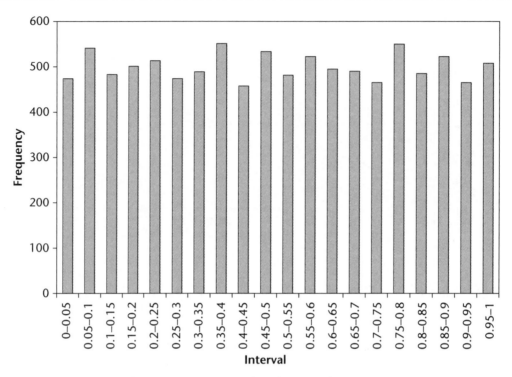

Figure 6.A.2 Frequencies of 10,000 =RAND() numbers from Excel

extremely low because of the high degree of precision of Excel (for example, Excel will not round the value 0.000,000,000,000,001 to zero).

Appendix 3 Converting Uniform Random Numbers to Numbers From Other Distributions

The Excel function = RAND() produces numbers that are uniformly distributed between 0 and 1. Usually, you will need to use numbers distributed in other ranges in a simulation model. There are a number of Excel functions that can generate numbers with other distributions. For example:

- To generate random numbers that are uniformly distributed between a and b, use the formula $= a + (b - a) * RAND()$.

- To generate random events that occur with probability p, use the formula
  $= IF(RAND () < p,1,0)$.

- To generate random numbers that are exponentially distributed with mean m, use the formula $= -m * LN(RAND ())$.

- To generate random numbers that are normally distributed with mean *m* and standard deviation *s*, use the formula = NORMINV(RAND(),*m*,*s*).

- Excel also has the functions = BETAINV, = GAMMAINV, and = LOGINV to generate random numbers that are beta, gamma, and lognormally distributed, respectively.

- Some special simulation add-in packages such as @Risk and Crystal Ball can generate random numbers from many other known distributions.

You can also simulate numbers by looking them up from a table of historical values. In Excel this would be done using database functions like = VLOOKUP().

Appendix 4 "Random" vs. "Uniformly Distributed"

A frequent source of confusion for people encountering simulation models for the first time is the distinction between the terms *random* and *uniformly distributed*. Numbers are uniformly distributed if the histogram is flat—that is, if the proportion of the total sample that falls into each equally sized interval is roughly the same. The histogram shown in Figure 6.A.2, for 10,000 values of = RAND(), shows a uniform distribution. Thus, the Excel function = RAND() yields numbers that are *random* and *uniformly distributed*.

Other methods for generating random variables, such as those described earlier, result in numbers that are *random* but *not uniformly distributed*. Why are these numbers random? Because they are all created as functions of = RAND(). Since you don't know what value will be produced from by the function = RAND(), you also don't know the value in any cell that contains a formula that is based on = RAND().

Try this experiment. In cell A1, type = RAND(). In cell B1, type = RAND()+1. In cell C1, type = NORMINV(RAND(),0,1). Each time you recalculate the sheet, all three of these numbers will change. Since the number in cell A1 is random, the values in cells B1 and C1 must also be random.

Appendix 5 Using Excel Data Tables to Generate Simulation Results

Sometimes, a simulation model can be run many times by copying and pasting a result down a row, as was done to simulate coin tosses or multiple instances of = RAND(). However, this is not always convenient for complicated models that involve many random numbers and several intermediate calculations before reaching a final output of interest. For example, a simulation model that simulates the performance of a portfolio of stocks, bonds, and derivate contracts could include several random variables representing the returns on the several items in the portfolio, as well as general market conditions. In these situations, we need a method of simulating just the final output, which in this case, would be the performance of the portfolio as a whole.

To simulate many events, use an Excel Data Table. The Data Table records values of a model output for various levels of a model input. To use a Data Table to generate simulation results, the model input will just be a counter to keep track of the number of times that the model is simulated.

Consider the following example. Suppose we want to compute the sum of three random numbers with different distributions. In cell A1, type = RAND(); in cell B1 type = –LN(RAND()); in cell C1 type = NORMINV(RAND(),0,1); and in cell D1 type = A1+B1+C1. Then, to simulate this result 10 times, we would form a data table as shown in the sequence in Figure 6.A.3.

	A	B	C	D
1	=RAND()	=-LN(RAND())	=NORMINV(RAND(),0,1)	=A1+B1+C1
2				
3			=D1	
4		1		
5		2		
6		3		
7		4		
8		5		
9		6		
10		7		
11		8		
12		9		
13		10		
14				

	A	B	C	D	E
1	0.3	0.534	-2.8553842	-2.01	
2					
3			-2.0127684		
4		1			
5		2			
6		3			
7		4			
8		5			
9		6			
10		7			
11		8			
12		9			
13		10			
14					

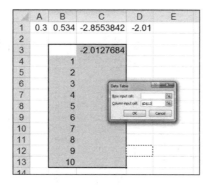

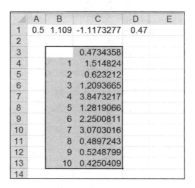

In the first step, we create the basic model and set up the shell of the data table, which includes a link to the model output in D1. In the second step, we begin to create a data table by highlighting the table area. In the third step, we specify the data table. We leave the "Row Input Cell" blank, since the table has been set up in columns, and set the "Column Input Cell" to be any cell on the sheet that is not used in our model. The last step shows the result—10 "runs" of our simulation model.

Why does this work? The Data Table works by substituting the column input cell into a specified cell. Each time this is done, the sheet is recalculated and a new output value is obtained, and this value is recorded in the table. Since the column input cell is just a blank cell, only the random numbers change, but not any other model parameters.

Appendix 6 Brief List of Commercially Available Simulation Software Packages

(abstracted from "Simulation Software Survey," *OR/MS Today*, October 2007. Online at http://www.lionhrtpub.com/orms/surveys/Simulation/Simulation1.html, accessed July 28, 2009.)

Software	Vendor	Typical applications of the software	Primary markets for which the software is applied
@RISK	Palisade Corporation	@RISK is a risk analysis tool using Monte Carlo simulation to show all possible outcomes, and their likelihood of occurrence.	Manufacturing, energy, finance, insurance, six sigma, medical, agriculture, transportation, government, academic, environment
Arena	Rockwell Automation	Facility design/configuration, scheduling, passenger and baggage-handling processes, patient management, dispatching strategy	Airports, healthcare, logistics, supply chain, mfg., military, business process, call centers, steel, paper, mining, ports
AutoMod	Applied Materials Inc.	Discrete event simulation to improve the design, configuration and optimization of material handling processes	Distribution centers, warehouses, automotive, airports, equipment, shipping, semiconductor, and manufacturing
Crystal Ball	Oracle's Crystal Ball Global Business Unit	Business planning and analysis, cost/benefit analysis, risk management, petroleum exploration, environmental assessment . . .	Financial services, environmental, oil and gas, pharmaceuticals, telecom, manufacturing, energy, utilities, insurance . . .
Emergency Department Simulator	ProModel Corporation	Emergency Department throughput, staffing, patient flow, and efficiency analysis.	Emergency Department Performance Improvement
ExtendSim Suite	Imagine That Inc.	Professional 3D modeling of continuous, discrete event and discrete rate processes.	When impressive presentations count. 3D modeling of manufacturing, logistics, business, government, education, engineering...
GPSS/H	Wolverine Software Corporation	Queuing models	General purpose

Process Simulator	ProModel Corporation	Lean, Six Sigma, value stream mapping, process mapping, flow chart simulation, continuous process improvement	All
ProcessModel Professional	ProcessModel, Inc.	Business process improvement - all areas	All
SIMPROCESS	CACI Product's Company	Combines process mapping, flow charting, discrete event simulation, activity based costing in a single easy to use product	Commercial, government, military, education, public, private
SIMUL8	SIMUL8 Corporation	Optimize throughput, maximize resource utilization, identify bottlenecks, reduced risk decisions, process management, learning and training. For comprehensive, easy to build simulations requiring power features.	Business processes: call center, manufacturing, supply chain, logistics, healthcare, financial, education
The DecisionTools Suite	Palisade Corporation	Risk & decision analysis: cost estimating, resource allocation, Six Sigma & quality analysis, supply chain distr., and more.	Manufacturing, energy, finance, insurance, Six Sigma, medical, agriculture, transportation, government, academic
WITNESS Simulation	Lanner Group	Strategy validation, operational planning and process improvement	Manufacturing, aerospace & defense, federal, homeland security, pharmaceuticals, energy, aviation, health, IT

Practice Questions

1. Develop two simulation models of tossing two six-sided dice (numbered 1 through 6 on the six faces).

    Model 1: Simulate rolling a single die twice and add the total.

    Model 2: Simulate a combined roll of two dice, giving a number from 2 through 12 with appropriate probabilities.

2. An advertisement in the newspaper offers a new car for sale or lease. The purchase price of the car is $43,240, or the car can be leased for 24 months for a monthly payment of $458, with a $7,500 down-payment. Under the lease option, there is a charge of 24 cents/mile for mileage above 30,000 miles for the 24 months, and a $550 security deposit, which is refundable at the end of the lease, must be deposited with the dealer. The car may be purchased at the end of the lease for $29,732. All other charges (taxes, maintenance, plates, etc.) are the same under both options.

    Develop a simulation model to compare the net present value of buying or leasing the car for 24 months. To compare the two options a number of assumptions must be made. Assume that:

    *   The mileage driven over the 24 months can be approximated by an exponential distribution with mean 25,000 miles.

    *   The best estimate of the interest rate over the next 24 months is a normal distribution with mean 8.5% and standard deviation 1%.

    *   The value of the car at the end of 24 months is the same under both options (that is, if the car is purchased, the realizable value at the end of month 24 is $29,732 less 24 cents/mile for each mile over 30,000).

    Use your simulation model to assess the probability that the lease option results in a lower net present value than does the purchase option.

3. A narrow (single lane) bridge over a railroad track slowed traffic on a busy road. During the rush hour, vehicles traveling south were observed to arrive at the north end of the bridge at a mean rate of 4 vehicles/minute. Vehicles traveling north were observed to arrive at the south end of the bridge at a rate of 3.5 vehicles/ minute. In both cases, vehicle inter-arrival times were well approximated by exponential distributions. Traversing the bridge took a single vehicle between 10 and 20 seconds, with any time in this interval equally likely. If a "batch" of vehicles traversed the bridge (in the same direction!), each vehicle in the batch added 3 seconds to the traverse time (that is, if a batch of five vehicles crossed the bridge in line together, the time taken was the time of the first vehicle, plus 15 seconds).

One group of bridge users believed that the bridge should alternate vehicles. That is, the first vehicle to arrive at the bridge should cross first. If, immediately after this vehicle had crossed, there was a vehicle waiting to cross *from the opposite direction*, then this vehicle had priority. If there was a queue of vehicles at either end of the bridge, then traffic on the bridge would switch direction after each vehicle.

A second group of users believed that traffic on the bridge should stay in the same direction until there were no more vehicles to cross. Once the bridge was free, vehicles traveling in the opposite direction could "capture" the bridge until the entire queue had crossed (by which time there would likely be a new queue of vehicles coming from the other direction).

A third group of bridge users suggested that the only "fair" discipline was strict "first to arrive, first to cross": vehicles should cross the bridge in strict order of their arrival at the bridge, regardless of direction.

Develop a simulation model to show the impact of these three different "scheduling rules" for the bridge on the waiting times of vehicles at the bridge.

Recommended Cases

Babcock and Wilcox (Ivey)

TriDev Realty Partners (Ivey)

Research and Development at ICI: Anthraquinone (Ivey)

Brilux: The FOT-320 Decision (Ivey)

Birch Resources (A) (Darden)

Enron Weather Derivatives (A) and (B) (Darden)

Superior Grain Elevator (Ivey)

Yangarra Resources (Ivey)

Gold Claim at Sturgeon Lake (Ivey)

Dofasco Lance Desulfurizing Plant (Ivey)

Oakville Hydro Optimum Engine Selection (Ivey)

Ohio Poymer (Ivey) *and* ProBut Hydrocarbon (Ivey)

Marsh and McClelland (Harvard)

Columbus-America Discovery Group and the SS Central America (INFORMS)

Charles River Jazz Festival (Harvard)

Deloitte Recommends Client Selection to Regency Bank (Ivey, 9B11E005)

CHAPTER 7

SIMULTANEOUS DECISION PROBLEMS

Management decision problems are often complex. Consider the following:

> Dow Chemical has devised one of the more sophisticated systems for juggling international production schedules. Using a computerized linear programming model that it began developing five years ago, the company weighs everything from currency and tax rates to transportation and local production costs to identify the cheapest maker of each product. For example, in making chloralkali and its derivatives, some of which require several intermediate chemicals, Dow's network chooses among factories on three continents to supply customers throughout the world. (*Source*: *Fortune*, March 14, 1988)

Good solutions for many such complex management problems can only be derived when the values of several (perhaps many) decision variables are determined simultaneously. We will call this type of problem a *simultaneous decision problem*.

The decision tree model presented in Chapter 3 copes with complexity by structuring a complex problem as a series of sequential decisions. Often, however, a number of dependent decisions must be made where an attempt to address each decision sequentially will produce a poor solution. Here are two examples where making decisions one-at-a-time will likely produce high cost results:

1. Suppose that we must decide how many units of several different products to produce this week. First, we might look at our most profitable product and decide a production quantity for that product, then move on to our second most profitable product and decide how many of that product to produce, continuing until we have moved through our entire product line.

2. The marketing manager might decide to tour the company's sales territories by traveling to the closest territory first, then the next closest, and so on.

Note that a simultaneous decision problem is a problem where there are benefits to making multiple decisions simultaneously, even though the decisions may be implemented over a period of time. Production scheduling is a common example where most firms achieve significant benefits by deriving a schedule for some time horizon (often weekly) simultaneously, even though the production levels derived are implemented sequentially.

We can improve our decision making if we develop the skills to recognize simultaneous decision problems, and also the capability to solve these problems simultaneously. Following, we provide examples to present the concept of a simultaneous-decision problem.

Examples of Simultaneous-Decision Problems

The kinds of decisions where a simultaneous solution approach has resulted in major profit or productivity improvements are widespread. Some examples are:

- American Airlines's decisions about what aircraft to use on which flights, and which flight crews to assign to each aircraft.

- The U.S. Department of Defense's decisions on how to transport the necessary personnel and materiel for the Gulf War from existing locations to the Gulf.

- The Chessie Rail System's decisions on the purchase and repair of more than $4 billion worth of freight cars.

- Hydro Quebec's decisions on which reservoirs to use to meet the demand for electricity each day.

- The Federal Land Banks of the Farm Credit System's decisions on how to refund maturing bonds and sell new bonds to generate new funds (amounting to some $6 billion annually) for growth.

- American Edwards Laboratories' decisions concerning which artificial heart valves to produce to best meet the available demand.

- EXXON refineries' decisions around adapting its refining capacity to adjust to the legislated changeover to no-lead automobile fuels.

- North American Van Lines's decisions on how to dispatch thousands of trucks each week.

- A Quebec health care authority's decision about where to locate a number of breast-screening clinics on the Island of Montreal and must also decide the capacity of each clinic.

These are just a few examples where organizations have improved processes and, in some cases, saved millions of dollars through understanding the need for simultaneous thinking. Small firms can also use these techniques; although the savings will not be as large for a small firm, they can still have an important impact on the bottom line.

Characteristics of Simultaneous-Decision Situations

While these examples occur in different industries, different sectors, and involve different issues, they do have several common features:

1. They involve many decision variables (often thousands, sometimes millions) that are interrelated.

2. There are some scarce resources that must be allocated among competing uses.

3. There are constraints on what can be achieved or what the manager wants to achieve.

4. There is a fairly clear and definite objective.

5. The decision problem is fairly well understood.

The approach used to solve such simultaneous decision problems goes by the general name of *optimization* or *mathematical programming* (MP) (the term "mathematical programming" has nothing to do with computer programming—the approach predates the computer). To understand MP, we need to take a look at a more rigorous statement of the problem.

A very general statement of the MP problem is:

The MP problem seeks to find values for a set of decision variables which maximize (or minimize) a single objective, and which satisfy a set of constraints.

We motivate our discussion with an examination of a hypothetical company called AB Company.

A Representative Example: The AB Company

The AB Company will produce only two products this week: Product A and Product B. Management must decide how much of each product to produce (in tons). Product A yields a contribution margin of $25 per ton and product B $10 per ton. All products produced will be sold.

Products A and B are made by mixing materials from inventory. For this week, there are three materials available in the following amounts:

Material 1:   12,000 tons

Material 2:   4,000 tons

Material 3:   6,000 tons

Product A is made up of 60% material 1 and 40% material 2.

Product B is made up of 50% material 1, 10% material 2, and 40% material 3.

A sequential approach to try to decide how much of each product to produce might first examine the product that has the highest contribution margin. This is Product A; if we try to produce the maximum possible amount of Product A, we are limited by the quantity of material 2, which makes up 40% of Product A. If we use all 4,000 tons of material 2 to produce Product A, we can produce (4000/0.4) = 10,000 tons of Product A, for a contribution of $250,000. This consumes 6,000 tons (= 10000*0.6) of material 1, leaving 6,000 tons of material 1, no material 2, and 6,000 tons of material 3 unused. Since we need material 2 in order to produce Product B, we can produce no Product B. The decision would be to produce 10,000 tons of Product A and no Product B, for a contribution of $250,000.

But there is a better solution: if we produce 6,250 tons of Product A and 15,000 tons of Product B, we make a contribution of $306,250. The materials requirements are:

For Product A,

60% Material 1 (.6*6,250)	3,750 tons
40% Material 2 (.4*6,250)	2,500 tons

For Product B,

50% Material 1 (.5*15,000)	7,500 tons
10% Material 2 (.1*15,000)	1,500 tons
40% Material 3 (.4*15,000)	6,000 tons

Total Materials used:

Material 1: 3,750 + 7,500	11,250 tons
Material 2: 2,500 + 1,500	4,000 tons
Material 3: 6,000	6,000 tons

Therefore, we use up all of materials 2 and 3 but have 750 tons of material 1 left over.

Those with some knowledge of algebra will recognize that this solution is found by solving equations simultaneously. This is a simple example of the value of simultaneous thinking over sequential thinking. By attempting to solve this problem sequentially, *$56,250 (roughly 20% of the initial solution) was "left on the table."* A competitive firm will not last long if it continues to make mistakes like this! Twenty percent is a significant lost opportunity.

An essential skill for every manager is the ability to recognize situations where sequential decision making fails to deliver a competitive decision. It is also important to have some understanding of how to derive a better solution.

Formulation for the AB Corporation

The problem is to decide how many tons of Product A and how many tons of Product B to produce. Therefore, we choose our decision variables as:

Let A be the number of tons of Product A to be produced, and

B be the number of tons of Product B to be produced.

Since the contribution from Product A is $25/ton and from Product B is $10/ton, we can formulate our objective as the maximization of contribution or:

MAXIMIZE CONTRIBUTION = $25 A + $10 B

We are prevented from making huge amounts of Products A and B (and, hence, huge contributions) by limitations on the amounts of available materials. The quantities of materials available will, therefore, be the constraints. To complete the constraints, we must identify the coefficients: that is, how many tons of each material is used up producing one ton of each product.

Since 60% of Product A is made up of material 1, then production of A tons of Product A consumes 0.6A tons of material 1. The remaining 40% of product A (0.4A tons) is material 2.

Similarly, production of B tons of Product B consumes 0.5B tons of material 1, 0.1B tons of material 2, and 0.4B tons of material 3.

The total amount of material 1 consumed (producing A tons of Product A and B tons of Product B) is, therefore:

0.6A + 0.5B

which cannot exceed the 12,000 tons of material 1 available. Our first constraint is, therefore:

0.6A + 0.5B ≤ 12,000 (material 1 supply constraint)

Following similar logic, we derive material supply constraints for materials 2 and 3:

0.4A + 0.1B ≤ 4,000 (material 2 supply constraint)
0.0A + 0.4B ≤ 6,000 (material 3 supply constraint).

We now restate the complete formulation (leaving out the 0.0 coefficient):

MAXIMIZE CONTRIBUTION = 25 A + 10 B

S.T.

0.6A + 0.5B	≤	12,000
0.4A + 0.1B	≤	4,000
0.4B	≤	6,000

with A ≥ 0, and B ≥ 0.

This problem can be solved to find those values of A and B that maximize the objective while satisfying the constraints, using any of a large number of computer programs.

A General Problem Formulation

By restricting the algebraic form of the objective and the constraints, various more limited MP problem types emerge. The most important of these is the *Linear Programming Problem (LP)*. The LP problem is one limited version of the general MP problem.

If we define $X_1, X_2, X_3, X_4 \ldots X_n$ ("the X_js") as the set of decision variables (or activities), then the LP problem is stated in the form of MAXIMIZING a linear objective function subject to a set of linear constraints or:

Objective function:

$$\text{MAXIMIZE } Z = c_1 X_1 + c_2 X_2 + \ldots + c_n X_n$$

Constraints:

SUBJECT TO:

$$a_{11}X_1 + a_{12}X_2 + a_{13}X_3 + \ldots + a_{1n}X_n \leq b_1$$

$$a_{21}X_1 + a_{22}X_2 + a_{23}X_3 + \ldots + a_{2n}X_n \leq b_2$$

$$a_{31}X_1 + a_{32}X_2 + a_{33}X_3 + \ldots + a_{3n}X_n \leq b_3$$

$$\vdots$$

$$a_{m1}X_1 + a_{m2}X_2 + a_{m3}X_3 + \ldots + a_{mn}X_n \leq b_m$$

where:

- $c_1, c_2, \ldots c_n$ (the c_is) (which appear in the objective function only) are the values attached to a unit of each decision variable in the objective function,
- $b_1, b_2, \ldots b_m$ (the b_is) are called the "right-hand sides" (or "rhs") and denote the total amounts of each of the constrained resources that can be taken up, and
- $a_{11}, a_{12}, \ldots a_{mn}$ (the a_{ij}s) are called the "coefficients" and denote how much of each resource is taken up by a unit of each decision variable.

Relating these to the formulation of the LP for AB Company above, $c_1 = 25$ and $c_2 = 10$; $b_1 = 12{,}000$, $b_2 = 4{,}000$, and $b_3 = 6{,}000$; $a_{11} = 0.6$, $a_{12} = 0.5$, $a_{21} = 0.4$, $a_{22} = 0.1$, $a_{32} = 0.4$.

For many applications, it is common to add a set of non-negativity constraints to the formulation. That is, we insist that:

$$X_1 \geq 0,\ X_2 \geq 0,\ X_3 \geq 0,\ \ldots X_n \geq 0.$$

The presence of these non-negativity constraints is often dictated by common sense: for example, employees cannot work a negative number of hours. Note that non-negativity is not always necessary. For example, in some financial applications, such as portfolio optimization, you may wish to allow negative values to represent short-selling, and in some supply chain management applications negative values may be useful to represent back-orders.

The LP problem can be written more succinctly as:

$$\text{MAX } Z = \sum_{j=1}^{n} c_j X_j$$

S.T.

$$\sum_{j=1}^{n} a_{ij} X_j \leq b_i \text{ for } i = 1,2, \ldots m.$$

$$X_j \geq 0 \text{ for } j = 1,2, \ldots n.$$

For a MINIMIZATION problem, note that Minimizing Z is equivalent to Maximizing $(-Z)$. To formulate a minimization problem, we change the signs of the c_is. (We don't actually have to do this, since most software for solving the LP problem can handle both maximization and minimization.)

While the general statement of the LP problem is formulated in terms of decision variables X_j (for $j = 1,2, \cdots n$), it is usually helpful to use meaningful variable names that clearly identify the decision variables in the real problem. For instance, the use of "A" and "B" in the AB Company example would probably be more intuitive than saying "Let X_1 be the number of units of A produced and let X_2 be the number of units of B produced."

Solving the LP

It can be proven mathematically that the optimal solution to an LP is at a *corner point*—that is, a point at the intersection of two or more constraints. This fact dramatically reduces the number of solutions that must be considered when solving an LP. There may be an infinite number of solutions that satisfy all of the constraints for a given problem, but only a handful of corner point solutions. Thus, many tools for solving LPs are based on finding the optimal corner point solution. There are three general approaches.

- If the LP involves only two or three decision variables, then it can be solved *graphically*. This approach is shown in many introductory operations research and management science textbooks. The approach involves plotting all of the constraints on a graph and then finding the corner point that yields the optimal value of the objective function. Solving problems in this way may yield some insights about the mathematical properties of LPs but it is not very practical. The graphical approach is only feasible for LPs with up to three decision variables (since it is impossible to draw a graph in more than three dimensions), whereas a large-scale LP could involve more than a million decision variables and several million constraints. Thus, additional solution procedures are needed to quickly and efficiently identify corner point solutions.

- The *Simplex Method* was initially developed by George Dantzig during the 1940s. Several variations and improvements are commonly used today. In this method, the solution procedure starts at a corner of the feasible region. Adjacent corners are inspected to see if the objective function can be improved by moving to an adjacent corner. If this is found to be the case, a procedure called a *pivot* is undertaken, which moves the solution to the adjacent corner that lies in the direction of the most rapid increase in the objective function value. The procedure terminates when no adjacent corner has a higher objective function value than the present solution. This approach can be thought of as choosing a path that will systematically search over all possible corner point solutions until the optimal solution is found.

• *Interior Point Methods* were initially developed by Narendra Karmarkar in the 1980s. These methods differ from the simplex methods in that intermediate solutions are developed which lie in the interior of the feasible region. Starting at a feasible solution, the interior point procedure generates new solutions across the feasible region in the direction of the optimal solution.

Examples of software for solving LPs and other types of MPs include GAMS, LINDO, What's Best, or CPLEX, while spreadsheet programs such Microsoft Excel also contain "solvers" that can solve LP problems. Problems involving very large numbers of decision variables (several thousand or more) take some time to solve, and a great deal of development effort has gone into producing fast LP computer codes. Frontline Systems' Premium Solver add-in for Microsoft Excel can solve problems with 2,000 variables and 1,000 constraints.

Using the Excel Solver Add-In

We illustrate how to formulate and solve an LP by formulating the AB Company example with the Excel Solver add-in.

Step 1: Build a General Spreadsheet Model

First, we lay out a spreadsheet, using good model building principles discussed earlier, with the "Data and Assumptions" listed separately from the "Model" (as shown in Figure 7.1; formulas are shown in Figure 7.2). The "Data and Assumptions" section merely contains all of the relevant information from the statement of the problem. We build a model by identifying our *objective* (total contribution), *decisions* (amounts produced of products A and B) and *constraints* (amounts used of the three materials), using formulas to refer to the data wherever possible. At this stage, we don't know the amounts produced—we will be using the model to provide insight about this—so we simply fill in any possible values. At the end of this step you will have a model in which you could use trial and error to change the amounts produced and change the total contribution.

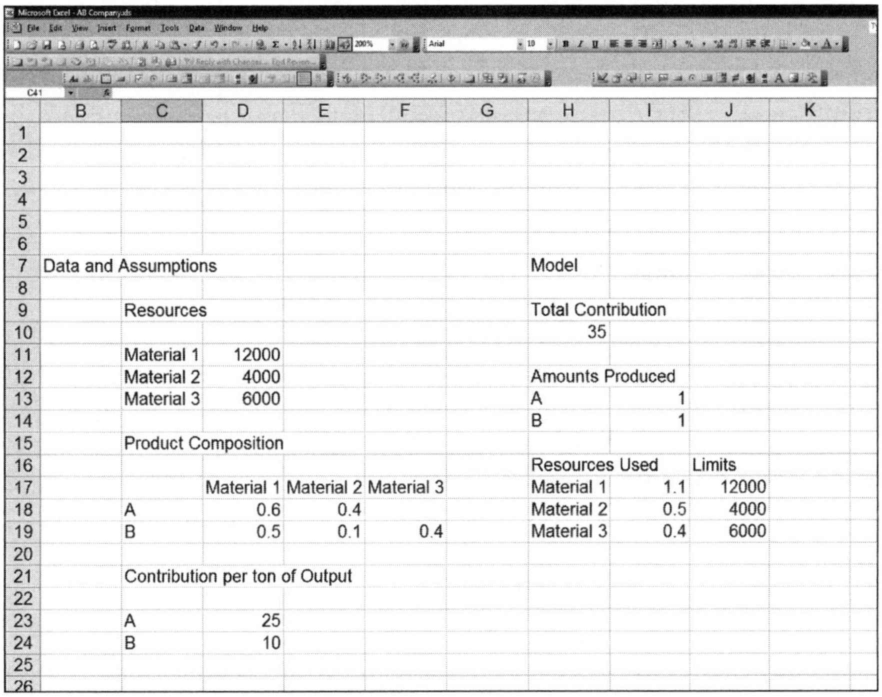

	B	C	D	E	F	G	H	I	J	K
1										
2										
3										
4										
5										
6										
7	Data and Assumptions						Model			
8										
9		Resources					Total Contribution			
10							35			
11		Material 1	12000							
12		Material 2	4000				Amounts Produced			
13		Material 3	6000				A	1		
14							B	1		
15		Product Composition								
16							Resources Used		Limits	
17			Material 1	Material 2	Material 3		Material 1	1.1	12000	
18		A	0.6	0.4			Material 2	0.5	4000	
19		B	0.5	0.1	0.4		Material 3	0.4	6000	
20										
21		Contribution per ton of Output								
22										
23		A	25							
24		B	10							
25										
26										

Figure 7.1 Excel model for AB Company

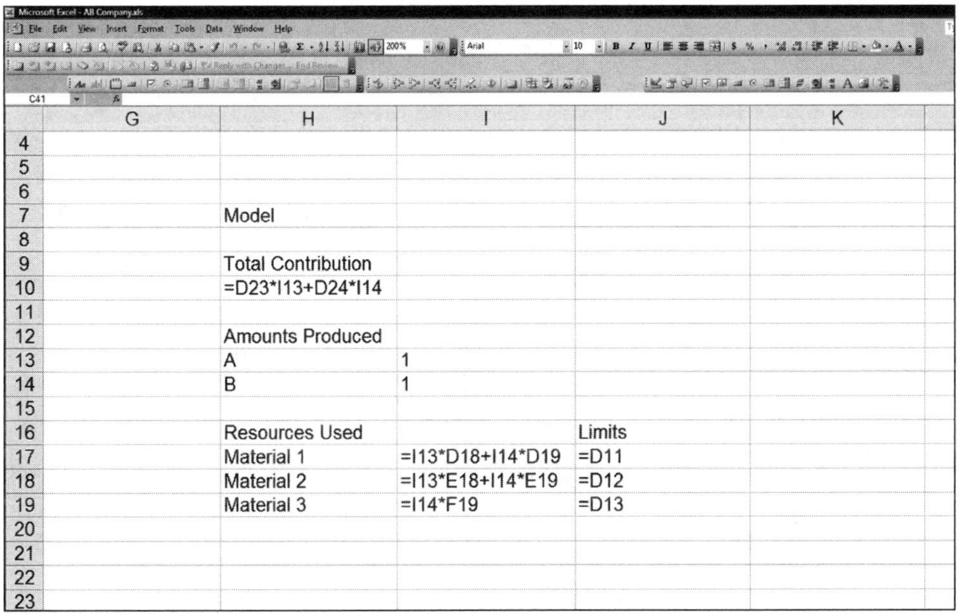

	G	H	I	J	K
4					
5					
6					
7		Model			
8					
9		Total Contribution			
10		=D23*I13+D24*I14			
11					
12		Amounts Produced			
13		A	1		
14		B	1		
15					
16		Resources Used		Limits	
17		Material 1	=I13*D18+I14*D19	=D11	
18		Material 2	=I13*E18+I14*E19	=D12	
19		Material 3	=I14*F19	=D13	
20					
21					
22					
23					

Figure 7.2 Excel model for AB Company showing Formulae

Step 2: Enter the Relevant Information in Solver

Open the Excel Solver (Tools–Solver in Excel 2003; Data–Solver in Excel 2007). With the Solver window open, enter the objective function cell (H10, in this case) in the "Target Cell" text box and the decision variable cells (I13 and I14, in this case) in the "By Changing Cells" text box. The changing cells can be entered as a row or column or they could be entered individually and separated by commas. To enter constraints, click the "Add" button next to the constraints window. The "Add a Constraint" window will appear (Figure 7.3).

Enter constraints in the add-a-constraint window. Constraints can be added individually or in rows or columns. This spreadsheet model was set up so that it is convenient to enter the constraints as columns, as shown in Figure 7.4. This illustrates the benefit of spending some time thinking about the layout of the spreadsheet before building the model. Click OK when all constraints have been entered, returning to the main Solver window.

From the main Solver window click the "Options" button (Figure 7.5). If the decision variables are *all* non-negative, click "Assume Non-Negative." We click this box for this example since amounts produced must be positive. If you are solving a linear model and using the basic Solver add-in, you should also click "Assume Linear Model." If you are using a version of the Premium Solver add-in, Assume Linear Model does not appear and you will have to select "Standard LP" from the main Solver window. Indicating that the model is linear is important if you wish to do any *sensitivity analysis* (to be discussed later).

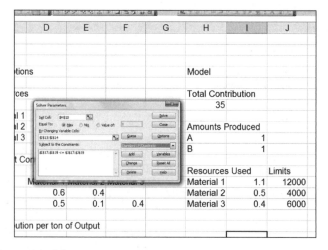

Figure 7.3 Solver Parameters Menu

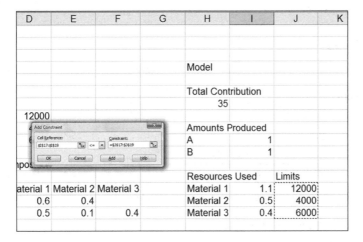

Figure 7.4 Adding Solver Constraints

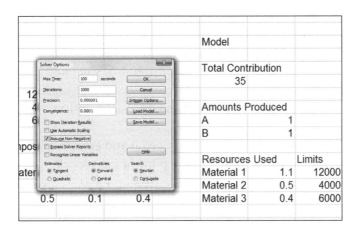

Figure 7.5 Solver Options Menu

When all of this has been done, click "Solve."

Step 3: Analyze and Interpret the Solution

After you click "Solve," a result window will appear. If the Solver was able to successfully solve the problem, then a success message will appear (Figure 7.6). Otherwise some form of error message will appear. If you are satisfied with the solution and want to examine it, click OK to keep the current solution.

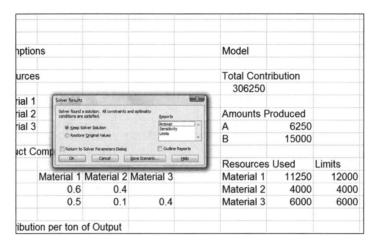

Figure 7.6 Solver Solution Dialog Box

How do we interpret the solution? In this instance the *optimal solution* is to produce 6,250 tons of A and 15,000 tons of B, yielding a total contribution of $306,250. This solution uses all of materials 2 and 3 but not of material 1. In the language of MPs, constraints 2 and 3 are *binding*, while constraint 1 is *not binding* and has *surplus*.

We make four important observations about the optimal solution:

1. You might have been able to find it using trial and error. However, this would probably take a very long time and involve a lot of guesswork.

2. Even if you did identify a solution with trial and error, and if you were unable to improve upon it, you would have no assurances that it was in fact the optimal solution. That is, you would not know if your solution had "left money on the table." By formally setting up the problem as an LP, you know that the final solution is, in fact, optimal.

3. If there were more than two decisions (say, tons of products A, B, C, . . . Z to produce), it would almost certainly be impossible to find the optimal solution using trial and error. In fact, as the number of decisions increases, it sometimes becomes difficult to just identify a feasible solution.

4. The optimal solution is usually not obvious, in that there is nothing in the original description of the problem that would immediately suggest that the solution shown in Figure 7.6 is optimal. For this reason, it is particularly important that managers be able to identify these types of problems where analytics can greatly improve upon intuition.

Properties of the Optimal Solution

There are three important properties of the optimal solution to an LP.

Property 1: The optimal solution (as denoted by the quantities of the decision variables) may not be very sensitive to changes in the objective function coefficients (that is, changes to the c_js).

Recall that the optimal solution is always at a corner point where constraints intersect. The slope of the objective function determines which of the many corners is optimal, and this slope is determined by the relative values of the c_js in the objective function. These coefficients often have to be changed considerably before the slope of the objective function changes sufficiently to switch the optimal solution to an adjacent corner. When this does occur, the values of the decision variables may change considerably.

An example: For the AB Company: if we increase the contribution from Product A, the slope of the objective function becomes increasingly negative (the objective function becomes more vertical). The geometry of linear constraints suggests that the objective function will have to reach a slope parallel to constraint 2 for the optimal solution to switch from the current corner (A = 6,250, B = 15,000) to the corner at (A = 10,000, B = 0).

We conclude that for any contribution for A between $25 and $40 (with the contribution of B held at $10), the contribution maximizing solution is to produce 6,250 tons of A and 15,000 tons of B. Note that if the contribution of A increases to exactly $40, both corner solutions (A = 6,250, B = 15,000) and (A = 10,000, B = 0) are optimal, as are all solutions that lie on the constraint joining these two corners: we have an infinite number of optimal solutions. This leads to Property 2.

Property 2: There may be a large number of optimal solutions to the LP problem, but one or more corners will always have the same objective function value as any optimal solution not at a corner.

Multiple optimal solutions arise when the slope of the objective is identical to the slope of a constraint bounding the feasible region. Knowing about multiple optimal solutions is important because there may be reasons for preferring one solution to another which were not part of the LP problem formulation (e.g., one solution may be easier to implement than the others).

Property 3: The optimal solution to an LP problem has two types of constraints: active and inactive.

The optimal solution is at the intersection of the set of active or binding constraints. The quantities of resources represented by the right-hand sides of the active constraints are fully utilized. In general, any change made to an active constraint will affect the optimal solution: the optimal solution will become infeasible if an active constraint is "tightened" (for example, the amount of a scarce material is reduced) or will generally become non-optimal if an active constraint is "loosened" (for example, more of a scarce material is made available).

Inactive constraints represent resources where there is slack or surplus. Changing the value of the right-hand side of an inactive constraint by a small amount will not generally change the optimal solution.

Post-Optimality Analysis

After an LP has been solved, we are often interested in further exploring some of the properties of the optimal solution. Many of these properties have important managerial implications. Two topics of interest include *shadow prices*, and *reduced costs*.

Recall that a constraint represents an upper or lower limit on a scarce resource. The *shadow price* of a constraint is that value by which the optimal value of the objective function would increase if there were one more unit of that resource available. There are two general possibilities: the shadow price is zero or the shadow price is not zero. If the shadow price is zero, then adding one more unit of the scarce resource will not change the objective function. This only happens when the constraint is not binding. Why? When the constraint is not binding, there is surplus of that particular resource. More could have been used, but was not. Since it was not optimal to use everything that was available, adding more cannot improve the value of the objective function.

The objective function coefficients (the c_js) represent the contribution per unit of activity j. If activity j did not occur (that is, if $X_j = 0$ for some j), then the *reduced cost* indicates the amount by which the objective function coefficient would need to improve before the optimal product mix would change and X_j would become positive.

Both shadow prices and reduced costs are associated with an *allowable increase* and an *allowable decrease*. These values, along with the current value of the shadow price or coefficient, give the range over which the shadow price or reduced cost is valid. In the case of shadow prices, the shadow price is valid from the current value of the constraint minus the allowable decrease to the current value of the constraint, plus the allowable increase. In the case of reduced costs, the reduced cost is valid from the current value of the objective function coefficient minus the allowable decrease to the current value of the objective function coefficient of the constraint plus the allowable increase.

Example: Post-Optimality Analysis of the AB Corporation

After solving the AB Company model, we are given the option of selecting three types of reports. We select "Sensitivity" and obtain the report shown in Figure 7.7.

The shadow prices are the values of one extra unit of each scarce resource (materials 1, 2, and 3, in this case). The shadow price for material 2 is 62.5, indicating that if we had one more unit of material 2, the objective function value would increase by 62.5. This can be verified by returning to the original spreadsheet, increasing the number of units of material 2 by 1, and re-solving. The allowable increase and decrease give us a range within which each unit of material 2 is worth 62.5. Specifically, each unit is worth 62.5 within the range (4000 − 2500, 4000 + 500) = (1500, 4500). Thus, 1 unit of material 2 is worth 62.5; 2 units are worth 2 × 62.5 = 125, and so on. If we lost a unit of material 2, the objective function would decrease by 62.5. This interpretation would only hold if the total number of units gained or lost were such that the final number was within the allowable range (1500 − 4500 in this instance).

The shadow price for material 1 is zero. Why? Because in the optimal solution, we are not using all of the material 1 that is available. If we are already not using all available units of material 1, then gaining one extra unit will be of no benefit.

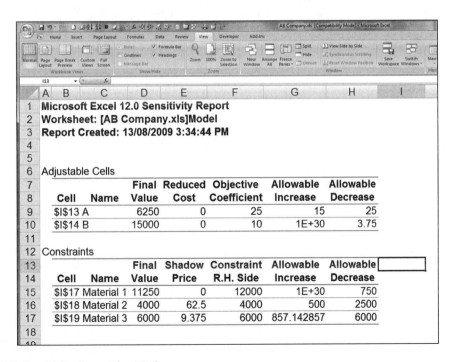

Figure 7.7 Sensitivity Report for AB Company.

This example illustrates a second common interpretation of shadow prices: they represent the most that a company would be willing to pay for one extra unit of the resource. In this case, AB company would be willing to pay at most $62.50 for one extra unit of material 2, $9.37 for one extra unit of material 3, and nothing for one extra unit of material 1.

The reduced cost for both products, A and B, is zero. This is because, in the optimal solution, AB Company produces some of each. If there was a product that was not produced in the optimal solution, then the reduced cost would indicate the amount by which the objective function coefficient would need to improve before that product might be part of the optimal solution.

Integer, Binary, and Mixed Integer Programming

The integer programming (IP) problem is identical in form to that of the LP problem except that one or more variables are restricted to having integer values (e.g., they can only take on whole numbered values, like 1, 2, 3, etc.). Examples of such problems are those that involve indivisible resources such as vehicles, airplanes, or people where an optimal solution that requires a fraction of the resource is not implementable.

Solving integer problems as LP problems and then rounding the values of the decision variables to integers sometimes gives good (near optimal) integer solutions . . . but sometimes it does not. This approach can easily produce integer solutions that violate one or more of the constraints: that is, the integer solution is not feasible.

IP problem formulation is identical to the LP formulation, with the additional constraint that one or more decision variables are restricted to integer values. Although most commercial solvers have IP functionality included, IP problems are *significantly* more difficult to solve than are LP problems. These solvers use a variety of rules-of-thumb and, for most problems, the solutions arrived at are very close to optimal but, in general, there is no way of knowing whether a better solution can be found. IP problem solvers generally take longer to reach a solution than LP solvers, thus, integer constraints should be used only when absolutely necessary.

An important subset of integer programs is that of binary 0/1 programs. Binary variables are convenient to represent events that either do or do not happen as part of an optimization problem.

Some example problems:

- "Assignment problems" such as assigning aircraft hulls to flights: the decision variables take on value 1 if the hull is assigned to a particular flight, and zero otherwise.

- The "truck loading" problem: should this load be placed on this truck or on some other truck?

- Investment problems: should we invest in this stock or not?

- Bidding problems: should we bid on this issue or project or not?

Formally, a model involving binary variables is specified by adding the constraint that one or more of the X_i variables must be binary.

Problems that include a mixture of liner, integer, and binary variables are referred to as *mixed integer programs (MIPs)*.

Nonlinear Programs

Nonlinear programs (NLPs) are a class of MPs in which the objective function or constraints involve nonlinear functions. In general, these problems are difficult to solve and require specialized techniques. When faced with such a problem, it may be worthwhile to try to approximate the problem by an LP or MIP form and arrive at a good solution by solving the approximation. The spreadsheet solvers can solve small nonlinear problems, but care is needed. Although a solver might terminate and indicate that it has found a solution, there is no guarantee that it has found the optimal solution.

A special case of the NLP is the quadratic program, in which quadratic functions are permitted. This type of problem can easily be solved on many commercial software packages.

Two important applications of nonlinear programming are portfolio optimization and revenue management. Revenue management has become such an important topic in analytics that we devote a separate chapter to the topic (see Chapter 8).

Multiobjective Programs

In the corporate world, most optimization problems can be reduced to a single objective: maximizing or minimizing some financial measure. In other arenas, particularly the public sector, multiple objectives are common. For example, many political funding decisions involve trading off dollars spent for lives saved; the more money spent (for example on ambulance or fire services), the more lives are saved. Recall that the optimization model has only a single objective, but there are many ways of incorporating multiple objectives.

The simplest of these are weighted "scoring" methods where each objective is given a weight and the overall objective is to maximize the total weighted score of all the objectives.

Another widely used approach is called *goal programming*. where a target value (or a "goal") for each objective is formulated as a constraint, with a penalty cost included if the constraint is not met. The optimization objective is then to minimize the penalty cost of not meeting the stated set of objectives.

Optimization in Action

Swift and Company Transformed Its Business with the Aid of Optimization

Swift and Company, a major international beef and pork company with annual sales exceeding $8 billion, used to be a supply-driven operation. That is, Swift would buy whatever beef and pork was available, process it, and then figure out how and where to sell the products. At the start of each week, only a small proportion of the product would be sold and the production schedule could not easily change to accommodate marketing opportunities.

With the aid of optimization, Swift transformed to a demand-driven operation, where product demand was forecast in advance, and optimizations were run to determine how many animals to buy, which are the best animals to purchase, and how they should be processed to most profitably meet demand. This very complex process is now optimized using an integrated suite of 45 linear programming models that dynamically schedule Swifts beef production at five plants in real time as orders arrive. Order fulfillment, on-time delivery, and production-to-order have all improved and the application achieved a 200% return on investment in the first year of operation (*Source*: A. Bixby et al., "A Scheduling and Capable-to-Promise Application for Swift & Company," *Interfaces 36*, 1).

Scott Paper Used Linear Programming for Forest Resource Allocation

Scott Paper operated a pulp mill and two sawmills, and also supplied roundwood and wood by-products to about 40 privately owned sawmills, another pulp mill, and a hardboard plant. Scott Paper faced the problem of how to allocate the wood resources available to the company to its own plants and those of its customers, in order to maximize profits.

Scott Paper obtained wood to supply these plants from three sources: logs cut on company-owned or leased land, roundwood purchased from landowners, and wood chips purchased from various sawmills. The availability of logs was dependent on the amount of forest available to harvest, and the availability of skilled wood crew labor.

A linear programming model was used to determine what tonnage of each type of wood (hardwood, softwood, pulp or sawlog, chips, or bark) should be harvested from each of 162 forest compartments, or purchased from Scott Paper's or privately owned sawmills or pulp mills, over a five-year time horizon. The objective was to maximize net profit for Scott Paper and all their customers, where net profit was calculated as selling price less cutting and transportation costs. Constraints in the model included the availabilities of wood in each area of forest and of labor to harvest the wood, as well as the demand for roundwood, chips, and bark at each plant. The model developed included 2,200 activities and about 800 constraints.

The model enabled Scott Paper's management to determine which operations were the most or least profitable, to evaluate the impact of a shortage of skilled woods labor and some measures to cope with this shortage, to determine a value to place on wood chips, and to determine the overall impact of management decisions that imposed annual cut restrictions in certain forest areas. The model was used for more than seven years, during which time it also provided valuable insight into the long-term effect of a severe inventory shortage resulting from spruce budworm infestation, and the economic feasibility of building a third Scott sawmill (*Source*: T. B Nickerson, "Forest Resource Allocation for Scott Paper," in *Successful Operational Research in Canada*, Peter C. Bell (Ed.), Canadian Operational Research Society, 1984).

Optimizing Vehicle Routing Problems

Optimization is routinely used by a great variety of organizations to solve various routing problems. There are a number of these problems that, while they have some similarities, are different enough to require special solution techniques. While most of these problems can be formulated as integer or mixed integer mathematical programming problems, these problems often become very large when realistic size problems are considered. For this reason, the solution techniques used often make use of a variety of heuristics to assist the optimizing software. Close-to-optimal solutions have been found and implemented for most of these problems using available software, or with the aid of consulting services from vehicle routing specialists.

1. *The Traveling Salesman Problem (TSP).*
    A traveler (vehicle or person) must visit a number of locations and wants to minimize the cost of travel or the time spent traveling. In the single TSP, there is only one traveler. In the multiple TSP, there are several travelers, each constrained as to the number of locations that can be visited.

2. *The Package Delivery and/or Pickup Problem.*
    A delivery organization must deliver (and/or pick up) objects to (and/or at) several different locations. Many complexities to this basic problem are common in practice: more than one vehicle may be required as a result of vehicle capacity or time-worked constraints, mixed pickup and delivery may require consideration of

vehicle loading patterns, a schedule of one-time pickups or deliveries may have to be merged into a schedule of fixed routes operated periodically, or vehicles may operate from a single depot or multiple depots.

2a. *The Package Delivery Problem with time windows.*

The package delivery problem becomes significantly more difficult if deliveries (or pickups) are constrained to occur only within certain times of the day that vary by location.

3. *The Haulage Problem.*

Quantities of materials (which may be multiple loads) must be moved from existing locations to new locations using a fleet of trucks.

4. *The School Bus Problem.*

Children living at known locations must be bused to school on vehicles that travel fixed routes at fixed times and have maximum capacities.

5. *The Mass Transit Problem.*

People need to be carried on a daily basis around a geographic area (usually a city or town) by a fleet of vehicles running on fixed schedules along predetermined routes.

6. *The Real-Time Dispatching Problem.*

Calls are received requiring pick-up of a person or object from one location and delivery to another location. The vehicles being dispatched may be spread out over a city (e.g., taxi cabs) or a country (e.g., long range road haulage).

7. *The "7-Up" Truck Problem.*

This is a delivery problem except that the driver sells from the truck. The size of each delivery is not known until the truck visits a location where a sale is made.

8. *The Traveling Lunch Problem.*

A mobile canteen vehicle must plan a day's operations. The sales made at each location visited depend on the time of day that the visit occurs.

9. *The Garbage Truck/Mail Delivery Problem.*

A route system must be derived in which every location in a given area is visited each time period. (The vehicle may, or may not, have to be on the same side of the street as the location being serviced.)

10. *The Transportation Planning Problem.*

A regional authority must plan new roads, railtracks, canals, dock facilities, etc., in order to allow for an integrated transportation policy.

Mathematical Programming at Military Airlift Command

Air transportation for the U.S. Department of Defense is provided by Military Airlift Command (MAC), whose corporate headquarters is at Scott Air Force Base near St. Louis,

Missouri. MAC used 5,000 pilots to fly some 700,000 hours annually, with 1,700 aircraft operating from 850 locations in 24 countries. On a typical day, MAC would fly 1,700 flights, move 5,000 passengers and 1,000 tons of cargo, fly nine rescue missions, and move 200 patients on medical evacuation flights.

The commander-in-chief of the MAC (a four-star general) had a group of 23 analysts who were actively employed in decision making involving mobilization of MAC's air fleet. This analysis group had to make the best possible decisions in the time available: their continued existence hinged on their performing credible, responsive, timely analyses.

This group has used linear programming (LP) extensively to arrive at efficient solutions to large and complex problems. Examples include:

Optimizing Scheduled Cargo Flights

MAC spends 35% of its flying hours for C-5, C-141, and C-130 aircraft flying regularly scheduled cargo flights over a global network. However, the volume of cargo to be transported exceeds the capacity of MAC's fleet; consequently, significant amounts of cargo capacity must be purchased from commercial air carriers. The problem facing the analysis group is to derive a network of scheduled cargo flights that minimizes the cost of purchased cargo capacity.

This problem is formulated as an LP problem with 18,000 variables and 13,000 constraints. The variables specify the number of times each month to fly a particular aircraft on a particular route. The problem takes about an hour to solve using a fast commercial interior-point LP code.

Solution of this problem has yielded impressive benefits. In 1988, $164 million was spent to buy commercial cargo capacity and it is expected that this can be reduced by about 15%. In addition, improved routing has eliminated the need to purchase at least one additional airplane (valued at $3.5 million).

Cargo Distribution in the USA

Some 650,000 cargo shipments originate at 10,000 locations in the continental United States and must be shipped (by air or truck) through MAC terminals and on to overseas destinations through the MAC scheduled global network. The problem is to find a low-cost set of MAC ports, combined with the global network, that takes into account where cargo originates and where it is going.

The problem is formulated as an LP problem with 60,000 variables and 6,000 constraints and takes about 20 minutes to solve. The variables specify the number of times each month to fly a particular aircraft or drive a truck on a particular route. The solution suggested a major change in operations of the port system: eight major ports were reduced to five, one primary port for each overseas destination, leading to more timely cargo delivery and financial gains from closing ports.

Patient Evacuation

Wartime medical evacuation will, in the future, be carried out by Boeing 767 aircraft of the Civil Reserve Air Fleet. The problem is to find an optimal set of distribution hubs that are near hospital bed concentrations in the United States, and to determine an optimal set of routes to these hubs from potential overseas locations.

The LP problem formulation has 250,000 variables, specifying the number of casualties to be transported on a particular route, the number of beds required in U.S. hospitals, and the number of aircraft that should fly particular routes. The 90,000 constraints involve casualty and hospital bed availability by type (burn, orthopedic, etc.), and aircraft capacity and ranges. The problem takes about four hours to solve.

As a result of this modeling, an ideal set of nine hubs has been chosen from 52 possible hubs, so as to minimize the average distance patients must travel to reach an appropriate hospital bed (*Source*: Robert Roehrkasse, "Linear Programming in Operations Research," *IEEE Potentials*, December 1990).

Summary

Simultaneous decision problems are very common in business and are difficult to solve intuitively.

Simultaneous decision problems have an objective, a number of decision variables, and a number of constraints. Simultaneous decision problems often involve large numbers of decision variables that compete for scarce resources. Problems with millions of decision variables and constraints are becoming increasingly common.

For smaller problems, it may be possible and appear intuitive to solve these problems as sequential problems. However, this approach ignores the interactions among variables and constraints and can lead to sub-optimal solutions.

Many companies now use optimization regularly and have had great success in improving their operations with this type of model. It is, thus, important for managers to be able to recognize, formulate, and understand such problems.

What the Manager Must Know

Optimization using mathematical programming techniques (particularly linear, integer, or mixed integer programming) are valuable competitive tools. To apply these tools effectively, the manager must:

- Be able to recognize these problem types within the organization.

- Be able to formulate these problems in a sensible way in order to attain the highest possible benefit from use of the available tools.

- Understand how to obtain an optimal solution for these problems.

- Be able to interpret the solutions and understand how the results obtained can be used to improve the firm's competitiveness.

When the problems are large and solved repeatedly, the manager will likely not solve these problems personally, but rather the manager's role switches to that of supervision. In this role, it is important that the manager can explain how the problem is to be solved (the objective, the constraints, etc.), and can validate the solution derived. Validation requires that the manager be able to inspect the output from the solver and determine that the formulation was correct and that the solution is feasible and implementable. Validation also requires an assessment that the data used in the model was correct and up-to-date.

When the optimization is performed repeatedly over time, particularly if the model is large, the manager must also take responsibility for the introduction and control of some form of data management system. Such a system ensures that the data required for the model is kept available, and the data is maintained to ensure that the model is always solved using current data. The manager also must know enough about the structure of the formulation to be able to recognize when the model requires reformulation.

Appendix: Technical Details

Objectives, Decisions, and Constraints

All optimization problems share three characteristics. They all have an *objective*, a set of *decisions*, and one or more *constraints*.

The *objective* is a function that you seek to *minimize* or *maximize*. This will typically be something like maximize revenue, minimize costs, or maximize contribution. However, other objectives are possible, such as minimizing inventory levels, maximizing market share, maximizing the total sales area covered, and many others.

Decisions represent values or levels that are under management control. These are what the manager decides in a simultaneous-decision situation. These may include sales price per unit, units of each product manufactured, hours worked by each employee, percentage of effort devoted to various tasks, or amount of raw material to blend into final product. Sometimes it is convenient to use decisions to represent calculated or intermediate quantities. These are not directly decided upon by the manager but are the result of other decisions. A common example would be the level of inventory to carry from month to month.

Constraints represent limits on *scarce resources*. Common types of constraints include availability of raw materials, production capacity, and upper or lower limits on demand. They are often represented as being less than something (e.g., production must be less that capacity) or greater than something (e.g., quality of the finished product must exceed some minimal level).

The mathematical programming problem can then be stated as follows: The manager must make *decisions* to optimize some *objective* while satisfying a set of *constraints*. When stated in this way, just about everything that a manager does can be thought of as a mathematical program!

General LP Formulation

The linear programming (LP) problem is one version of the general MP problem. We define $X_1, X_2, X_3, X_4 \ldots X_n$ (the X_is) as the set of decision variables (or activities); $c_1, c_2, \ldots c_n$ as the contribution per unit of activity j; $b_1, b_2, \ldots b_m$ as the available units of scarce resource j; and a_{ij} as the number of units of resource j consumed for each unit of activity i.

Then, the LP problem is stated in the form of MAXIMIZING a linear objective function subject to a set of linear constraints and can be written more succinctly as:

$$\text{MAX } Z = \sum_{j=1}^{n} c_j X_j$$

S.T.

$$\sum_{j=1}^{n} a_{ij} X_j \le b_i \text{ for } i = 1,2, \ldots m.$$
$$X_j \ge 0 \text{ for } j = 1,2, \ldots n.$$

The non-negativity constraints, $Xj \ge 0$, are common in many applications (for example, an employee in general cannot work a negative number of hours), but there may be applications where they are not required. When they are needed, they must be specified so that the software used to solve the linear program can find the correct answer. Although it may seem obvious to you when they are and are not needed, they are not obvious to a computer solver!

Note that the form of the LP problem is that of a linear objective function with linear constraints; hence, the name linear programming.

Linear vs. Nonlinear Models

A linear model is one in which all expressions (i.e., the objective function and constraints) are linear in the decision variables. If X_j is a decision variable and c_j is a constant coefficient, then the only types of expressions that are linear are of the form $c_1X_1 + c_2X_2 + c_3X_3 + \ldots + c_nX_n$.

What is not linear?

- Anything where two decision variables are multiplied together, such as $X_1 \times X_2$.

- Anything that involves dividing by a decision variable, such as c_1/X_1. (In some cases, there are techniques to remove this problem. This might involve doing some algebraic manipulation to write the model in a slightly different way.)

- Anything where a decision variable has an exponent other than 1, such as X_1^2, X_1^3 or $\sqrt{X_1}$.

- Anything involving the transcendental functions or trigonometric functions, such as $\log(X_1)$, $\exp(X_1)$, $\cos(X_1)$, or $\sin(X_1)$.

- Any combinations of the above.

Does this mean that the concept of linear models is very restrictive? Yes and no. Yes, they are restrictive in that they do not allow the full flexibility to formulate a model in any desired way. However, the answer is also no, in the sense that many business and real word applications are linear. Consider these examples:

- If X_1, X_2, X_3, ... X_n are the hours worked by employees 1, 2, ... n and c_1, c_2, c_3, ... c_n are their hourly wages, then $c_1X_1 + c_2X_2 + \ldots + c_nX_n$ is a linear equation for total payroll.

- If X_1, X_2, X_3, ... X_n are the number of units sold of items 1, 2, ... n and c_1, c_2, c_3, ... c_n are the revenue per unit, then $c_1X_1 + c_2X_2 + \ldots + c_nX_n$ is a linear equation for total revenue.

- If X_1, X_2, X_3, ... X_n are the amounts, in kg, of raw materials mixed together in an industrial process and c_1, c_2, c_3, ... c_n are the costs per kg, then $c_1X_1 + c_2X_2 + \ldots + c_nX_n$ is a linear equation for total.

If there is a loss of flexibility associated with linear models, why do people use them?

There are some strong mathematical results that enable one to find optimal solutions for linear models, even in the case of very large-scale problems, and that guarantee that these solutions will be optimal. In general, no such theory exists for nonlinear problems. The ability to solve problems quickly and the guarantee that the optimal solution will be found are two important reasons for using linear models. In fact, linear models are so important that there are several "tricks" used by experienced modelers to convert nonlinear problems into equivalent or nearly equivalent linear problems.

To summarize, linear models are quite flexible and they are a natural way to express many business and real world applications. There may be some loss of flexibility associated with using linear models, but the gains are ease of understanding and the ability to solve very large-scale problems quickly and accurately.

Terminology: Mathematical Programs vs. the Excel Solver

Mathematical programming was developed before the computer software that is used for solving MPs. As we have seen, all MPs have an objective, decisions, and constraints. Different software may use different terminology to refer to these items. The Excel Solver add-in refers to the objective as the "target cell," the decisions as "changing cells," and constraints as "constraints."

Modeling Tip: "Soft Coded" Constraints

Suppose you have a constraint of the form cell G15 ≤ 10. There are two ways that you can enter that as part of a model using the Solver.

Method 1 (Hard coding): When adding constraints, enter G15 ≤ 10 in the Solver constraints input box.

Method 2 (Soft coding): Enter the number 10 in another cell (e.g., H15). Then enter the constraint as G15 ≤ H15.

What is the advantage of method 2?

Suppose that after some time working with the model you decide that the right hand side of the constraint (i.e., the number 10) should actually be a different number. Or suppose you decide that you are not sure what number it should be. If it is hard-coded, then you must manually change the constraint using the Solver dialog box each time you want to evaluate a different possibility. However, if it is soft-coded, then you merely need to change the number on the spreadsheet before re-evaluating.

Beyond this convenience, there is an even more important reason for soft coding. By soft coding, you can identify the number 10 as a constraint or assumption on your spreadsheet and document to other users what the source was for the assumption. If your constraints are hard-coded, then a user would need to open the Solver model and go through all of the constraints in order to identify all of your assumptions. Since there is no text in the Solver input boxes, it may be difficult for another user to understand the reasons for the particular right-hand-side values in the constraints. Thus, soft coding makes it easier to do sensitivity analysis and to explain your model to others—both of which have tremendous value.

Solver vs. Goal Seek

In earlier chapters, we encountered the Goal Seek function in Excel. At first glance, Goal Seek may appear to be quite similar to the Solver, but there are three important differences:

- With Goal Seek, you do not optimize; you merely set a target cell equal to something. With the Solver, you can maximize, minimize, or set a target cell equal to a specific value.

- With Goal Seek, only one cell changes when searching for the solution. With Solver, several cells can be designated as changing cells.

- With Goal Seek, there are no constraints. Thus, the changing cell may take on any value. With Solver, the optimal solution is the set of changing cell values that satisfies all of the constraints.

Exercises

1. A car dealership can offer a $36,000 car under a special promotion with four years financing at 0%, or can offer a discount off the price of the vehicle if the buyer finances the sale at 0.5% monthly over the four years. What discount off the purchase price results in the buyer making the identical monthly payment under either purchase option?

2. A steel mill produces two types of steel alloy: boral and chromal. Production of each alloy requires three processes: Box anneal, Cold Roll, and Strand anneal. Production capacities are:

   Box anneal: 4,000 hours/month
   Cold Roll: 500 hours/month
   Strand anneal: 1,000 hours/month

Production rates in tons per hour are:

	Box anneal	Cold roll pass 1	Strand anneal	Cold roll pass 2
Boral	4	72	11	36
Chromal	2	Not required	20	24

The maximum demand for boral is 10,500 tons/month and for chromal 6,000 tons/month. The contributions/ton are boral: $25, and chromal: $35.

What combination of boral and chromal maximizes total monthly contribution?

3. The director of advertising for a retail chain is considering how to allocate her $200,000 budget for television advertising among four programs (A, B, C, D) on three channels (1, 2, 3). Market research studies have shown that the chain's customers can be broken down into two groups: "High-end Achievers" and "Aspiring Achievers." High-end Achievers spend twice as much in the store as do Aspiring Achievers. The director wants to maximize the total in-store spending potential of the audience but must have at least three ads on each program, and cannot spend more than 50% of the budget on any one channel. The audience by program and the ad costs are:

Channel	Program	Expected Audience	% High-End Achievers	% Aspiring Achievers	Cost/Ad
1	A	100,000	25	75	$7,500
1	B	50,000	60	40	$4,000
2	C	90,000	40	60	$6,500
3	D	80,000	50	50	$5,000

1. What is the most effective ad purchase ignoring the fact that the number of ads on any one program must be integer?

2. Include an integer constraint on the number of ads and re-solve.

3. Compare the two solutions.

Recommended Cases

Red Brand Canners (Stanford)

Northwest Newsprint (Ivey)

New England Feed Supply (Ivey)

TransTech Venture Partners (Ivey)

Bloomex.ca Logistics Optimization (Darden)

M2 Universal Communications (Ivey)

Mars Inc.: Online procurement (Ivey)

Dofasco Fuel Gas Allocation (Ivey)

AgrEvo International Inc.

Toronto Rehab (Ivey)

Vytec Corporation: Warehouse Layout Planning (Ivey)

S.C. Johnston; Planning Coupon Promotions (Ivey)

Ai Li Industrial Company (Ivey)

Arthur Hill & Company Realty Services (Ivey)

Long Wang Sha Tan Ku Company (Dragon King Shorts Company) (Ivey)

Kuwait Al-Manakh Stock Market (INFORMS)

Hooker Group Insolvency (Ivey)

ATT Telemarketing Site Selection (A) and (B) (INFORMS)

Vytec Corporation: Warehouse Layout Planning (Ivey)

Canning Consultants: The OPAC Assessment (Ivey)

Foulke Consumer Products (Darden)

Buckeye Power and Light (Darden)

Gartland Steel (Harvard)

DD Traders; Sourcing for DEMDACO (Ivey)

CHAPTER 8

REVENUE MANAGEMENT AND SCIENTIFIC PRICING

Prior to about 1985, analytics had focused on the cost side of the firm and had recorded a great many outstanding successes in improving corporate profitability through reducing costs and improving efficiency. In the mid-1980s, this changed when analytics professionals turned attention to the revenue side of the firm and since that time analytical thinking has pioneered a number of new business practices aimed at enhancing the firm's revenues. These business practices and the analytics that supports them are known collectively as *revenue management*. The part of revenue management that supports pricing decision-making is known as *scientific pricing*.

Revenue management has developed to a point where it is revolutionizing markets and challenging what were once considered to be good management practices. Many previously successful firms have been victimized by revenue management systems: these systems have proven time and again to be extremely effective competitively.

A Brief History of Revenue Management

Revenue management (RM) first appeared in the North American airline industry shortly after deregulation in 1979. In this new intensely competitive industry, carriers struggled to gain a competitive edge or even survive, and American and Delta began experimenting with variable fares. Over the next 15 years, first American and later Delta, United, and USAir invested very heavily in developing revenue management systems.

Revenue management was an innovative concept: for years firms had worked very hard to manage and control costs but the revenue side of the financial statements remained largely unmanaged. For the most part, firms simply posted product prices and relied on the market to determine the numbers of units sold and the resulting revenues to the firm. The airline industry was the first to recognize that managing revenues could produce returns at least as great as cost cutting or downsizing.

The impact of revenue management on the airline industry has been dramatic: Robert Crandall, chairman, president, and CEO of American Airlines, has stated:

> I believe that (revenue) management is the single most important technical development in transportation management since we entered the era of airline deregulation in 1979. (*Source*: B.C. Smith et al., "Yield Management at American Airlines," *Interfaces*, *22*, 1)

Crandall has also provided an idea of how much revenue management has contributed to American's financial success:

> We estimate that yield management has generated $1.4 billion in incremental revenue in the last three years [*by*] creating a pricing structure that responds to demand on a flight-by-flight basis. (Smith et al.)

In assessing the impact of revenue management at American, it is important to recognize that the $1.4 billion over three years is *incremental revenue*: American did not have to buy more planes, or undergo any kind of "downsizing" or structural reorganization, or even incur any major costs. This added revenue came from cleverly extracting higher revenues from customers for each seat-mile flown. By 1998, Tom Cook, president of Sabre Decision Technologies, had revised this estimate upwards:

> We have estimated that the yield management system at American Airlines generates almost $1 billion in annual incremental revenue. (*Source*: T.M. Cook, "SABRE Soars," *OR/MS Today*, June 1998)

Customers also benefitted: revenue management lead to fuller planes and consequently lower costs per passenger, savings which were passed on to passengers through lower fares.

The impact of revenue management on the airline business was dramatic. Major carriers that implemented revenue management survived, while many others failed (see example of Peoples' Express Airline at the end of this chapter). Revenue management has emerged as a formidable competitive weapon.

From the airlines, RM spread rapidly to other service industries (rental cars, hotels) and manufacturing.

> Ford Motor Co. has quietly been enjoying a huge surge in profitability . . . 1995 and 1999, U.S. vehicle sales rose just 6 percent, from 3.9 million units to 4.1 million units. But revenue was up 25 percent, and pretax profits soared 250 percent, from about $3 billion to $7.5 billion. Of that $4.5 billion growth, Ford's Lloyd Hansen, controller for

global marketing and sales, estimates that about $3 billion came from a series of revenue management initiatives. (*Source*: Leibs, "Aided by New Software, the Automaker is Using Revenue Management to Boost the Bottom Line," *CFO Magazine*, August 2000)

Defining Revenue Management

The objective of revenue management is not necessarily to stimulate product demand directly, but rather to better convert existing demand into higher revenues. *Revenue management (RM) is the science and art of enhancing firm revenues while selling* essentially *the same amount of product.*

There are five distinct concepts that drive the development of revenue management:

- **Scientific pricing**, which involves changing prices optimally and frequently to respond to changing market conditions.

- **Product protection**, whereby units of product that are in inventory are withheld from sale in anticipation that more revenue can be created from their sale at a later date. Implementations of protection include discount allocation and some methods for managing dynamic pricing.

- **Managed Overselling** (also known as overbooking), where the firm deliberately takes orders for more product than it has available because it expects that some customers will not show up to collect their order.

- **Planned trading-up**, where the firm plans in advance to meet demand for a lower-priced product by providing the customer with a higher-priced product at the lower price.

- **Short-selling**, where the firm sells product that it does not have, knowing that it can obtain the necessary units later. In the airline industry this is known as replaning.

Each of these concepts has been demonstrated to be a proven revenue producer.

Scientific Pricing

The most innovative single component of RM is a new approach to the pricing of products and services. Product prices are a critical marketing variable and many books and articles have been written on how the firm should price its products. Deciding on product prices has been an intensively human problem, where managers and groups of managers argued and discussed whether a product should carry a $10.49 or $10.99 price sticker, or whether discounting should be used to clear out excess inventory. This view that setting prices was such a critical and complex activity that it had to be done by humans began to be challenged in the 1980s when computer systems that performed product pricing began to appear.

Before revenue management, the common view was that it was the product that had value to consumers. Pioneer revenue managers rejected this simplistic view by recognizing that there is a time component to the value of a sale. This time component may surface in several ways:

- A consumer may attach a different value to the same product at different points in time. For example, a customer will generally attach a higher value to a product needed immediately than to the same product needed in several months.

- The product itself may change over time, such as the case of perishable, seasonal, or fashionable products.

- The firm may attach value to "locking in" sales early, since this reduces uncertainty and may lead to cost savings.

To illustrate these concepts, we will look some examples of time-dependent demand. Note that when demand is high, customers buy more of the product at the same price, or in periods of high demand we can sell the same amount of product at a higher price.

Examples of Time-Dependent Value

The demand for airline tickets (and many other forms of event tickets) provides an example of customers attaching different values to the same product at different points in time. A typical demand pattern is illustrated in Figure 8.1.

Some customers like to be very organized and attach a high value to having their tickets in-hand very early. These customers, along with a variety of speculators who hope to take

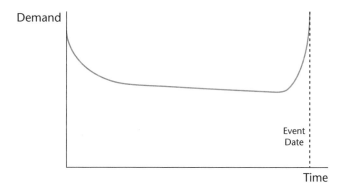

Figure 8.1 Typical Demand Pattern for Event of Trip Tickets

advantage of later unsatisfied demand, buy their tickets very soon after an event opens for booking. There then follows a period when demand is distinctly lower: customers who are more "flexible" will shop around looking for "good deals," and will not finalize their plans until much later. Finally, as the event date becomes imminent, there are customers who, for various reasons, attach a very high value to traveling on one particular flight or attending the event. These customers will pay a substantially higher price for a ticket "at the gate."

In the case of sporting events, theatre, pop concerts, and many other "events," it is very common for this "at the gate" peak demand to be met by "scalpers." "Scalpers" are arbitrage agents who buy tickets early, when demand is often lower, and bet that they can resell the tickets later when demand (and price) is higher. In some jurisdictions, such "scalping" is a legal way of meeting peak demand "at the gate," but the profits from "scalping" rarely return to the owner of the event.

The demand for Christmas items (such decorations, toys, gifts, etc.) initially follows a similar pattern to that of airline tickets (Figure 8.2). Some shoppers will pay higher prices for the comfort of having their holiday shopping completed early when the best selection of goods are available. These shoppers will buy as soon as the holiday goods appear on the shelves. After the initial "rush," demand slows but then grows to a peak as the date approaches. Last-minute shoppers will pay a high price, delighted that they have found the right gift at last. Unlike airline seats, however, Christmas items have value after Christmas: some customers will buy Christmas decorations for next year on Boxing Day. Interest, however, quickly wanes after the holiday season.

Other examples of items which consumers value differently at different points in time include fashion items, such as spring fashions in clothes, fast food (where the demand for hamburgers and fries is typically strongest over the lunch hour and the dinner hour), and perishable items, including produce and dated groceries where demand declines as the

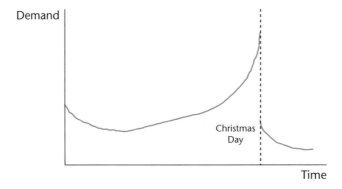

Figure 8.2 Typical Demand Pattern for Christmas Items

product ages. These examples all illustrate the key fact that the same product can have different values at different points in time. In effect, each point in time represents a different *market segment*. Understanding market segmentation requires a review of what we mean by a market.

Markets and Market Segmentation

A market is simply a place where we sell a product. Global firms see the world as their market. Others focus on a single country, state, province, or town. Small local firms such as landscapers or hairdressers might see just part of a town as their market. In all these cases, economists summarize the market by plotting a curve that shows the basic relationship between the prices they charge for their product and the quantity of product that they expect to sell (Figure 8.3). In general, as price is increased, the quantity sold decreases: at some (high) price, no units will be sold. As price decreases, the quantity sold increases with demand, becoming very large at very low prices. As economists are fond of saying: "The demand for a free good is infinite."

We can represent this demand model using a demand curve, which is a function that relates Quantity Sold (Q) to Price (P) or:

$$Q = F(P)$$

A demand curve exists for a period in time. This could be a year, a month, a week, an hour, or a minute. In the past, marketing people have been concerned with demand over quite long periods (weeks or months or years), since prices were set and held for these long periods.

The demand curve focuses on the relationship between Quantity Sold and Price charged, but the demand for a product on a given day depends on many outside or "exogenous" factors. Hot weather can turn a "low demand" day at the ice cream parlor into a "high demand" day, or if our competitor slashes prices, our "high demand" day can quickly turn

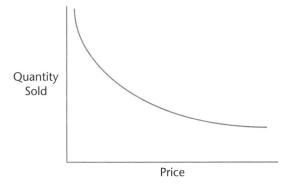

Figure 8.3 A Typical Demand Curve Representing a Market

into a "low demand" day. Advertising spending, swings in public opinion, even the latest news can have an impact on the location of a demand curve on a particular day (Figure 8.4). We can include these external factors (X_1, X_2, . . .) in the demand function:

$$Q = F(P, X_1, X_2, . . .)$$

In practice, demand curves are often more confused than this suggests, in part, because it is difficult to "see" a complete demand curve. If each day has a different demand curve, and if we set only a single price each day, we only ever see one point on the demand curve: it is difficult to construct a whole curve from a single point!

A common practice in marketing is the segmentation of single markets into a set of smaller market segments (Figure 8.5). There are multiple reasons why market segmentation can contribute to improved marketing. For example, a national magazine might decide to publish regional issues so that it can include more local features, a car manufacturer might

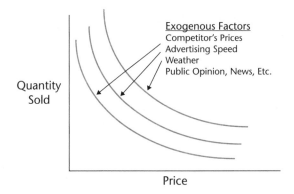

Figure 8.4 Many Exogenous Factors Influence the Location of a Demand Curve

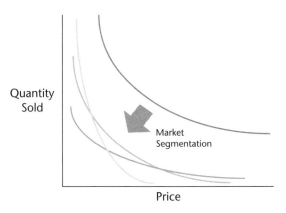

Figure 8.5 Market Segmentation

produce various "custom editions" to appeal to different kinds of buyers, or a manufacturer selling through retail stores and www-sites might offer a slightly different product through these different channels recognizing that www-shoppers and retail shoppers are different kinds of people.

Marketers have used a wide variety of variables to segment a single market into multiple sub-markets or customer "clusters." These include customer characteristics (seniors, students, or income level), sales channel ("clicks" and "bricks"), customer's size (discounts for large customers), delivery time (for example, a premium for overnight delivery), and time of purchase (for example, a discount for early purchasers.)

We can represent market segmentation as follows:

$$Q = F(P, X_1, X_2, \ldots) \text{ becomes } \begin{cases} q_1 = F_1(p_1, X_1, X_2 \ldots) \\ q_2 = F_2(p_2, X_1, X_2 \ldots) \\ . \\ q_i = F_i(p_i, X_1, X_2 \ldots) \\ . \\ q_N = F_N(p_N, X_1, X_2 \ldots) \end{cases}$$

where q_i represents the quantity and p_i the price in the $i = 1, 2, \ldots N$ different market segments.

RM uses the fact that if we can successfully segment a market into a number of segments differentiated by customer cluster and time of purchase, *and can market to each segment separately*, we can both serve our customers better and enhance our revenues. We improve our service to our customers by better meeting the needs of each customer segment *at each point in time,* while we add to our own revenues by making product available to each market segment optimally. Figure 8.6 illustrates how the revenue manager might segment the market illustrated in Figure 8.1 for event or trip tickets into seven different segments (or periods) with a view to controlling the price and units of product available for sale in each period.

Figure 8.7 illustrates the point that demand at each point time for each customer cluster creates RM market segments.

The first step in scientific pricing is to determine how many units are available for sale over the sales horizon, or what the sales target is for this period. Step two is to define multiple market segments where the product is to be sold. Step three is to build a demand model or a set of demand curves, one for each segment (more later on methods for doing

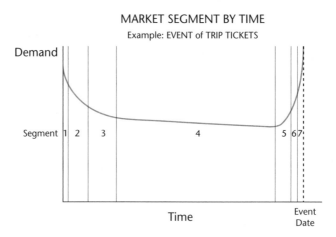

Figure 8.6 Revenue Management Market Time Segmentation

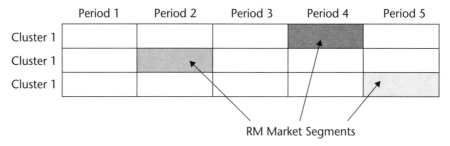

Figure 8.7 Revenue Management Market Segmentation

this). Step four is to calculate prices for each segment. The three RM approaches to calculating pricing are:

1. Fixed (or "traditional") pricing.
2. Variable pricing.
3. Dynamic pricing.

To illustrate the three approaches, we assume that we have I units available for sale, N customer clusters, and T time segments, so we have $N \times T$ total market segments. For each segment (n,t), we have a demand curve $Q_{n,t} = F_{n,t}(P_{n,t})$, which relates the price we set in that segment $(P_{n,t})$ to the quantity sold in that segment $(Q_{n,t})$.

Fixed Pricing

The fixed-pricing method requires a single price be set and held for the entire T period selling horizon. This price (P) is set to maximize total revenue while selling the required total amount of product. In words, we want to find the price (*P*) that maximizes total revenue (or the price multiplied by the total number of units sold across the *N* x *T* segments) while ensuring that our inventory available for sale (*I*) is sufficient to meet demand over all the segments. This is an optimization problem that can be written as:

$$\text{Maximize: } \textit{Total Revenue} = PQ_{1,1} + PQ_{1,2} + \ldots + PQ_{1,T} + PQ_{2,1} + PQ_{2,2} \ldots + PQ_{N,T}$$

Where $Q_{n,t} = F_{n,t}(P)$ for each customer cluster *n* = 1,2, . . . , *N* and each period *t* = 1,2, . . . *T* and we require: $Q_{1,1} + Q_{1,2} + \ldots + Q_{1,T} + Q_{2,1} + Q_{2,2} \ldots + Q_{N,T} \leq I$

The output of this optimization is a single *optimum fixed price* that we plan to post to all market segments for all time periods.

Under fixed pricing sales will vary significantly from segment to segment: over time, this will mean there are rush periods and slow periods. For example, the typical supermarket maintains fixed prices leading to very busy Saturday mornings when addition cashiers must be hired, and slow weekdays when fewer cashiers are needed.

We have assumed that demand was known, but in reality demand is uncertain. To accommodate uncertain demand, in practice, inventory is usually checked toward the end of the sales horizon and a "sale" price posted if it is found that demand has been less than expected and there is likely to be product left over.

Variable Pricing

Under variable pricing, we set a separate and potentially different price for each market segment. Prices are set to maximize total revenues, while selling no more than the available inventory. Again, finding prices $P_{n,t}$ (for each clustert *n* = 1,2, . . . ,*N* and each period *t* = 1,2, . . . *T*) is an optimization problem that can be written as:

$$\text{Maximize: } \textit{Total Revenue} = P_{1,1} Q_{1,1} + P_{1,2} Q_{1,2} + \ldots + P_{1,T} Q_{1,T} + P_{2,1} Q_{2,1} + P_{2,2} Q_{2,2} \ldots + P_{N,T} Q_{N,T}$$

where $Q_{n,t} = F_{n,t}(P_{n,t})$ for each cluster *n* = 1,2, . . . , *N* and each period *t* = 1,2, . . . *T*

and we require: $Q_{1,1} + Q_{1,2} + \ldots + Q_{1,T} + Q_{2,1} + Q_{2,2} \ldots + Q_{N,T} \leq I$

Variable pricing will increase prices in market segments with high demand that will reduce sales in these segments. To compensate, prices in segments with slow demand will be reduced, resulting in an increase in sales in these segments. The result is a set of prices that produce the same total sales over the *N* x *T* segments, but with the important result that revenue will almost always increase. Note that the fixed price solution [*P* = $P_{n,t}$ for all *n* and *t*] is a possible solution to the variable price optimization, and so if the variable price optimization results in different prices for different segments then total revenue must increase.

The set of variable prices that produces the highest possible total revenue is the *optimum variable pricing plan*. Finding this plan is an optimization problem that can be solved using Solver. The optimum variable pricing plan has the highest possible revenue for the given demand conditions.

The two important effects of variable pricing are:

- First, revenues generally increase while selling exactly the same quantity of product. Results from practice suggest that moving to variable pricing increases revenues 2–7% depending on the number of segments and the demand conditions. In general, the more pricing segments and the more variable the demand, the greater the revenue gain from moving from fixed to variable pricing.

- Second, the variable prices will smooth out the demand from segment to segment and over time. This reduced variability of sales often saves the firm selling expenses. For example, a supermarket that switched to variable pricing would have reduced prices on weekday mornings, leading to more customers and increased prices on Saturday mornings reducing the rush period and the need to hire additional cashiers on Saturdays.

The incremental revenue gain provides a strong financial incentive to move to variable pricing, since this additional revenue is achieved while selling the identical quantity of product and consequently there is almost no increase in costs. For this reason, incremental revenue has a disproportionate effect on profits:

For example, if a firm under fixed pricing might make a $5,000,000 profit on sales revenues of $100,000,000. If the firm switched to variable pricing and increased sales revenues by 5% while selling the same units of product, profits would double.

Conclusion: Setting higher prices in customer clusters with high demand and lower prices in clusters with low demand can significantly add to revenues while selling the same volume of product. Such variable pricing may also smooth out demand and this may have the additional benefit of reducing selling costs.

Examples of Variable Pricing

There are many examples of variable pricing of everyday items in the news. For example:

- McDonald's in January 2008 was offering coupons good for special prices for hamburgers on Wednesdays, cheeseburgers on Sundays, and chicken nuggets on Mondays. The effect of the coupons was to reduce prices during low-demand periods.

- Coke Cola chairman Doug Ivester was quoted with respect to a soda vending machine that could raise the price of a can of soda in hot weather when demand was high. The company later issued a press release that denied that the company planned implementation.

- Insurance companies in Europe vary the price young drivers pay, according to their driving habits. Drivers can opt to have an electronic monitoring device installed in their car that measures speed, breaking severity, cornering, and the types of roads driven at various times of the day. The data is transmitted to the insurer, who assesses driving performance and assigns the driver to a customer cluster. The cluster assigned determines the insurance premium paid. According to a report on the BBC News website (http://www.bbc.co.uk/news/technology-16969509 February 10, 2012), detection of "extreme speeds would be greeted with a stern email to the driver . . . and all the anecdotal evidence suggests that people who have installed the system have about a 30% better claims experience—in other words, less crashes—than those who don't."

Dynamic Pricing

The optimum variable prices derived above represent *a plan* developed using forecasts of demand. In practice, errors occur in our demand forecasts, with the result that executing the variable pricing plan will often result in stockouts or excess inventory and unexpectedly reduced revenues. Often there are also increased costs associated with customers denied product or liquidating unsold inventory.

Dynamic pricing requires that the market be segmented over time: prices are modified over time to reflect observed market conditions. If, for example, the first period's demand is lower than expected and, consequently, we sell fewer units than planned, we reduce the price for the remaining periods in order to avoid being left with inventory at the end of the sales horizon. Alternatively, if demand in the first period is higher than expected, we increase prices for the remainder of the selling horizon to avoid a stockouts in the last period. In *dynamic pricing*, the variable pricing plan is modified over time as actual demand varies from planned demand: dynamic pricing adapts prices to respond to observed errors in demand forecasts.

Optimum dynamic pricing follows the same general principal as dynamic pricing, except that a new set of prices are computed each period, such that total revenue from all future periods is maximized while liquidating the inventory. Optimum dynamic pricing requires the solution of a new optimization problem each period:

At the start of the sales horizon, the variable pricing problem is solved and the first period's price (or several prices if there are multiple customer clusters) are posted into the marketplace.

At the end of the first period, the market returns *actual* quantities sold for each customer cluster. The inventory is reduced by the amount of actual sales in the first period.

The variable price optimization is now re-solved for periods 2 through T to find a new set of variable prices for periods 2 through T that maximize revenue while selling the remaining inventory of products.

This process is repeated at the end of each future period: inventory is reduced by actual sales to-date and a new set of prices for future periods are computed to maximize revenues while selling the remaining units of inventory.

After the price(s) for the final sales period are posted, there remains the possibility of forecast error in the last period and there may be stockouts or unsold product. However, if the last period is quite short the magnitude of the forecast error is limited and the cost of shortage or excess inventory will be small.

Conclusion: Adjusting prices dynamically over time in response to differences between actual sales and planned sales provides a way to maintain revenues while using prices to control inventory to zero over the selling horizon. The new prices can be calculated so that revenue over the remainder of the sales horizon is maximized.

Examples of Dynamic Pricing

- Airlines and rental car companies change effective ticket prices frequently in response to demand and remaining capacity.

- It is common practice in retail stores to discount merchandise toward the end of the sales period when inventories are thought to be excessive.

- Supermarkets often offer unsold inventories of perishable products (such as day-old bread) at a discount.

- Scalpers will change the price of tickets up or down as game time approaches.

- Time of day electricity metering provides an almost-perfect platform to revenue manage electricity prices.

Summarizing RM Scientific Pricing Problem

The basic elements that make up the scientific pricing problem are:

- The **Selling Horizon** is the fixed time period, during which the product will be on sale.

- The starting **Inventory** or **Capacity** is the number of units of product we wish to sell during the Selling Horizon.

- **Customers are clustered** into different market segments that will see potentially different prices at the same point in time.

- The **review periods** are the points in time that separate the time-based market segments. At the review periods, we will compare actual sales (or equivalently, the actual remaining inventory level) with planned sales (or planned inventory) to determine whether we need to solve a new problem and adjust prices.

- **Product prices** are the variables we are going to compute and implement.

- **A demand model** is required to enable us to estimate what effect price changes will have on sales and hence on remaining inventory.

- **Optimization software** is required to calculate the set of future prices at each review period that maximizes revenue subject to an inventory or maximum sales constraint.

Here are some examples to illustrate how real problems match this framework.

The *first set of problems* appears in the service industries, where a service that is not delivered on a particular date represents a lost-revenue opportunity since it cannot be recovered or carried over.

Examples that fit this first category include:

- *Airline seats*: Once an aircraft has been assigned to a flight, the air carrier has a fixed inventory of seats (business class and economy) to sell between the date the flight "opens" for sale (usually 270 days prior to flight date) and the day of the flight. Seats not sold by the flight date are non-revenue producing (or "waste"). Since almost all the costs of flying the plane and staffing the airline are fixed, the air carrier's objective is to maximize the revenue produced by each flight.

- *Hotel rooms*: Hotel room sales closely match the framework. There are a fixed number of rooms available for each night, unsold rooms are "waste," and costs are mostly fixed.

- *Rental cars, cruise ships, holiday packages* (such as Club Med), and *telecommunications* also have fixed product availabilities, limited selling horizons, and lost revenues from unsold product.

- *Transportation services* including passenger trains, road freight, overnight delivery services, all have the same problem characteristics.

- *Utilities*, including gas and electricity, are subject to variable demand according to weather or season, with fixed quantities available for distribution.

- *Cinemas, theaters, stadiums, theme parks, recreational facilities, toll roads, parking lots, etc.* all have finite capacity, a limited selling horizon, and are unable to inventory unsold product. These area all problem characteristics that fit the revenue management framework.

The *second major set of problems* involve *perishable products*. Examples include fruits and vegetables, dairy items, frozen foods, baked goods, any time-dated grocery items, pharmaceuticals, etc., and even blood. Once we have acquired a stock of a perishable product, our objective is to sell the stock before the end of the product's useful life since out-dated product may have a very limited "salvage" value, or even be worthless. If all our acquisition costs are "sunk," then maximizing revenue is the appropriate objective is setting prices.

A *third large group of problems* involve *fashion items*. Fashion items do not perish on a particular date, but their selling horizon is strictly limited. For example, a dress shop must sell-off its spring fashions before the summer stock arrives. In addition to fashion clothing, fashion items would include, for example, seasonal clothing such as winter coats and boots, concert t-shirts, some electronic items, Christmas and Hanukah seasonal items, and fad items with a short shelf life.

Restaurants, fast food outlets, medical clinics, gas and lube stations, golf courses, and *electronic or automobile repair shops*, are just a few examples of facilities where operating costs are largely fixed and idle capacity cannot be easily recovered.

As these examples illustrate, the list of products and services that lend themselves immediately to the application of scientific pricing. This includes a very large segment of the total national economy.

A large proportion of the remaining pricing problems involve re-stockable products: that is there is no fixed inventory of product to sell over a fixed time period. In some cases, these situations are addressed by setting sales or market-share targets and using scientific pricing to achieve these targets. In other cases, the problems are addressed by maximizing contribution instead of revenues (more about this later).

A Revenue Management System

We can now review the basic elements and functioning of a revenue management system (Figure 8.8). Historical data on prices and quantities sold is collected and used to develop a demand model (Figure 8.4). The demand model is used to forecast demand for each sales period at each possible price, and then optimization procedures are used to compute revenue maximizing prices for the current sales period and all future sales periods. Current prices are posted into the marketplace. As sales data is collected, it is added to the historical database, but is also used to refine the current demand forecasts and adjust inventory or space available levels. At the end of each sales period, a new set of prices are computed and posted into the marketplace.

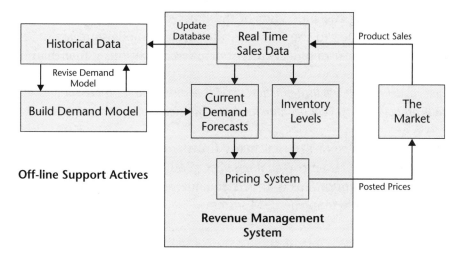

Figure 8.8 A Revenue Management System

The Demand Side of Revenue Management

Successful scientific pricing requires current, accurate estimates of demand conditions, which are a critical input to the pricing system. The pricing routines use the demand forecasts to determine revenue-maximizing prices for each market segment. These prices are then set in the marketplace and generate new demand data that feeds back into the demand forecasts to produce revised forecasts for the following period.

Demand forecasting, as illustrated in Figure 8.8, can be broken down into two components:

- Developing and maintaining the underlying demand models.

- Incorporating the most recent demand data into the models to generate new demand forecasts.

Human experts can develop the demand models over a period of time, off-line from the RM task. However, since most revenue management systems handle a large number of products with short (e.g., daily or hourly) price review periods, the task of updating the forecasts to reflect the most recently available demand data must be programmed into the revenue management software. These updating routines must be *fast*, *sensitive*, and *robust*:

- *Fast*, because we are going to be executing these routines for every product, every period, and our computers have to be able to handle this computational load in real time.

- *Sensitive*, because a key success factor for revenue management is the ability to pick up and exploit period-to-period differences in demand conditions.

- *Robust*, because we do not want to be reacting to "off-the-wall" forecasts very often.

An important task facing the supervisor of the RM system is to ensure that, as the new daily demand data is added to the database, the demand models are maintained and, if possible, improved, in order to reflect current demand conditions rather than history.

Good demand modeling will produce practical, useful demand curves that will enable the firm to price optimally and effectively. Poor demand modeling may lead to ineffective revenue management.

We know from the practice of RM that many firms are very good at estimating demand conditions. Unfortunately, the firms that are very good at this are reluctant to reveal their methods to the outside world. This is understandable, since this is part of the competitive advantage that they derive from their RM systems.

Demand modeling is a real craft: there are no correct or incorrect ways to do this. The objective is to construct demand curves by observing the impact of changing prices on quantity sold across market segments, and then somehow "modeling" demand across several periods and segments. Ideally demand modeling begins with data, but most "traditional" firms change product prices fairly infrequently, and so have little historical data to use to estimate demand. A new firm introducing RM for the first time is at a distinct disadvantage over one that has been using these techniques for some time. The established RM firm will have a large database of price and quantity observations to use for demand curve estimation. The competitive advantage in this case clearly lies with the first firm in the industry to adopt RM.

In the absence of data on the sensitivity of the quantity sold to changes in price, it is possible to use management experience and opinion to arrive at initial demand curve estimates. To do this, we would want to tap the opinion of someone close to the market who had a good feel for the dynamics of the market place. Consulting such an expert could provide estimates of demand curves. For example:

- A linear demand curve can be constructed from opinions on quantities that would sell at two different prices: If we expect to sell Q_1 units at price P_1 and Q_2 units at price P_2, then an estimate of the quantity sold (Q) at any price (P) is given by:

$$P = P_1 + (P_2 - P_1)/(Q_2 - Q_1) * (Q - Q_1)$$

An experience-based approach such as this will allow us to start up our RM system, but once we are underway and generating a price/quantity database, there is an opportunity to use this data to refine our demand models. This will usually require the uses of statistical methods such as regression, or the statistical estimation of demand elasticities. If the demand forecasting procedures of the RM system are able to pick up and react to major differences between expected and actual demand, the revenue gain from dynamic pricing over fixed pricing will increase.

Incorporating Additional Constraints

The above example allows the price optimization to set any price on any day. There are a variety of instances where such unconstrained prices are not acceptable, but these situations can generally be included without great effort, although generally at a cost in terms of a diminution of revenue below the maximum attainable. Here are some examples:

Maximum or Minimum Prices

Management may decide that there is a minimum price that they are prepared to set for the product. For example, if a product has a "salvage value" if unsold at the end of the selling period, it certainly makes sense not to sell the product during the selling period at less than the salvage value. In certain instances, setting maximum prices may also be sensible taking into account the overall image of the firm.

Maximum or minimum prices for single periods, or all periods, are easily incorporated into the pricing model by simply adding constraints that force prices into the acceptable range. If, however, the addition of price constraints changes the solution, there will be a loss of revenue. If price in any period matches the minimum imposed price, there will generally be a loss in revenue, but there may also be product unsold at the end of the selling period (since prices could not be reduced low enough to clear out the inventory).

Planned "Fire Sales" (or any Required Price in any Period)

A planned "fire sale" (such as "50% off on Boxing Day") is easily incorporated into the pricing model by simply adding a constraint that fixes the price for the required period. The optimization will maximize revenues from the remaining periods while accepting whatever revenue arises from the fixed-price periods. If the fixed-price period is near the end of the selling period, then the price optimization may "short" the "fire sale" period, attempting to mitigate the revenue loss that results from the fixed price.

Non-Increasing Prices

Some firms are happy to accept "constantly falling prices" but have a difficult time raising prices in the way that the pricing algorithm may suggest. Adding a set of constraints that the price in any period cannot be greater than the price a period earlier obviates this problem, although this will result in a loss of revenue.

The "non-increasing" price revenue maximizing solution is common in retail where it is called *markdown optimization*. Special purpose markdown optimization software is available.

The Amount of Product to Inject into the Marketplace

In traditional pricing, a price is set and the market returns the quantity sold: making a profit depends on selling enough units. In scientific pricing, the situation is reversed: management decides how much product to sell over a given selling horizon and the pricing algorithms attempt to sell that inventory: the market returns the revenue received. Under scientific pricing, making a profit depends on getting high enough prices. The general level of prices depends on how much inventory we inject into the market: the more inventory, the lower will be the average price level. This makes choice of the amount of product an important management decision. An extreme example of the consequences of mismatched product quantity and demand occurred after 9–11 when air passenger demand was dramatically reduced but the air carriers were slow to reduce their capacities. As a consequence, the pricing algorithms cut prices as far as possible to try to fill all the available seats, resulting in huge losses for the airlines.

A number of different situations can be identified:

- Situations where the quantity is fixed by physical limitations: for example, the number of seats in a stadium or theater, the capacity of a cable link, or the number of cabins on a cruise ship.

- Situations where the quantity is fixed in the short run but variable over the longer term: for example, the number of rental cars on the lot or holiday vacation packages available, the number of seats on an airplane or train (it is usually possible to change to a larger or smaller plane, or to add coaches to a train), or the number of rooms in a hotel/motel, or spaces in a parking lot.

- Situations where the quantity is quite variable at the time of purchase; for example, the amount of milk, broccoli, or dated foodstuffs that we purchase or the number of fashion or seasonal items that we purchase for resale.

When the inventory quantity can be varied, choice of this amount is a critical management decision for the revenue manager: how much product should be injected into the marketplace each selling period? Solving this problem technically appears quite straightforward: we might simply add the inventory amount into the optimization as a decision variable. However, it is also important to consider the cost of changing the initial inventory and also the risks associated with overstocking or understocking. The basic scientific pricing model often does not tell us enough about *profitability,* particularly if there is no cost of buying the inventory included in the model. (There are several ways in which contribution, or profits, or can be included in the model, but these will not be presented here.)

In summary, the quantity of product chosen to sell and the length of the selling horizon will have a major impact on prices and profitability. These decisions should be reviewed carefully by managers who understand the market place with the maximum amount of assistance from the RM system.

To this point, we have considered only the pricing aspect of RM, which depends on the ability to develop demand forecasts and to use these to compute revenue-maximizing prices. Revenue managers have developed a number of other ideas to grow firm revenues including product protection, overbooking, trading-up and shortselling.

Product Protection

A key idea that emerged from an analytical approach to revenue enhancement is the idea that sometimes revenues can be enhanced by *not* selling a unit of product, even when the unit is stock and a customer is there requesting a unit. The idea here is that units in inventory can be *protected* from being purchased by certain customers. This practice is revenue enhancing when the customer is requesting the product for a lower price than the price that the firm can anticipate receiving from sale of the unit at a later date. Implementations of protection include *allocating product among various price classes* (or market segments) and the allocation of product among various packages (or *discount allocation*).

Allocating Inventory to Multiple Price Classes

There are a number of instances where firms face the problem of allocating a fixed supply of product among two or more different customer classes who pay different prices. Since an important input to the RM system is the inventory available for sale to each customer class over the selling horizon, the firm must determine how many units of product to allocate to each different product inventory.

For example, the airlines fly several different fare classes in the same seats. "Full-fare economy," advance reservation, and "supersaver" ticket holders all fly side-by-side in the main cabin of the airplane but there may be different conditions attached to the tickets (refundable, change penalties, baggage fees, etc.). A customer trying to purchase a "supersaver" or other discount fare often finds out that this class is sold out, although full-fare economy seats are still available in the same cabin (at a higher price). From the airline's perspective, the seats allocated to the low-fare classes on that flight are all sold, although there is still space available for customers willing to pay higher fares; in the words of RM, a number of seats are *protected* for higher fare classes. How do we determine how many seats to allocate to each fare class? Here is the theory.

Suppose we have three products to sell from the same inventory over a selling horizon. We will consider these to be a $1,000 product, a $600 product, and a $300 product. The problem is to find the number of units to reserve for the $1,000 product, and the $600 product, with the balance going to the $300 product.

If P_N is the probability of selling the Nth unit of the $1,000 product, then we expect P_N to become smaller as N increases: that is the probability of selling the 100th unit at $1,000 is smaller than the probability of selling the 5th unit. We will assume that the revenue received from selling a $1,000 unit is $1,000, whether this is the 1st, 50th, or 100th unit. The *marginal revenue* received from each unit that we sell is, therefore, $1,000. The *expected marginal revenue* for the Nth unit of $1,000 product is the marginal revenue ($1,000) multiplied by the probability of selling that unit (P_N) or:

Expected marginal revenue from Nth unit of $1,000 product = $1,000 P_N

Since P_N declines as N increases, expected marginal revenue declines as N increases. This situation is illustrated by the top line in Figure 8.9. As we reserve more inventory for the $1,000 product, the probability of selling the last unit declines to zero and with it the expected marginal revenue from the last unit reserved.

The same analysis applies to the $600 product. The expected marginal revenue of the first unit reserved for this product is close to $600, since the probability of selling one unit is (presumably) close to 1. As we reserve more of the inventory for the $600 product, the expected marginal revenue declines to zero as the probability of selling the last unit declines to zero (the middle line in Figure 8.9). The same analysis determines the shape of the expected marginal revenue curve for the $300 product (the bottom line in Figure 8.9).

We can now determine our product allocations. We allocate inventory to the $1,000 product up to the point where the expected marginal revenue from the Nth unit falls below the

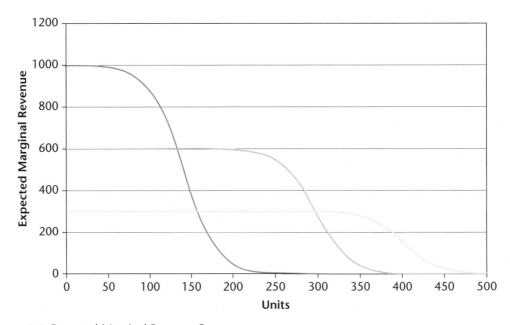

Figure 8.9 Expected Marginal Revenue Curves

expected marginal revenue from the $600 product: in Figure 8.9, where the top line crosses the middle line, which is at 140 units. We reserve inventory for the $600 product as long as the expected marginal revenue for the $600 product is greater than that for the $300 product, or to the point where the middle line in Figure 8.9 crosses the bottom line (at 300 units).

We now have our allocations: reserve 140 units for $1,000 customers, 160 (= 300-140) units for $600 customers, and the balance for $300 customers. We now *protect* 140 units for $1,000 customers, 160 units for $600 customers, and allow $300 customers to fill the remainder of the plane. Of course, we revise our calculations over time as reservations appear and change the protection levels, if warranted by observed differences in the number of customers of each class who have appeared and the number that we expected to appear.

Protection levels form the basis of airline RM: airlines do not change prices, but move seats among fare categories as protection levels evolve over time. In general, there are six or seven fare classes travelling in the economy cabin. Seats generally sell from the low-price categories first and so, at any point in time, the three of four low-fare classes will be sold out but seats will be available in the higher-fare categories. If the plane is filling up on schedule, the price of an available seat increases as fare classes are sold out. However, if demand is slower than expected, the airline will reduce the protection levels in the higher-fare categories, which has the effect of pushing available seats into lower-fare categories and so reducing the price of available seats.

Product protection is also a feature of discounting. Many products are offered in a variety of discount packages. Properly managed package discounts can increase rather than decrease revenues. Here are some examples of typical discounts:

- Airlines, theaters, etc., often offer lower rates for large groups of travelers.
- Car rental companies offer a host of different discount plans for longer-term rentals.
- Parking lots offer lower rates for "all day" or longer-term parking.
- Amusement parks and restaurants may offer family rates and group rates.
- Formal clothing rental stores will offer a lower rate for the whole wedding party.
- Cell phone companies will offer lower rates if the buyer commits to more call time.

Managing discount pricing is an important revenue enhancing opportunity. As a simple example, suppose an item is offered in singles or at a discount in packages of ten. Presumably, the 10-pack is offered because there is a market for 10-packs and it is optimum to price the 10-pack at less than 10 times the cost of a single. Under these conditions, it is important to optimize the pricing so that the single unit and 10-pack are priced to maximize revenues. It is also important for maximum revenue that a quantity of the inventory should be *protected* for single unit sales. This would be particularly true if the demand for 10-packs occurred earlier than did the demand for singles, when without product protection all the single units would be sold in 10-packs and the demand for singles (the high revenue sales) will be lost.

Revenue managers recognize that appropriate discounting, coupled with product protection, can enhance revenues. To illustrate the revenue enhancing potential of discounts, we examine one of the discount allocation areas that has attracted a lot of attention: this is managing the pricing of hotel rooms.

A typical hotel in a major city has a peak demand midweek when it is usually full of business travelers staying one or two nights, but business travelers go home over the weekend. If the hotel posts a daily rate, good for any night of the week, it ends up being busy and profitable during the week but below capacity over the weekend. To increase occupancy and revenues, hotels will offer a variety of discount rates. For example, a hotel can offer a weekly rate that represents something less than seven times the daily rate, or they can offer a weekend special rate, again at a discount off the daily rate. Clearly, many other pricing opportunities are possible, including short notice walk-in rates, special "any three nights" rates, etc., each aimed at a different market segment.

The skill in designing a set of discount packages and rates is to use the discounts to enhance revenues when the hotel is below capacity, while avoiding the discount rates

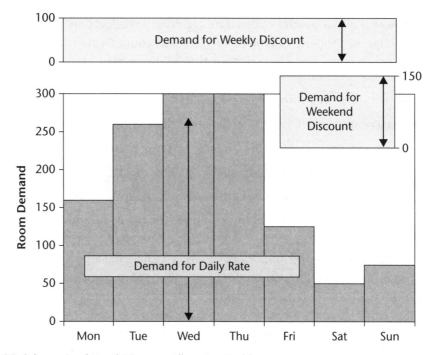

Figure 8.10 Schematic of Hotel Discount Allocation Problem

cannibalizing the high-value daily rates when the hotel is full. Figure 8.10 illustrates the problem for the case of a 300-room hotel offering daily, full-week, and weekend rates that all use the same rooms. In this example, the daily rates could be set to fill the hotel mid-week (the histogram bars in Figure 8.10), but this would leave empty rooms five days of the week. There is a demand for a full-week discount rate and the size of this demand depends on the rate (rectangle), but accepting rooms at the weekly rate will squeeze out some daily rate customer on the busy nights. There is also demand for a weekend rate and there seems to be space available, but accepting too many weekend bookings will squeeze out full-week customers.

We can begin to see why this type of discount scheme is potentially revenue-enhancing from Figure 8.10. If the hotel sells only a single weekly discount package, and offers no other discounts, it will lose just two nights at the daily rate and replace these with seven nights at the weekly discount rate. As long as the weekly rate is greater than twice the daily rate, we will gain both revenues and occupancy. The figure also illustrates that if we offer a weekend (Friday, Saturday, Sunday) discount package, and no other discounts, we can sell up to 180 of these packages without cannibalizing the daily rate business at all, since maximum daily demand on these days is the 120 nights on Friday.

Figure 8.11 illustrates a possible solution to the discount allocation puzzle: occupancy is greatly increased and with optimized pricing revenues will be considerably higher. The attraction of such discounts is easy to see: apart from a small amount of variable cost in cleaning rooms, linen, etc., any new revenues received from these discount packages goes straight to the "bottom line," since the great majority of the hotel's costs are fixed.

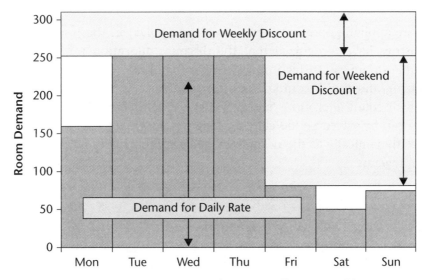

Figure 8.11 Schematic of One Solution to the Hotel Discount Allocation Problem

In the past, the design of these discount schemes was a hit and miss affair. Clearly many tradeoffs must be considered simultaneously. Here are some examples:

- If we sell too many weekly packages, or price the weekly discount package too low, we are going to displace more daily rate business than we gain in weekly discount business.

- At the same time, if we offer too many weekend packages, we can lose both weekly discount business and daily business rate business leading to higher occupancy (and higher costs) but lower revenues.

- Depending on how many weekly discount packages we sell, there is an opportunity to enhance revenues by raising the daily rate, since otherwise we will be turning away more customers mid-week.

Reasoning through an evaluation of these tradeoffs runs into the fundamental difficulty that the demand for the various full and discount rate packages depends upon the price of the package. We must, therefore, specify a price and a maximum room allocation for each discount package, and must try to do this in a way that maximizes revenues.

With the application of RM pricing in the hotel industry, the discount allocation problem becomes both more complex and potentially more important. Each day during the booking period, we must decide what price to offer for each discount package, and how many rooms to allocate to each discount package or, alternatively, how many rooms to protect for the high-paying customers at the non-discount rate (who are often business travelers who book much later than do travelers booking for the whole week or the weekend.) By solving this problem dynamically and optimally, we maximize the revenues to the hotel.

Those who are applying optimum dynamic pricing (ODP) in the hotel/motel/resort and similar industries have recognized that the discount allocation problem can be solved using the same optimization techniques used to compute optimum dynamic prices. In fact, the pricing and the discount allocation problem can be solved simultaneously to provide both discount allocations and prices that together maximize revenues. Further, this problem can be solved periodically as bookings appear, so that prices and protection levels change dynamically as the occupancy dates approach so that the hotel can be full at maximum revenue.

Managed Overselling (Also Known as Overbooking)

Overbooking appeared in the 1970s as a response to the "no-show" customer. A "no-show" is a customer who commits to take units of product during the sales period but does not show up to collect the product on the delivery date. In the hotel business, a customer who books a room a month in advance but does not appear to claim the room is a "no-show."

"No-shows" can be a significant problem. In some instances, "no-show" rates for rental cars approach 50%: that is, if no steps were taken to address this problem, car rental companies would have half their cars idle on the lot.

These are many examples of products where customers may buy or order the product for "delivery" on a future date:

- Airline seats, and passenger train seats, are usually booked in advance of the date of travel.

- Rental cars can be reserved ahead of the day of rental.

- Hotel rooms and campsite spaces are usually reserved in advance.

- Seats for stage shows, sports events, and concerts are sold in advance.

- Package vacations and cruises are usually booked in advance.

- Tuxedos, cut flowers, some baked goods, etc., are commonly booked for future delivery.

Managed overselling is now a routine part of RM for products, such as these, where at least some customers "book" the product ahead of the delivery date. If the firm reserves product for a "no-show" customer, then two bad things may happen. First, the firm may be stuck with product that it cannot sell within the inevitable short notice that results from a "no-show" customer. Second, other customers who wanted to buy the product may have been turned away because the supply of product was fully booked, leading to disappointed or unsatisfied customers.

"Overbooking" simply means that we take more bookings or reservations for product than we have product available. "Managed overselling" implies that we do this carefully and thoughtfully in order to minimize the impact on our customers. This impact is made up of three different items:

- The **probability** that we have to tell a customer who has booked the product that there is no product available.

- The **costs** that we incur as a result of a customer who had a valid booking but who could not be provided with product.

- The **revenues** that we receive from sales of additional units of product.

The *probability* that a "booked" customer has to be denied a product depends upon the volume of overbooking that we accept, and, if we overbook, the probability that other customers will be no-shows. Customers may not show up to collect their product for a variety of reasons, some of which are uncontrollable by the customer, and some controllable. Uncontrollable reasons include sickness, weather, travel delays, job layoff, etc. Controllable reasons include the availability of a better deal elsewhere, or a change of plans.

Figure 8.12 illustrates the interplay between the three items that determine the number of units to oversell. The revenue from sale of product increases with the number of units sold, although the ODP algorithms will generally reduce the price per unit if we inject additional units into the marketplace. For this reason, the "Sales Revenue" curve in Figure 8.12 exhibits decreasing revenue/unit as sales increase.

We incur no "overbooking cost" unless we take bookings above capacity. As we increase bookings above capacity, our *expected overbooking cost* increases (the *Overbooking Cost* curve in Figure 8.12). The *expected overbooking cost* is the cost we expect to incur as a result of customers who have reservations but cannot be accommodated, multiplied by the probability of us having more customers than product available.

The probability of having one or more overbooked customers increases with the number of reservations taken in excess of capacity (the *overbook quantity*).

Example: If we have 500 rooms in our hotel, and we take 501 reservations for the same night, then only one of 501 customers must be "no-show" for us to have enough rooms for everyone that shows up. If however, we take 600 reservations, then 100 customers must be "no-show" for us to avoid unsatisfied customers. Clearly, the probability of

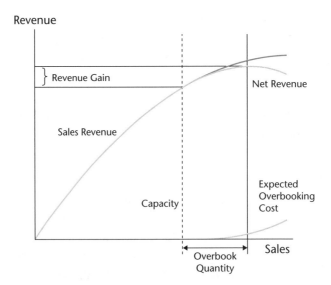

Figure 8.12 Determining Optimum Overbooking Quantity

having 501 "shows" (that is one overbooked customer) in 600 booking is much greater than the probability of having 501 "shows" in 501 bookings.

The optimum *overbook quantity* (Figure 8.12) is determined by subtracting the *Overbooking Cost* from the sales revenues at each booking level. This gives the *Net Revenue* curve (Figure 8.12). The sales level at which the net revenue reaches a maximum gives us the revenue maximizing quantity to book.

The *Revenue Gain* from overbooking is given by the difference between the revenue achievable by selling at the overbooking level and the revenue achieved by selling at capacity (Figure 8.12).

To achieve this revenue gain over the long term, the firm will need to pay attention to managing the overbooked customer and will need to put in place a set of procedures to look after the customer with a valid reservation for product who shows up when no product is available. There is a short-term cost in handling such customers, since alternate, and often more expensive product, is usually provided, but there is also a longer-term cost in terms of customer goodwill. Ideally, the overbooked customer should be treated in a way that encourages customer loyalty, and maintains, perhaps even strengthens, the customer's relationship with the supplier.

The cost to the firm of an overbooked customer depends critically on how the customer is handled. Typically, such actions include "trading up," or meeting the customer's order with a higher-valued product (usually at the same price as the ordered product), and/or some form of compensation. Here are some examples:

- Airlines have had good success offering travel coupons to ticketed customers in order to persuade them to take an alternate flight when space is needed for overbooked passengers. Such coupons have the advantage of having a real value to the customer but an often quite-low cost to the air carrier, particularly if the customer can be persuaded to use the coupons on a flight that would not normally be full.

- Some airlines offer cash, conducting an auction to persuade the required number of passengers to give up their seats and take a later flight.

- Hotels will trade up overbooked customers to rooms on the executive floor.

- Rental car companies will substitute a higher class of car at no extra charge, or if no such car is available, will make arrangements for a substitute car with a competitor.

The first few overbooked customers can probably be handled at low to modest cost, but as we overbook in greater numbers, the cost of processing these unsatisfied customers generally increases very sharply. It is one task to free up one or two seats on a plane, but much more difficult to find 20 or 30 seats! Similarly, a hotel may be able to accommodate a few over-booked tourists on the executive floor at quite low cost, but when the executive floor is full, the costs could increase dramatically.

Overbooking is not a business practice that is universally well received, but when carefully managed, overbooking can be source of considerable benefits to both the firm and its customers. The firm benefits from enhanced revenues, while few customers who book an "economy" class airline seat are angry when they are asked to travel "business class" because no "economy" seat is available. Few customers who book a "sub-compact" rental car are disgruntled when they are offered a "compact" or medium-sized car (at the same price) because no sub-compact is available. In cases such as these, overbooking can be managed so that the costs of overbooked customers are paid by the firm, and not by the customer.

A second important management task when overbooking is to do whatever is reasonable and possible to encourage customers not to be "no-shows," or to cancel their bookings as soon as they know that they will not be collecting the product. Management practices to discourage "no-shows" are not new: in some businesses, "no-shows" have been a costly problem for some time. Here are some examples of the types of practices that have been used to discourage "no-shows":

- Require payment at the time the booking is made, perhaps offering an early payment price reduction. This is a common practice in the package vacation industry and in educational courses. Payment may be non-refundable or may be partially or fully refundable if cancellation is received far enough in advance of the delivery date for the supplier to re-sell the product.

- Require payment in full at some prearranged time in advance of the delivery date. If payment is not received, the supplier cancels the booking. Hotels routinely require a credit card number to guarantee a booked room beyond a certain time. If the customer "no-shows," at least one night's room rate is charged to the card.

- Customer deposits are often taken at the time of booking. These may be partially or wholly refundable on cancellation, if sufficient notice is received. Airlines, hotels, vacations, formal rentals, etc., now often require some form of deposit to reserve product.

- Fees may be charged if a booking is changed. Airlines charge $100 or $150 if a customer wants to switch to a different flight. This discourages customers from reserving a flight at a high price and then switching to a lower-priced ticket if such a ticket becomes available on that or an equivalent flight.

Planned Trading-up or Managed Upgrades

Planned trade-ups are an RM practice where the firm plans in advance to meet demand for a lower-priced product by providing the customer with a higher-priced product at the lower price. In some cases, this upgrade may be transparent to the customer, as when a supersaver air traveler is upgraded to economy class, but in other case trade-ups can be both highly visible and revenue enhancing.

Consider the example of a retail store selling running shoes. The store would have shoes for the major brands at several price points: One brand of training shoes might be available at $99.95, $119.95, $139.95, $159.95, and so on. A customer selects the $119.95 shoe but after checking the storeroom, the assistant finds that the shoe is out-of-stock in the customer's size. At this moment, store management faces a decision: How do they handle the customer? Traditionally, the assistant would tell the customer, "Sorry, not available in your size," and stand there as if the stock-out was somehow the fault of the customer, who might then leave the store and the sale is lost. RM, however, recognizes that under some circumstances, revenues will be enhanced if the store offers the customer a higher-priced shoe (in this example, the $139.95 if it is available) at the same price as the shoe originally selected.

Let us assume that the markup on running shoes is 100%. If the store sells a $119.95 shoe, it makes a margin of about $60. If the store sells a $139.95 shoe at $119.95, it still makes a margin of $119.95 less 50% of $139.95, or about $50: that is, the store only loses about $10 of margin as long as it can manage inventory so that it does not lose a future sale of the $139.95 shoe at $139.95. Further, making the sale and offering the customer a good deal will lead to a content customer and enhances customer relations for the store.

A store policy where the store will meet requests for shoes that are out of stock by trading the customer up to the next price point at the store's expense appears to make economic sense. An additional advantage of the adoption of a trade-up policy such as this is that this enables the store to reduce its inventory: the store no longer must stock shoes in every size at every price point, but would want to ensure that it had a complete inventory at every second or third price point (depending on how many price points it is prepared to trade-up).

The additional complexity in this analysis is that often a customer faced with an out-of-stock situation will "trade" themselves up to the next price point voluntarily. If the store trades-up a customer at the store's expense when the customer would have bought the higher priced shoe at the regular price, then margin will be lost. Here then is a simple trade-up decision rule:

Let: R_H = revenue from high-priced product

   R_L = revenue from low-priced product

c_H = cost of high-priced product

P = probability the higher-priced product will be sold at the list price, either to the rejected low-priced customer or to another customer (if inventory is short.)

Then trading up is revenue enhancing if the margin obtained on the trade-up is higher than the expected margin on the sale of the higher-priced product at the list price:

$$(R_L - c_H) > P(R_H - c_H)$$

Or we should trade-up the customer if the probability of selling the higher priced product in the future at the list price is low:

$$P < (R_L - c_H)/(R_H - c_H)$$

Managed upgrades are a common business practice in many service industries (hotels, rental-cars, cruises) and are beginning to appear in retail. The "theory" suggests that we will likely see more of this.

Short-Selling and Replaning

Short-selling and replaning are practiced when the firm sells product that it does not have, knowing that it can obtain the necessary units later. Short-selling involves selling something that you do not have but know that you can obtain. For example, the concierge at a hotel might sell you a theatre ticket she does not actually possess, knowing that tickets are available for that particular show and she can easily get one. Short-selling is revenue-enhancing when the revenue from the short-sale exceeds the cost of obtaining the product.

Replane Inc. was incorporated on May 21, 2003, with former American Airlines analytics group head Tom Cook as CEO. The company was formed to market "replaning" as "the next step forward in revenue enhancement for the airlines." Here is how replaning works. Suppose that a flight is closed (or oversold to the maximum level that the airline will accept) some days prior to flight date. Now suppose that a customer appears prepared to pay $1,000 for a seat on the closed flight. If the airline can identify a passenger with a seat on the closed flight, and can "incentivize" the passenger to happily change to a different flight where space is available, then the airline can make a revenue gain: perhaps as high as $1,000, less the value of any incentive given if there is no cost to re-accommodating the passenger on the alternate flight. Cook has estimated that such "replaning" could produce additional revenues of $100 million annually for a large carrier such as American Airlines.

"Replaning" could also be practiced in many other revenue management application areas, although the name might have to be generalized. For example, one might have a reservation for the theatre and receive a call offering an incentive to move to a different performance.

We have presented scientific pricing, product protection, overbooking, planned upgrades, and short-selling separately although these are all highly interrelated. For example, for an airline, the overbooking level, protection level for full-fare economy passengers, whether or not the airline is planning upgrades, and/or planning replanings all determine the inventory of product for sale and, hence, the current prices. In reality, airlines must solve a complex series of interrelated optimizations frequently if they wish to optimize revenues.

A search for "revenue management" on the internet will find many RM providers offering the five major concepts presented above but also a range of other revenue enhancing practices which are variations of the five major ideas. For example:

- Markdown optimization (which is common in retail) is dynamic or variable pricing with non-increasing prices.
- Enterprise profit optimization is a merger of scientific pricing and supply chain optimization where product prices and demand models are included in the optimizations that set ordering, production scheduling, and transportation decisions.

Requirements for Successful RM

Successful revenue management requires good information technology in order to have up-to-date reliable information on sales and inventories, strong analytical skills in order to build appropriate demand models, calculate prices, and outstanding management skills. The firm that implements RM in a way that upsets its customers is unlikely to see the expected revenue gains.

Strong management of RM includes setting the correct quantities of product to launch into the pricing systems, updating the demand models and RM systems frequently, and monitoring these systems carefully to avoid surprises and ensure that revenue gains materialize. It is also important to communicate the aggregate benefits of RM to the customers and avoid a backlash that could reduce demand and cut revenues.

Revenue Management in Action

Peoples' Express Airlines

The history of Peoples' Express (PE), which is well documented in a series of Harvard Business School case studies, is that of a highly successful airline that grew rapidly following deregulation of the North American airline business. PE paid particular attention to six precepts that closely matched some of the common management fads of the day. These precepts were:

1. Service: commitment to the growth and development of our people.
2. To be the best provider of air transportation.
3. To provide the highest quality of leadership.
4. To serve as a role model for others.
5. Simplicity.
6. Maximization of profits.

PE was very "people oriented" and stressed "customer service." Founded in the summer of 1980, the strategy seemed to work, as PE grew to annual revenues of almost $1 billion in 1985. Contemporary writings from the mid-1980s suggested that PE had some problems, but no one anticipated that PE would be facing bankruptcy by the end of 1986. The development of revenue management methods at American and Delta was not seen as a significant competitive threat at the time. After the fact, it is generally agreed that its inability to come up with a competitive response to revenue management drove this successful air carrier out of business in just a few short months. Donald Burr, founder and CEO of PE:

> believes that major carriers' use of sophisticated computer programs to immediately match or undercut his prices ultimately killed People Express. (*Source*: J. A. Bryan, "Donald Burr May Be Ready to Take to the Skies Again," *Business Week*, January 16, 1989, pp 74–75)

Using "sophisticated computer programs" to adapt product prices to changing market conditions is the essence of revenue management.

The teaching note, which provides a guide to use of the Harvard PE cases, provides an independent assessment:

> The major carriers met People Express's pricing structure . . . and used their reservations systems to achieve optimal pricing and yield management. PE's performance, in essentially all dimensions, immediately declined . . . The end was swift. (*Source*: G. Loveman & M. Beer, "People Express Airlines: Rise and Decline," *Teaching Note*, Harvard Business School 5-491-080, 1991)

Many other airlines faced significant financial problems at about this same time, including TWA, Pan American, Eastern, Continental, Braniff, and the list goes on. It is tempting to conclude that revenue management, as practiced at American, was responsible for these bankruptcies, but the evidence is not that strong. What is clear is that American, Delta, United, and USAir made a strategic decision to invest in the development of revenue management capability, and that this proved to be a successful strategy. Other airlines that followed different strategies did not survive, or else survived only as niche carriers.

Revenue management is now universally applied across the airline business; a modern airline simply cannot survive without revenue management. There is broad recognition that RM is now a critical part of airline operations:

> It is worth emphasizing that a reservations system, with its yield management capacity, is arguably the single most important strategic asset of an airline. (HBS case 9-490-012)

Sources: "People Express Airlines: Rise and Decline" (1993) Harvard Business School 9-490-012; "People Express" (March 1984) (1986), Harvard Business School 9-487-043; "People Express" (May 1985) (1986), Harvard Business School 9-487-044; "People Express Update," 1/89 (1989), Harvard Business School 9-489-022; "People Express" (A) (1995) Harvard Business School 9-483-103.

National Car Rental

In 1992, National Car Rental (National) was losing millions of dollars every month. General Motors (GM), National's parent company, was forced to take a $744 million charge against the ownership of National. Despite cutting costs and reducing staff, the company was still unprofitable, with the result that morale was very low. GM stated that if National did not become profitable, so that it could be sold, it would be liquidated and all 7,500 employees would lose their jobs.

Turnaround specialists Jay Alix and Associates were called in, and Larry Ramaekers was assigned to lead the turnaround and act as president. Looking to the airline industry, Ramaekers noted the success of their new RM technology and decided to go for a revenue-based turnaround, as opposed to a cost-cutting turnaround: RM offered the potential to increase revenues without a significant increase in costs. Time was short: a working system was needed in only three months.

After conducting extensive meetings with several top consultants in the hope that they could provide the required RM tools to save the sinking company, National turned to Aeronomics, a consulting company from Atlanta that employed several former Delta Airline RM specialists. Aeronomics assignment was straightforward: save the company.

National Car Rental was essentially bankrupt when it introduced its new RM system. The impact was dramatic:

> "(Revenue management) basically saved National Car Rental. And you can go from the CEO of National on down, and they will all say: 'just applying these models made the life or death difference for this company,'" wrote Kevin Geraghty of Aeronomics Inc. (*Source*: M.K. Geraghty & Ernest Johnson, "Revenue Management Saves Car Rental," *Interfaces 27*, 1997, pp 107–127).

Scientific Pricing Examples

- A **major transportation provider** priced shipments by origin and destination and did not have sufficient capacity to handle all the shipments that appeared early in the week but had excess capacity at the end of the week and during the weekends. By firming up prices during the busy times and offering discounts off-peak, revenues increased and capacity utilization was smoothed out (examples: long-haul freight, ready-mix concrete, ocean containers). (*Source*: Container Transportation Company. Ivey Publishing)

- **7-Eleven Inc.** noticed that when it fought to "beat down" certain costs, so its convenience stores could reduce some of the prices they charged consumers, the effort wasn't always worthwhile, says Kay Trapp, manager for merchandise pricing. It turned out that several items with newly lowered prices saw no change in sales. The chain bought price-optimization software to get such insights in advance. "We decided it made us smarter," Trapp says. (*Source*: *USA Today*, April 27, 2007 http://www.usatoday.com/tech/products/2007–04–27–2143056104_x.htm)

- An **electronics retailer** priced batteries the same all over, until SAP's Khimetrics software showed that consumers in Dallas were generally willing to pay more for batteries than were people in Boston. The data revealed another strange twist: The battery that had the highest "price sensitivity" in Dallas had the lowest price sensitivity in Boston. In other words, while Texans would buy this particular battery only within a narrow price-range, Bostonians were far less picky about it. The store altered its prices accordingly, sold more batteries, and made more money at it. (*Source*: *USA Today*, April 27, 2007, http://www.usatoday.com/tech/products/2007–04–27–2143056104_x.htm)

- A **manufacturer in China** faced a highly seasonal demand that it partially accommodated by expediting shipping: the reduced shipping time extended the interval over which the firm could produce product to meet peaks in orders. However, the air freight cost for the expedited shipping consumed about 40% of the firm's annual profit. The firm moved to offering a small discount (2%–3%) to customers who would take delivery of product earlier. Air freight costs were greatly reduced and the firm's profits increased. (*Source*: Case *Long Wang Sha Tan Ku Company (Dragon King Shorts Company)*. Ivey Publishing 9B09E008)

- The CEO of *Albertson's grocery stores* told analysts in 2005 that the chain was reaping "big dividends" after pricing software advised charging less for such items as paper towels, toilet paper, ketchup, and soup. For now, the software is enough of a competitive advantage that chains are reluctant to publicize their experiences. Still, it's clear that price-setting software and similar, more-established technologies such as markdown optimization figure to make stores more efficient and savvy at promoting precisely what consumers want. Or at least what we think we want. (*Source*: Brian Bergstein, "Pricing Software Could Reshape Retail," *USA Today*, April 28, 2007, http://www.usatoday.com/tech/products/2007–04–29–24371588 59_x.htm)

- **ALDO Group Inc.**, a Canadian shoe company with stores worldwide, began selling two kinds of sneakers it wanted off shelves by the end of June. One pair was $29, the other $49. According to Bob Raven, ALDO's vice president of finance, the $29 version was a smash and figured to sell out by May. The $49 pairs seemed to be doing so-so. So a merchandise manager, following his instinct, prepared to cut the price, perhaps all the way to $29, until the company cranked up its new markdown-optimization system from Oracle. The verdict: Keep the shoes at $49. The software showed that based on current and historic sales figures, the shoes would still sell out by June. (*Source*: Brian Bergstein, "Pricing Software Could Reshape Retail," *USA Today,* April 28, 2007, http://www.usatoday.com/tech/products/2007–04–29–2437158859_x.htm)

Summary

Revenue enhancement is now a major application area for analytics.

A number of important revenue-enhancing ideas have appeared from the analytics literature and been translated into new business practices. The objective of these new practices is to raise additional revenues while selling essentially the same units of product, which differentiates them from traditional marketing with its focus on increasing the number of units sold.

Analytics has led to new ways of pricing products where prices are flexible and dynamic responding to demand and inventory conditions. Product protection, overbooking, planned trading-up, and short-selling are new business practices that are leading to increased revenues for many organizations.

RM methods have been very successful at enhancing revenues for many firms but others have not done so well. Often the difference between success and failure is the ability of management to maintain customer loyalty in a world of flexible prices and restricted product availability.

What the Manager Must Know

- Revenue management seeks to grow revenues while selling essentially the same quantity of product. Managers need to understand and be able to recognize the use of the five basic RM tools and variants of these.

- Use of these tools provides the opportunity to grow revenues while maintaining the same volume of business: such incremental revenues have a marked effect on profitability.

- While simple RM ideas can be implemented with little analytics (for example, "price high when demand is high, price low when demand is low," or planned upgrades), in general capturing the benefits of RM requires investment, application, and management over a significant period of time.

- Successful implementation of RM requires competent information technology, good analytics, and great management.

- RM has proven to be a dynamite competitive weapon: many firms have struggled or gone out of business because they could not compete with RM.

Exercises

Perishable Product Pricing

We have 3,000 units of product to sell over a five-day period. From historical sales data, we have estimated the following demand curves:

P = price/unit in $,

Q = number of units sold.

Day 1: $P = 10 - 0.01Q$

valid for prices between $3 and $8.

Day 2:   same as Day 1.

Day 3: $P = 15 - 0.01Q$

valid for prices between $6 and $10

Day 4: $P = 20 - 0.01Q$

valid for prices between $6 and $12

Day 5:   same as Day 1.

Assignment

- Formulate as a Solver problem in Excel. What are the revenue maximizing prices for days 1–5? What is the maximum possible revenue?

- If the price must be the same on each day, what is the revenue-maximizing price? What is the revenue? What is the revenue penalty for operating a fixed-price policy?

- Suppose that on Day 1, we post the optimal price (from 1 above) but sales are 10% above estimated demand. Re-solve the problem computing new optimal prices for days 2–5, assuming demand is 10% above expected each day except the last day. What is the revenue?

- Repeat Q3 with an assumption of a fixed single price for the 5 days. What is the revenue? Again, compute the revenue penalty for operating a fixed price policy.

- Is 3,000 the optimal number of units to order? Would you order more, or fewer?

- Repeat questions 3 and 4 under an assumption that demand is 10% below expected each day except the last. Assume inventory-clearing prices on the last day. What is the revenue penalty from fixed pricing?

Hotel Room Pricing

A hotel has 500 rooms. During a typical week in the holiday season, the hotel is busy on Monday, Tuesday, Wednesday, and Thursday nights, primarily with business people, but there is generally space available on Friday, Saturday, and Sunday nights.

Hotel management provided the following demand estimates, as shown in Table 8.1:

Assume linear demand functions over the range of all non-negative room rates and demands.

Table 8.1: Demand Estimates

Room Rate	Days	Estimated Demand (rooms/day)
$160	Mon, Tue, Wed, Thur	500
	Fri, Sat, Sun	200
$175	Mon, Tue, Wed, Thur	350
	Fri, Sat, Sun	125

Assignment

- What is the revenue-maximizing room rate if the hotel posts only a single rate good for any day of the week? What weekly occupancy results?

- What are the revenue-maximizing room rates if the hotel posts a "mid-week" rate good for the peak demand period (MTWT), and a different "weekend" rate good for Friday, Saturday, or Sunday. What is the new weekly occupancy? What is the revenue increase?

- Another option is for the hotel to offer a discounted weekly rate in order to attract vacationers who will stay for the full week. Management estimates that demand will be 40 per week at $900/week and 160 per week at $800/week. Again assume a linear demand curve.

- If the hotel posts a weekly rate and a single daily rate (good for any night), what are the revenue-maximizing prices? What is the occupancy rate? What is the revenue gain?

- If the hotel posts three rates: a mid-week rate, a weekend rate, and a weekly rate, what are the revenue-maximizing prices? What is the occupancy rate? What is the revenue gain?

Overbooking

You have 100 hotel room/nights to sell at $300 each. The no-show rate for bookings is 10%. The cost of looking after a customer with a reservation whom you cannot provide with a room is $1,000. How many reservations should you accept?

Recommended Cases

Four Star Motorsports (Ivey)

Container Transportation Company (Ivey)

Long Wang Sha Tan Ku Company (Dragon King Shorts Company) (Ivey)

Craig Manufacturing (Ivey)

Northwest Newsprint (B) (Ivey)

National Car Rental (INFORMS)

Texas Children's Hospital: Contract Optimization (Ivey)

The University of Wyoming Men's Basketball Team (Ivey)

Craggier National Park (Ivey)

The Clonlara Hotel (Ivey)

CHAPTER 9

ANALYTICS AS A STRATEGY TO ACHIEVE COMPETITIVE ADVANTAGE

The number of corporations that view analytics as an important component of their corporate strategy is increasing. In this chapter, we examine some of these corporations, and the way they use analytics as a competitive weapon. Recall that *analytics* is a broad term that encompasses several techniques and disciplines, including operations research, management science, industrial engineering, decision sciences, data mining, statistical analysis, and many others.

Corporate Strategy, Competitive Strategy, and Distinctive Competencies: A Short Primer

Michael Porter defined *corporate strategy* as determining what business the corporation should be in and how best to manage the array of business units ("From Competitive Advantage to Corporate Strategy," *Harvard Business Review*, May–June 1990).

A *competitive strategy* is the method of creating competitive advantage at the level of the strategic business units. In assessing its competitive strategy, the firm must determine those products that its customers value which the firm is capable of delivering better than others, and which competitors cannot easily replicate. A successful competitive strategy is one that leads to a sustainable competitive advantage.

To execute a successful competitive strategy, the corporation must make use of its *distinctive competencies*. Distinctive competencies are the skills, knowledge, and organizational structures that are internal to the corporation, that cross functional boundaries, and that are not easily replicated. Distinctive competencies are difficult for competitors to imitate, make a significant contribution to the value the customer attaches to the product, and provide the corporation with the ability to compete in several markets. Distinctive competencies cannot usually be outsourced or purchased.

The example of Federal Express (FedEx) will help tie these ideas together:

- FedEx's **corporate strategy** is to be a major player in the international, overnight package business.

- FedEx's **competitive strategy** includes "absolutely, positively" overnight; guaranteed on-time delivery, with friendly staff, and low prices.

- FedEx brings a variety of **distinctive competencies** into this competitive strategy, including the configuration of its aircraft fleet, its hubs and package-handling systems, its package-tracking and customer support functions, and its analytics support.

Distinctive competencies provide the foundation of a successful competitive and corporate strategy: they enable a corporation to execute strategy more effectively than do other companies that might have the same or a similar strategy.

The use of information technology (IT) now provides a competitive advantage for many globally competitive firms, and has become a distinctive competence for these organizations. The potential strategic value of IT was first recognized in 1985:

> Until recently, most managers treated information technology as a support service and delegated it to EDP departments. Now, however, every company must understand the broad effects and implications of the new technology and how it can create substantial and sustainable competitive advantage . . . Information technology is changing the way companies operate. (*Source*: M. E. Porter & V. E. Millar, "How Information Gives You Competitive Advantage," *Harvard Business Review*, July–August 1985)

Analytics is a key component of IT.

> Today IT must be conceived of broadly to encompass the information that businesses create and use *as well as a wide spectrum of . . . technologies that process the information.* (emphasis added; Porter & Millar)

The strategic importance of information systems is recognized through the existence of senior appointments in IT in many major corporations, including many vice-presidential level "chief information officer" (CIO) positions. Historically, the average CIO has been an information systems' professional who has emerged from the data processing department, who paid much more attention to hardware and software management, and to how data is collected, rather than to how the data is used to achieve a sustainable competitive advantage. A number of analytics professionals have also achieved C-level positions at major corporations.

One important pioneer was Tom Cook, a former professor of analytics who rose to be a vice president at American Airlines, then president of Sabre Decision Technologies (SDT) (renamed from American Airlines Decision Technologies, AADT, following a 1994 reorganization that moved the Sabre reservation systems group from American Airlines to AADT). SDT was the analytics function for AMR, the parent company of American Airlines. Cook thought of the objectives of SDT's work in these terms:

> The things we are doing are designed to create a competitive advantage. (P. Horner, "Eyes on the Prize," *OR/MS Today*, August 1991)

American Airlines is one of a number of organizations where senior management recognizes their analytical capabilities as a distinctive competence, and consider these skills to be a strategically important asset.

We will define the term *strategic analytics* to mean analytics that achieves a sustainable competitive advantage. Strategic analytics is, therefore, a body of work that forms the basis of a distinct competence in analytics. As we examine several of the world's leading organizations, we will find many examples of strategic analytics.

Analytics Activities and Sustainable Competitive Advantage

The value of a distinctive competence to a corporation is that it creates a competitive advantage for the firm that is sustainable over a period of time. Competing firms must then react or else they will lose market share, and may eventually have to leave the business. Consequently, strategic analytics is accompanied by changes in industrial structure, including reorganizations and bankruptcies, and the appearance of new businesses that exploit the particular advantage. Often, these new businesses are spawned from the original innovator.

The existence of strategic analytics would be confirmed by finding examples of firms that are achieving a sustainable competitive advantage from their use of analytics, but evidence of a sustainable competitive advantage from any source is rarely directly observable. Instead, the existence of strategic analytics activities can be inferred from secondary evidence:

1. The CEO of the firm will know about the firm's analytics work and of its importance to the organization.

2. There will be analytics work being done which constitutes the "strategic asset," and this work should be identifiable and not easy to replicate.

3. The firm has an analytics team that has achieved strategic success and has been provided with a certain status within the company. This team will be involved in other major decisions on a regular basis.

4. There will be evidence of a response from the firm's competitors to the successful strategic analytics work, perhaps by attempting to copy this work.

5. There will be evidence that industrial restructuring has occurred, motivated by one firm's successful strategic use of analytics.

6. New business start-ups will appear offering to provide analytics to firms that do not have a capability to do the strategic analytics themselves.

We will review examples of each of these.

CEOs on the Importance of Analytics Activities

Many CEOs of major corporations have confirmed the importance of analytics to their organizations. Some examples include:

- Analytics has "given us a significant competitive advantage during the 'Up Front Market' (for TV advertising.) All the hard work and creativity that went into this project definitely has paid off. In fact, these new systems have an impact of over $50 million in annual revenues and have greatly boosted the productivity of the NBC sales staff. Thanks to GE's corporate research and development center, our network sales organization has seen firsthand how operations research methodologies can revolutionize how we work. We will continue to deploy these technologies across all functions as we grow and improve our business." (*Source*: Robert C. Wright, Chairman & CEO, National Broadcasting Company, Vice Chairman & Executive Officer, General Electric, http://www.scienceofbetter.org/can_do/testimonials.htm, February 2012)

- "[A]nalytics plays an important part of our ability to manage our diverse businesses . . . As we look to the future, analytics will continue to be a vital and necessary part of our organization and our goal to remain a world-class company, capable of competing against all comers." (*Source*: R. E. Howson, Chairman of the Board and Chief Executive Officer, McDermott International, Inc. Plenary Speech to the INFORMS Conference, New Orleans, October 1995)

- "We have developed the best scheduled railway model in the industry . . . The result has been huge gains in efficiency and productivity and better service for our customers. Our job, however, is never over . . . I learned that an awful lot of opportunities still exist for us in the area of revenue management and contract negotiations. We're continuously looking for new ways to improve, and operations research . . . [is] going to be crucial to our success in the future." (*Source*: Robert Ritchie, President & CEO, Canadian Pacific Railroad, http://www.scienceofbetter.org/can_do/testimonials.htm, February 2012)

- "The decision to implement (analytical choice models) was an unprecedented change in strategy for us. [Analytics] provided the modeling and analyses that enabled me and my executive management team to better understand the revenue risks. The overall risk ranged from $200 million to $1 billion in revenues. This is the kind of thing that kept me up nights! [The outcome] has been an unqualified success . . . (and) had leaped to $83 billion under management by the end of 2000 and accounted for $22 billion of net new money. And it allowed us to seize the initiative in the marketplace. We have moved forward like a bullet train and it is our competitors that are scrambling not to get run over." (*Source*: Launny Steffens, President, U.S. Private Client, Vice Chairman, Merrill Lynch and Company, http://www.scienceofbetter.org/can_do/testimonials.htm, February 2012)

- Analytics "plays a big role in the five-year . . . approximately one billion dollar expansion and modernization program that we launched in 1987. Under the program we have built 22 manufacturing plants—we would not have dared to undertake the expansion at all without analytics . . . San Miguel's Senior Management appreciates the vital role of analytics in attaining our corporate goals, and in implementing the strategies that enable us to achieve adequate growth and satisfactory returns for our various stakeholders." (*Source*: Francisco Eizmendi Jr., President, San Miguel Corporation, E. Del Rosario, "OR Brews Success for San Miguel," *OR/MS Today*, 1994)

- "Employing (analytics) techniques and modeling skills, the (analytics) department has played a role in the development of long-range plans for the past 17 years and was instrumental in determining the specific growth sequence that allowed FedEx to become the world's largest and most reliable air express carrier. Every major system change . . . [was] modeled . . . several years in advance of the actual system change. This enabled the company to grow smoothly . . . By modelling various alternatives for future system design, FedEx has, in effect, made its mistakes on paper. Computer modelling works; it allows us to examine many different alternatives and it forces the examination of the entire problem." (*Source*: Frederick W. Smith, Chairman, CEO, and founder of Federal Express Corporation (FedEx), P. Horner)

These examples point to several corporations that are candidates for possession of a distinct competence in analytics; however, the CEO's knowledge of the value of analytics work is a necessary, but not a sufficient condition, for analytics to be delivering a sustainable competitive advantage.

Analytics As a "Strategic Asset"

There are many examples of analytics work that has produced handsome returns. Few can match the examples of Zara or KeyCorp:

- Zara is one of the world's leading fashion retailers, with 2007 annual sales in excess of $8 billion. Zara spent between $150,000 and $250,000 redesigning its global supply chain that supplies 1,500 stores in 68 countries from two primary warehouses in Spain. The benefits of this work were estimated to include a 3–4 per cent increase in sales, which for 2007 and 2008 translated to an estimated $353 million in increased revenues and an estimated $233 million increase in profits. (An internal rate of return approaching 3,000%!) (*Source*: F. Caro et al., "Zara Uses Operations Research to Reengineer Its Global Distribution Process," *Interfaces 40*, 1)

- KeyCorp was a bank holding company in Cleveland with about 1,200 branches and assets of US$66.8 billion and equity of US$4.7 billion. KeyCorp invested "less than US$500,000" in an analytics project beginning in 1991, which was expected to reduce expenses by US$98 million over five years. This represents a payback period for this investment of less than 10 days, or an internal rate of return of about 3,500%! (*Source*: S. K. Kotha et al., "KeyCorp Service Excellence Management System," *Interfaces 26*, 1, 1996)

While these financial results are impressive (although it might be argued that $98 million over five years is not a great deal of money for a bank with $66.8 billion in assets), in order for these investments to be considered "strategic," they must have created an advantage that was sustainable for some period of time.

Earlier chapters include many examples of analytics works that have produced a competitive advantage, particularly a cost advantage, but in many of these examples it was difficult to sustain this advantage, since in many cases the work described was easily replicated. For example, a feed formulator can introduce optimization as a way of reducing the cost of its products but, if this firm prospers, competitors can quickly replicate the work and nullify any advantage. There are, however, some kinds of "strategic problems" that do appear to provide analytics with the ability to sustain an advantage over a long period of time.

One form of strategic analytics problem is the very large and complex operational problem that is theoretically "optimizable," but, for reasons of size and complexity, the optimum solution cannot currently be obtained. Successful analytics teams address these problems using a series of heuristics that constrain the problems to a size that can be solved in real time "at the leading edge" of available technique and technology. Once a constrained problem can be optimized, new heuristics are developed that relax the constraints to produce a new problem that, with further work, can be optimized to produce an even lower cost solution, at which point the heuristics are changed again and the process repeated.

Strategic analytics problems yield increasingly lower-cost solutions over a substantial period of time, as the solution procedures are refined and developed. The cost advantage is further sustainable if management intervention is required to implement the improved solutions as they are developed.

Sustainability of the competitive advantage, therefore, arises from two sources:

1. The analytics group has developed skills and knowledge (and perhaps hardware, databases, and code) that a competitor starting work on the same problem cannot easily replicate.

2. Management has adapted the firm's structure and operations to take maximum advantage of the low-cost solutions that the analytics group is producing. These structural changes may involve contracts, labor relations, or facilities design.

The competitor, sensing that a firm is achieving a competitive edge, must first find a way to replicate the analytics work. Even if it can do this quickly, it may not be able to implement the results because of structural issues (for example, the union contract might not permit the required changes in working hours or practices, or it may take several years and/ or many dollars to renegotiate the contract), or it may find that it obtains much smaller cost savings on implementation than the established firm.

An example of a strategic analytics problem is the *aircrew scheduling problem*. Crew costs are the second-largest cost item for an airline (after fuel) and amount to several billion dollars annually for a large airline. The problem of assigning flight crews to flights is solved as an integer program that selects the low-cost set of crew "tours," which covers all scheduled flights. A critical input for this assignment problem is a set of feasible crew "tours." Each crew tour is a work schedule for a crew: the tour starts at a crew base where the crew reports for work, works a feasible set of flights, and returns to the crew base. Developing feasible "tours" to input to the optimization is time consuming but critical: there are a huge number of possible tours. As new tours are developed and tried over a period of time, the cost-effective tours are retained, while others are replaced by promising newly developed tours.

A heuristic that makes this problem much more manageable involves limiting the crew tour lengths considered. The problem that has the fewest feasible crew tours is the "one-day" problem, where each crew is constrained to spend every night at its crew base. Over a period of time, good solutions to the "one-day problem" can be developed (even if the flight schedule is variable), since the skill and knowledge required to develop new tours can be developed and the database of good "one-day" tours can be extended. At some point, however, switching to a "two-day" tour heuristic, where a crew is allowed to spend one night on each tour away from the crew base, becomes possible.

The "two-day" problem is much larger that the "one-day" problem, since there are more flights and many more possible crew tours, but the "two-day" problem must have lower cost than the "one-day" problem (since a feasible solution to two "one-day" problems is a feasible solution to the "two-day" problem). It is even possible for a crude solution to the two-day problem to have lower cost that a near-optimum solution to the one-day problem. In time, with skill, an analytics group can develop near-optimal solutions to the two-day problem, but at some point, decreasing returns to scale set in. At this point, the even larger "three-day" problem looms, again with the promise of cost savings. After the "three-day" problem, there awaits the "four-day" problem, and so on. How far can this go? It took several years of work for American Airlines Decision Technologies/Sabre Decision Technologies (SDT) to achieve good solutions to the "three-day" problem (*Source*: Ranga Anbil et al., "Recent Advances in Crew-Pairing Optimization at American Airlines," *Interfaces 21*, 1).

Figure 9.1 illustrates how crew costs can be continuously reduced over a long period of time by improving solutions to the existing n-day tour problems and then switching to larger and more difficult ($n+1$)-day problem as analytical skills and knowledge improve.

As improved solutions to the n-day problem are developed, management can adapt the organization to take advantage of the promise of lower crew costs. Some fairly straightforward adaptations include changing the numbers of crews available, opening new crew bases, or closing existing ones. Others changes, such as rescheduling flights in order to make them less costly to crew, may involve complex tradeoffs and take considerable time to implement. Moving from n-day tours to ($n+1$)-day tours requires more management intervention, including, perhaps, renegotiated union contracts and possibly even changes in flight regulations, but the airline that can successfully manage these changes will gain

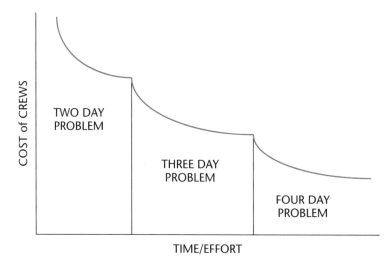

Figure 9.1 Continuous Improvement in Analytics Can Reduce Crew Costs Over a Substantial Period of Time.

greater advantage through lower operating costs. Over time, the operation of the airline becomes "tuned" to the crew assignment algorithms.

Even if a competitor were to "buy" the analytics expertise to solve this problem, it would still not be able to achieve the same crew efficiencies immediately, since considerable management and structural change would be required to implement the solutions at the same level of effectiveness. It is significant that at the same time American Airlines Decision Technologies (AADT) was developing advanced algorithms to solve this problem at American Airlines (AA), they were marketing software to their competitors that "solved" the same problem. Clearly, management did not believe that the software alone was sufficient to counter the cost advantage that American was obtaining.

Other large critical problems have a similar structure to the crew-scheduling problem, and provide opportunities for analytics to improve operations over a period of time. As one example, the Brazilian company Petrobras produces oil from about 80 offshore oil platforms and uses a fleet of 40 helicopters to transport some 2,000 employees daily between these platforms and the mainland. Since the 40 helicopters have different capacities, costs, and performance characteristics, it is cost effective to try to assign certain helicopters to particular flights. The complex large-scale optimization model developed by Petrobras has so far "reduced offshore landings by 18 percent, total flight time by 8 percent, and flight costs by 14 percent, resulting in annual savings of more than $20 million." The model currently solves in about an hour, includes a host of simplifying heuristics and is preloaded with a library of routes that have been found to be effective. As the model is used, the library of routes is expanded as new effective routes are found, leading to more effective solutions the next time around. Over time, new heuristics are found or former heuristics are abandoned leading to constantly improving solutions (*Source*: F. Menezes et al., "Optimizing Helicopter Transport of Oil Rig Crews at Petrobras," *Interfaces 40*, 5).

Other common problems that have these strategic characteristics are supply chain optimization (see Proctor and Gamble, following) for a major manufacturer or retailer, and the airline revenue management problem.

There is broad recognition that RM is now a critical, strategic, part of airline operations:

> It is worth emphasizing that a reservations system, with its yield management capacity, is arguably the single most important strategic asset of an airline. (*Source*: Harvard Business School case 9-490-012)

Wall Street Journal columnist Thomas Petzinger Jr. reported revenue management to be the number one "emerging business strategy" in his column on January 5, 1996. There is very strong evidence that AA generated a revenue advantage over its competitors for about a

15-year period through its ability to continuously improve its analytical approach to the dynamic pricing and seat allocation problem (for more details, see "American Airlines 1982–1996" at the end of this chapter).

In a few cases, major firms have turned their ability to solve a critical problem for them into a competitive asset through the use of analytics. FedEx designed their original "hub and spoke" distribution system using optimization, and through the consistent application of analytics to continuously improve operations of this system over many years maintained leadership in this market. UPS worked similarly in the ground transportation delivery market. SAS developed a strong internal expertise in working with large data and data mining and has now used this internal competence to emerge a major third-party provider of these types of analytics.

An interesting well-documented example is that of AT&T and telemarketing call centers. (The INFORMS cases: AT&T Telemarketing Site Selection (A) and (B) describe this problem and provide an opportunity to try to solve a small version.) Prior to deregulation of the North American telephone industry, AT&T made its profits by selling telephones and telephone calls, but after deregulation, telephones became low-margin items and new carriers moved in to cream off profitable sectors of the call business. AT&T's response was to package existing items (calls and hardware) together into revenue-producing products. One such package product was a *telemarketing product.*

A telemarketing product consists of one or more telemarketing centers, each containing a mass of telephone equipment and many lines to the network, where groups of people answer incoming telephone calls or originate new calls. These telemarketing centers are used to coordinate customer service, perform order processing for catalogue or direct response television sales, provide field sales staff support, or account management, and conduct direct telephone sales and opinion polling. It was estimated that 8 million people were employed in telemarketing in North America in the year 2000.

The telemarketing product offered by AT&T was rich in analytics (*Source*: T. Spencer III et al., "AT&T's Telemarketing Site Selection System Offers Customer Support," *Interfaces 20*, 1). The key to cost-effectiveness was to select the sites for the call centers and design the communications system so as to minimize the costs of labor, real estate, and communications, while providing a given level of service. AT&T used a large-scale mixed integer optimization to select minimum cost sites for the centers from the list of politically acceptable sites, and to assign originating calls to sites so as to minimize the total cost of the system. In 1988, AT&T used this optimization to help 46 customers who committed $375 million in annual AT&T long distance network services and $31 million in equipment sales from AT&T. Some consulting firms also offered a site selection service, but AT&T competed aggressively since it saw the product as the package, not just the site-selection problem: it was reported that DHL, an express package delivery service, would have had to pay US$240,000 to a consultant for advice on site selection for its call centers but AT&T provided the same advice for free in just 10 days (*Source*: AT&T, "The Old Order Changeth," *Focus Employee Annual Report*, 1991).

AT&T marketed "Call Center Solutions" for almost a decade and developed minimum cost systems for hundreds of customers. In doing so, AT&T developed the algorithms and software to solve this complex problem, but also accumulated and maintained a massive database of location data, including available office space, building costs, labor market data, and local taxes and wage rates. The combination of developed skills and experience together with algorithms, software, and databases provided AT&T with a competitive advantage in the "call center" business for a decade. This analytics work appears to have been a "strategic asset" for AT&T until a strategic decision at the AT&T Board level resulting in AT&T's exit from the call center business.

Analytics Groups That Are Broadly Involved in Corporate Decision Making

In companies where analytics has scored a strategic success, the analytics group will have gained significant credibility and, as a result, the input of the group will be regularly sought on important decision issues. Procter & Gamble, Federal Express, San Miguel Corporation, and McDermott International provide examples of analytics groups that appear to have gained this expected broad involvement in corporate decision making:

Procter & Gamble (P&G), the world's largest consumer goods company ($76 billion in annual sales, 138,000 employees, and operations in more than 80 countries in 2008), routinely collects massive amounts of data and uses this data to measure and optimize almost everything it does. A "central army of "quants" at P&G are arguably as important to its overall success as those storied P&G brand managers. The company has turned analytics "into a competitive edge that few others fully understand" (*Source*: CBS Money Watch, February 2008).

Glenn Wegryn, associate director of product supply analytics, and P&G's analytics group work continuously on optimizing P&G's complex global supply chains and a host of other problems. According to Wegryn, P&G doesn't make any changes to supply-chain structure without input from his team, because any change can have significant financial consequences. The success of analytics in designing and reforming P&G's supply chain begin in 1992, when Wegryn and a team of analytics professionals took on the challenge of streamlining and redesigning P&G's extensive North American supply chain. The team, which at one time included 30 managers and upwards of 1,000 employees around the country, devised planning tools that enabled multiple scenarios to be examined by decision-making teams. As a result, manufacturing plants were closed, production was relocated, warehouses were closed or relocated, and shipping patterns were reworked. The analytics group's recommendations generated more than $1 billion in cost savings. Following success with the North American supply chain, the group moved on to Europe, SE Asia, and around the world.

Success at streamlining manufacturing, optimizing shipping, and redesigning supply chain activities gave analytics the momentum needed to assume a much broader role in decision making at P&G. Material sourcing, online procurement through combinatorial auctions, inventory management, and the analysis of international trade flows and exchange rate risks are just a few of the issues where analytics is now routinely involved. Analytics has also developed human resource planning simulations that take into account attrition, retirements, job moves, etc., to help mangers with hiring, staffing, and promotion issues.

The analytics group also receives regular requests for help with one-off decisions. For example, when P&G was planning to introduce teeth whitening strips, Wegryn's group used decision analysis to give advice on the use of "Crest" as the brand name (Crest was a toothpaste; the strips were a new product for P&G where a new brand name might be sensible). Using a decision analysis that clarified the alternatives and uncertainties and analyzed the best available data, the recommendation was made that led to Crest White Strips.

Analytics at P&G is a cross-functional discipline applied to everything from executive compensation to inventory management: analytics provides input into strategic, structural, and operational problems. Methods used cover the full spectrum of analytics and include structured analytical modeling using spreadsheets, decision-analysis methods, optimization methods broadly defined, and simulation.

Analytics at P&G is highly integrated throughout the business. Wegryn says that the analytics group has "developed a reputation of having an unbiased view of how the business operates, and we've earned their trust."

(*Sources*: J. D. Camm et al., "Blending OR/MS, Judgment, and GIS: Restructuring P&G's Supply Chain," *Interfaces 27*, 1; T. Sandholm et al., "Changing the Game in Strategic Sourcing at Procter & Gamble: Expressive Competition Enabled by Optimization," *Interfaces* January/February 2006; I. Farasyn et al., "Inventory Optimization at Procter & Gamble: Achieving Real Benefits Through User Adoption of Inventory Tools," *Interfaces* January/February 2011; *CBS Money Watch*, February 2008)

Federal Express (FedEx) has had a successful OR group for many years, and this group has historically been involved on major decisions. For many years, Joe Hinson, general manager of Operations Research at Federal Express, chaired the corporate strategic planning committee. Hinson reported directly and regularly to CEO Fred Smith, and suggested:

> When you know that you'll be listened to, the weight of your work becomes a little bit heavier and more satisfying. It's nice to know that the answer that you come up with will not be muddled by the time it reaches the top. (*Source*: Horner *op cit.*)

An article produced by the Harvard Business School MIS History Project (*Source*: R. O. Mason, J. L. Mckenney, W. Carlson, & D. Copeland, "Absolutely, Positively Operations Research: The Federal Express Story," *Interfaces 27*, 2, 1996) provides much interesting commentary on OR at FedEx. Although this group had generally documented firms (such as American Hospital Supply, BankAmerica) where information systems provided a strategic they conclude that:

> FedEx is an archetype of a company that has succeeded by applying the scientific methods to its operations. Models and analysis have informed many of (FedEx's) crucial, business-shaping decisions. In cases in which OR wasn't used . . . the company performed poorly. (*Source*: Mason et al.)

Five reasons for the success of analytics at FedEx were provided:

- The air cargo industry is a "whole system" business, not easily managed separately.
- Fred Smith, the founder and CEO, is "devoted to the use of scientific inquiry in his business. [Analytics] is a voice to be heard at FedEx."
- Analytics has focused on crucial issues and has not been sidetracked in "the esoteric or bogged down in minutia."
- FedEx OR results and models were considered to be "living things, not imperial edifices cast in concrete . . . By means of continual dialogues between the [analytics] team and executive management, they jointly arrived at a shared understanding as to the problems they faced, the pros and cons of the models, and the strengths and weaknesses of what the model results were telling them."
- The analytics "team conducted itself as a learning organization, a center of knowledge and inquiry about the most important dimensions of the business. Captured in their models and databases are literally millions of items . . . that characterize all of the most important activities of the business." (*Source*: Mason et al. *op cit.*)

Hinson discusses how deeply his analytics group is ingrained in the activities of FedEx:

> An [analytics] department's effectiveness doesn't necessarily have to be measured by the one big home run that saves the company millions of dollars, but rather by giving

out lots of good results, providing answers to lots of questions every day and every week of the year, year after year." (*Source*: Horner *op. cit.*)

San Miguel Corporation's head of Operational Research, Elise del Rosario, was a corporate senior assistant vice president, and established her group as an integral part of corporate strategic decision making. Company President Francisco Eizmendi Jr. suggests the opinion of this group is broadly sought:

> In our strategic planning meetings every year, whenever a division or business unit manager presents a project, we always make sure that Operations Research has gone through the proposal. (*Source*: E. Del Rosario, "OR Brews Success for San Miguel," *OR/MS Today*, October, 1994)

The extent of OR involvement in activities at San Miguel was extraordinary: the OR group tackled 65 projects during 1985–86, and in 1992, ten analytics projects produced a bottom line impact of US$35 million. Further, San Miguel had "OR-type people throughout the organization: Senior vice-presidents, plant managers, production schedulers, economic analysts and so on. Many of these individuals at one time in their career worked in the OR department" (*Source*: E. Del Rosario).

Analytics at *Babcock and Wilcox (B&W)* (now part of McDermott International) achieved a significant success in the late 1960s when B&W's Nuclear Equipment Division was experiencing rapid growth. The resulting scheduling problems were leading to losses of about $15 million annually, prompting *Fortune* magazine to write (in November 1969) that the future of B&W was at stake. A simulation model to aid scheduling, developed by the analytics group, was implemented at a cost of about $8 million, and by the time the model was fully operational, the $15 million annual loss had been turned into a $17 million annual profit. As McDermott International CEO Howson states:

> When we acquired B&W, one of the buried treasures we discovered was a well-established, well-respected (analytics) group . . . Over the years, our [analytics] staff have used their quantitative, analytical methods to solve many other complicated problems around our company. (*Source*: Howson *op. cit.*)

In common with San Miguel Corporation, analytics group input is now institutionalized:

> Currently, our (analytics) staff is helping evaluate projects with a total value of over $1 billion. We are convinced that the application of quantitative methods to estimating and contract management increases our company's chances for success. Recently we issued a corporate policy which requires the use of these methods on major proposals and contracts. (*Source*: Howson *op cit.*)

Competitive Reaction to Successful Analytics

Successful strategic analytics provides a competitive advantage over a period of time to the instigator. Competitive corporations would be expected to notice this advantage through declining market shares, sales, or profits, and react. This reaction should be noticeable.

The clearest example of such a scenario is the airline business following the successful implementation of revenue management by AADT at American Airlines in the mid-1980s. One previously highly successful airline (People Express Airlines (PE)) was driven out of business because it could not come up with a competitive response:

> The major carriers met People Express' pricing structure . . . and used their reservations systems to achieve optimal pricing and yield management. PE's performance, in essentially all dimensions, immediately declined . . . The end was swift. (*Source*: G. Loveman & M. Beer, "People Express Airlines: Rise and Decline," *Teaching Note*, Harvard Business School 5-491-080, 1991)

Many other airlines (including Braniff, TWA, Continental, Eastern, Pan American) incurred large losses at this same time leading to bankruptcies and "Chapter 11" reorganizations. It is tempting to conclude that analytics work at AADT was the driver of these changes; however, these were established airlines that faced new and vigorous competition in this period from new carriers, such as PE, which appeared at the onset of U.S. airline deregulation in December 1981. Established air carriers faced a number of competitive pressures at this time. AMR, the parent company of American Airlines and AADT, reacted to this pressure by investing heavily in analytics and this proved to be a successful strategy. Others that followed different strategies were less successful and did not survive or survived only in greatly trimmed down form.

Competitive air carriers would be expected to respond to AADT's strategic analytics successes by attempting an accelerated analytics program. There is some evidence that this was the case as United, Delta, and USAir all invested significantly in analytics. In spring of 1995, USAir ran an advertisement attempting to add 40 professionals to its analytics department: "Based upon its past contribution, USAir's OR Department is growing by 40 professionals" (*Source*: USAir advertisement, *OR/MS Today*, April 1994). The advertisement stated:

> Our existing OR Department of 37 professionals provides management consulting and decision technology to all divisions of the airline. Grow with us as we find solutions to some of the most complex real-world problems in: . . . Transportation Scheduling & Routing, Revenue Management, Operations & Maintenance Planning.

By 1995, AADT had grown to more than 400 professionals, and so it is apparent that USAir with only 37 professionals (expanding to 77) was some ways behind. The problem areas listed in the advertisement were all areas where SDT had published highly profitable analytics applications, providing further evidence of "catch up" behavior by at least one competitor.

The 1990s began a "golden age" of airline analytics, with many different airlines publishing examples of successful analytical work.

The implementation of revenue management in the rental car and hotel industries followed similar paths, although the lead provided to the first mover was much reduced. Hertz, Avis, and National all invested in revenue management within a very short time span, and while Marriott appears to have been the first hotel group to implement revenue management, other major chains quickly followed suit.

A further example appears in television advertising. CBC appears to have been the first network to attempt revenue management for television advertising in 1992, although this was limited to a few programs where ad space regularly sold out. ABC and NBC followed a few years later, with much more sophisticated RM systems reflecting the larger scale of their advertising revenues.

Industrial Restructuring As a Result of Strategic Analytics

Analytics at ABB Electric has been credited (D. H. Gensch et al., "A Choice-Modeling Market Information System that Enabled ABB Electric to Expand Its Market Share," *Interfaces 20*, 1) with significant restructuring in the North American market for industrial transformers. ABB entered the electrical transformer market in 1970 and had almost reached a break-even state (with a 6% market share) by 1974. The total market for transformers was about 3,300 units in 1974, but fell to less than 1,000 units in 1975, as a result of events that included the formation of OPEC and the end of the era of cheap energy. Industrial giants Westinghouse, General Electric, McGraw-Edison, and the fledgling ABB were left to fight for a share of a market that remained in the 800–1,500 units annual range through 1988. By 1988, ABB had 40% of this shrunken market, and Westinghouse and General Electric no longer made industrial transformers.

Between 1974 and 1988, ABB undertook a series of innovative and sophisticated analytics projects that transformed the company and its markets. Noteworthy was work which, following the introduction of the industry's first five-year product warranty, enabled ABB to develop a manufacturing system to produce extremely high-quality transformers while at the same time becoming the low-cost producer in the industry. In addition, a series of market choice models enabled ABB to develop products that met customers' needs, and to target their marketing efforts toward those customers that promised the greatest returns.

While many factors contributed to ABB's success, president Daniel Elwing observed in a statement at the 1988 Board of Directors meeting at which time ABB sales had grown to exceed $100 million:

> Without the insights from our marketing models, it is unlikely we would have current sales of $25 million; in fact, without the use of these models, it is unlikely we would be here at all (Gensch et al.).

Turnarounds

Another form of corporate restructuring is the "turnaround": reviving a failing corporation or revitalized a lethargic one:

> Citgo invested some $20–30 million [in analytics] in 1984–85, which was instrumental in turning a loss exceeding $50 million annually in 1984 into a pre-tax profit exceeding $70 million in 1985. *John P. Thompson, Chairman of the Board of The Southland Corporation* (Citgo's parent company) said: "We have been very gratified at the success that this approach, with its heavy dependence on [analytics] and cooperative effort, has achieved at Citgo. The numerous systems that were developed . . . Have become an integral part of the Citgo operation, saving many millions of dollars . . . we look forward to further [analytics] developments which might provide even greater advantages to Southland in what is becoming an increasingly competitive business climate. (*Source*: D. Klingman et al., "The Successful Deployment of Management Science Throughout Citgo Petroleum Corporation," *Interfaces 17*)

National Car Rental (M. K. Geraghty, et al., 1; described in more detail in Chapter 8) also represents a turnaround largely attributable to analytics. The National Car Rental case appears particularly compelling: the analytics was a direct order from the CEO, and the company was apparently told that it faced liquidation by its parent company (General Motors) if profits were not significantly increased. "The main thing that we introduced and which is probably unique in most of the car industry, is demand-based pricing. Stop following the competitor's around."

Harris Corporation's Semiconductor division is another good example of an analytics-induced turnaround. Harris Semiconductor invested US$3.8 million starting in 1992 in an analytics project, which led to the installation of IMPReSS, a system which used state-of-the-art optimization to set production, delivery, and inventory levels in 22 manufacturing plants worldwide (R.C. Leachman et al., "IMPReSS: An Automated Production-Planning and Delivery-Quotation System at Harris Corporation—Semiconductor Sector," *Interfaces 26*, 1). In announcing the effort on company television, Jon Cornell, divisional president, emphasized how close to the brink the semiconductor division was: "[The division] will not survive unless we solve our delivery problem. If IMPReSS succeeds, we can succeed. If it fails, we will surely fail." After installation of IMPReSS, Phil Farmer, president and CEO, talked about the dramatic nature of the turnaround: "Our on-time delivery was running about 75%, which was not acceptable. IMPReSS raised our on-time delivery to 95%." Significantly, 75% represented the worst performance in the industry, while 95% represented about the best. The financial consequences were that a loss of US$100 million annually during 1989–91 was turned into profits of US$20 million in 1993, US$30 million in 1994, and US$42 million in 1995.

An example of what can be done at modest cost to revitalize a lethargic (or failing?) company is the case of Merit Brass (A. D. Flowers, "The Modernization of Merit Brass," *Interfaces 23*, 1, 1993). Merit Brass was a traditional firm in the pipe, valve, and fittings industry that recognized that its customer service had slipped and needed improvement. "The company had outgrown its people-intensive systems and needed to implement [analytics] methodologies to elevate it to the next level of performance." Merit invested just US$78,090 (this included the purchase of two personal computers) plus US$19,500 in continuing annual costs in some analytics work. The result was an increase in their service level on Class A items from 74% to 98% in less than one year, while simultaneously reducing inventories, to obtain a cost savings of $201,000 annually. Not surprisingly, the "entire top management team at Merit Brass supported these efforts wholeheartedly."

Finally, new corporate startups can catalyze structural change within industries. The story of the startup of FedEx provides compelling evidence of the strategic value of analytics:

On March 12, 1973, FedEx began its inaugural air-package service serving 11 major cities. After three days of operations, service was suspended because of a lack of business; the first day produced just six packages. Founder Fred Smith, however, would not give up. He formed an ad hoc "analytics team" to address the problem, and this group worked 18 to 20 hours a day for 15 days straight, analyzing the problem. The group concluded that FedEx had opened serving the wrong cities, and analyzed 112 cities to determine that were the best candidates for the new air-package service. Using an origin/destination flow model, the analytics team developed indicators of each city's market potential, which took into account the outbound parcel volume, types of businesses, and availability of air cargo service. A new network of 26 cities was defined that was quite different from the original 11-city network. On April 17, 1973, FedEx began serving its new 26-city network, and the rest, as they say, "is history." FedEx is now the world's largest express transportation company, delivering more than 2 million items to more than 200 countries each business day, employing 110,000 people, and operating 500 aircraft and more than 35,000 vehicles (Mason et al. 1996).

New Business Start-ups Providing Analytics Solutions

There is a rich documentation of the formation of new businesses serving analytics-intensive industries. These include firm's developing solvers (GAMS, CPLEX, ILOG, Express MP, Lindo, What's Best) and simulation packages (see list at the end of Chapter 6). There are also many examples of spin-offs and start-ups selling general analytics consulting or "solutions."

For evidence on the strategic use of analytics, we look for start-ups of firms supplying solutions to strategic analytics problems; for example, revenue management, air crew scheduling, and supply chain optimization.

After many successes at American Airlines, moving into the 1990s, AADT (later Sabre Decision Technologies) started marketing RM, crew scheduling, and other airline analytics to all comers and was joined by a host of other third-party providers (Aeronomics spun out from Delta Airlines, later became DFI, then Talus, PROS Revenue Management, etc.) selling packaged analytics solutions to the major airline problems. Even though these products required extensive data collection and customization, their acquisition and use over time diluted the competitive advantage from analytics. There is broad recognition that analytics is now a critical part of airline operations:

> It is worth emphasizing that a reservations system, with its yield management capacity, is arguably the single most important strategic asset of an airline. (*Source*: Harvard Business School case 9-490-012)

Supply chain optimization (SCO) has seen a host of start-ups (Manugistics, i2, JD Edwards, Logility, etc.), mergers and takeovers, and also the entry of some major internal users of SCO (IBM, UPS) into the out-sourcing marketplace.

The Path to a Competitive Advantage with Analytics

Many of the firms that are the strongest candidates for having a distinct competence in analytics have followed a common path, as analytics has grown to a position of strategic significance.

First, there has to be a corporate need that initiates the development of an analytics capability within the firm. This "need" has often appeared alongside an increasing level of competition with its accompanying uncertainty about the future. Deregulation of previously regulated industries has triggered a major expansion of analytics, particularly in the North

American Airline, banking industries, and electric power industries. Actual or impending business failure or the appearance of new and intense competition has catalyzed many analytics startups. Regulated or government-owned organizations are often poor candidates to have strategic analytics activities.

After the need has been recognized, analytics skills will have to be developed within the organization. In terms of the INFORMS descriptors (presented in the Introduction to this book), most organizations are able to use data to understand what happened (descriptive analytics), some firms will have to develop skills to use data to predict what will happen (predictive analytics), but most firms will have to invest significantly to be able to use data to determine how to better operate the business (prescriptive analytics).

Once established, the analytics group must capture senior management and particularly CEO attention. Those that have done this have successfully have generally moved through four phases:

- Begin by "cherry picking" a number of small problems where analytics can achieve a financial gain with low risk and minimal effort.

- Move on to use analytics to address one or more very large and very significant problems for the organization, and emerge as the internal expert on this problem and its solution.

- Use the credibility gained to encourage an analytics way of managing throughout critical parts of the organization.

- Begin marketing the developed special skills in analytics to others.

Investing in analytics as corporate strategy will change the culture of the firm. This cultural change requires senior management commitment and attention, and a host of management changes within the organization. Once implemented, this cultural change is difficult to reverse, and provides the analytics group with a position of "power" within the firm where they are looked to for solutions to existing problems, and also for help when new problems are recognized.

Analytics in the Not-for-Profit Sector

This chapter has focused on the strategic use of analytics in the private sector, but analytics has also been very important to government, health care, the military, and other not-for-profit organizations, although sustaining a competitive advantage is usually not a critical objective for this sector. In fact, there is a rich history of analytics use, beginning in World War II (as illustrated by Harold Larnder's reporting of the use of analytics by Winston Churchill; see Chapter 2). We can point to a great many other examples of analytics that have informed senior not-for-profit decision makers over a substantial period of time. These include:

- Using analytics to assign crews and develop crew schedules for public transit companies, and also to "cost out" proposals during contract negotiations.

- Optimization models used and continually updated to manage hydroelectric power generation from a system of reservoirs.

- The U.S. Military Airlift Command has used large-scale optimization models to schedule airfreight operations seven days a week for more than 20 years.

- Optimization was used to schedule the Hanshin Expressway at Osaka for more than 30 years.

- UK National Health Service uses advanced analytics to allocate some £25billion to health organizations in the UK and the models have been regularly maintained and updated.

- French railyways (SNCF) used scheduling and yield management models developed for them by Sabre Decision Technologies.

- Military "war games" make extensive use of large-scale simulation models.

There are also many examples where a "one-shot" advanced analytical model informed major policy decisions. For example:

- A single analytical study identified Diagnosis Related groups that are now a mainstay of medical administration and have saved the U.S. government many billions of dollars.

- An advanced analytical study initially showed the advantage of needle exchange programs in reducing the spread of HIV/AIDS, and this study has been replicated in many different jurisdictions with the same result. The resulting programs have produced large social benefits.

- New York City used a model to help it comply with a court-ordered 24 hours "arrest to arraignment." Once the city was in compliance, the need for the model went away.

- Optimization was used to define a new South African Army (SANDF) after independence.

- When the bubble of the Kuwait al Manakh Stock Market collapsed, optimization backed by law was used to resolve $94 billion in uncovered cross-payments.

As governments and not-for-profit organizations become more cost conscious, we will see more emphasis on data-driven decision making and the increasing use of analytics.

Strategic Analytics in Action

American Airlines 1982–1996

In 1982, American Airlines (AA) employed 12 operations researchers. By 1991, following a stream of highly successful projects under the direction of Tom Cook, a former professor of analytics, the number of analytics specialists employed had grown to more than 300. In 1988, the analytics group become a separate division of AMR, the parent company of American Airlines, known as American Airlines Decision Technologies (AADT), with Cook as president. In 1994, the Sabre information systems group was merged with AADT to form Sabre Decision Technologies (SDT). The Sabre Group conducted an initial public offering of 18% of its stock in 1996 and in 2000 spun out 100% from AMR.

Over the period 1982–1996, AADT worked exclusively for American Airlines, and analytics tools and systems developed by AADT resulted in huge cost savings for American Airlines. Large problems that have been addressed and where results have been published include:

Fleet Assignments—revenue gains of $75 million realized in 1988, as well as a 1.4% increase in operating margins.

Flight Crew Scheduling—annual savings realized in excess of $20 million.

Airline Crew Bid Generation System—productivity improvement of 600%.

Performance Analysis and Capacity Planning of Landing Gear Shops—the development of appropriate planning capabilities for future production increases of 100%–130% per year.

Repairable Part Management—one-time savings of $7 million, plus recurring annual savings of $1 million.

Arrival Slot Allocation System—reduction in annual air traffic control delays totaling 345,000 minutes, for a savings of $5.2 million per year.

Yield Management—revenues from overbooking improvements were $225 million in 1990; revenues from discount-fare controls were $313 million in 1990; productivity savings reached $1 million; the net quantifiable benefits from yield management improvements were $1.4 billion over three years.

AADT took the lead in demonstrating that analytics is fundamental in providing information and solutions to problems that are too large and complicated to be solved manually. The nature of the airline business, the regulations under which it operates, and the magnitudes of the variables involved (such as the numbers of aircraft, stations, and flights) lend themselves to modeling solutions. The cost savings from these solutions to an organization the size of AA made a significant resource commitment worthwhile, and models that AADT developed transformed the airline industry. AADT become recognized and respected by the highest level of AA management as one of the most profitable and successful parts of the AMR parent organization, thereby giving support and drive to further developments.

During this time period, AA was committed to low-cost operations through the use of analytics to address critical and competitively important problems. AMR saw the capabilities of SDT as one of its distinctive competencies.

Airline revenue management (called "Yield Management" by AA) first appeared as a strategic asset and producer of competitive advantage at AA. AA's innovative yield management systems developed by the analysts at AADT revolutionized air travel. The systems took the schedules and fare structure set by the planning departments and determined the product mix to be offered to the customers. Data such as the expected passenger demand, expected volume of cancellations, and other passenger behavior (such as reactions to being re-accommodated on another flight) were taken into account by the yield management systems.

AA's original yield management system (called DINAMO, Dynamic Inventory and Maintenance Optimizer) took into account overbooking, discount allocations, and passenger flight connections to other flights.

The DINAMO optimization model maximized the net revenue associated with overbooking decisions, and determined the optimal overbooking level as the point at which the marginal revenue gained from allowing an additional reservation was equal to the marginal cost of an additional oversale.

DINAMO uses an optimization model to allocate the available seats to the different fare classes. The model weighed the marginal value of a new fare request against the marginal value of all other fares, given the probability of receiving a future request for a higher-priced fare if the current request was rejected. Factors taken into consideration included the fact that the marginal value of a fare diminishes with the overbooking level, the probability of receiving another fare request diminishes the closer the scheduled flight is to the request day, and that the popularity of the flight affects the expected level of future requests.

About two-thirds of all passengers on a flight to a hub airport connect to another flight to continue to their destination. DINAMO took decisions on how to connect passengers and on the fare types to offer on each connecting flight. With the number of possible connections available, the number of possible desired connections, and the number of fare types, this could branch into an enormous number of options.

The Benefits AA Realized Through Yield Management

American Airlines reduced its spoiled seats (cancellations or no-shows) from the original estimate of 15% per flight to a 1990 average of 3%. The involuntary oversales were been reduced by 62% from 1980 to 1990.

Revenue opportunity is measured as the difference between the minimum revenue expected for a flight (no discount controls) and the maximum revenue expected (perfect discount controls). Performance is measured as the percentage of opportunity revenue actually achieved. The yield management group estimated that AA achieved 90% of the revenue opportunity resulting from overbooking in 1990, which equates to $225 million. The achieved percentage of revenue opportunity from discount-fare controls jumped from 30% in 1988 to 49% in 1990, representing earned revenue of $313 million for 1990 alone.

Before the implementation of DINAMO, yield management specialists had to review each flight individually but after implementation only those identified as critical needed to be manually reviewed. In 1990, this was only 5% of the flights: the productivity per analyst increased over 30%, representing an annual savings of $1 million.

AADT's yield management models allowed American to offer a greater variety of products for sale while maintaining control over discount seat availability. In 1998, Tom Cook, president of Sabre Decision Technologies, reported the benefit of yield management to AA as incremental revenue of $1 billion annually: far in excess of AMR's profits over this same period.

Robert Crandall, chairman, president and CEO of American Airlines, summed up AA's reaction to these developments:

> I believe that yield management is the single most important technical development in transportation management since we entered the era of airline deregulation in 1979 . . . (yield management) creates a pricing structure which responds to demand on a flight-by-flight basis. As a result, we can more effectively match our demand to supply. (*Source*: Smith et al., *Interfaces 22*, 1)

The success of analytics, and particularly RM, at AA promoted structural changes within the airline business and a massive competitive response. Several airlines went out of business (most notably People's Express, where Donald Burr, founder and CEO, recorded: "that major carrier's use of sophisticated computer programs to immediately match or undercut his prices ultimately killed People Express.")

Other airlines initiated RM analytics, and several outside RM analytics groups appeared marketing RM and other airline solutions. In this environment, Sabre started selling its yield-management and crew-scheduling systems to other airlines. Over time, as these alternative solutions were populated with local data and developed and customized, AA's competitive advantage faded. The decision to sell off the Sabre group, started in 1996 and concluded in 2000, was presumably in recognition that airline analytics was now widely integrated into airline operations and was no longer a competitive advantage to AA. (For a more compete history of AADT and Sabre visit http://www.sabre.com/home/about/sabre_history/.)

Sources: Helmut Richter, *Thirty Years of Airline Operations Research*, Jeph Abara, *Applying Integer Linear Programming to the Fleet Assignment Problem*, Ira Gershkoff, *Optimizing Flight Crew Schedules*, Russell D. Jones, *Development of an Automated Airline Crew Bid Generation System*, B. Vinod and B. N. Srikar, *Performance Analysis and Capacity Planning of a Landing Gear Shop*, Mark J. Tedone, *Repairable Part Management*, Alberto Vasquez-Marquez; all in *Interface 19*, 4. *American Airlines Arrival Slot Allocation System (ASAS)*, Ranga Anbil et al. *Recent Advances in Crew-Pairing Optimization at American Airlines*, Thomas A. Feo and Jonathan F. Bard, in *Interfaces 21*, 1. *Flight Scheduling and Maintenance Base Planning*, in *Management Science 35*, 12. Barry C. Smithet al., *Yield Management at American Airlines*, *Interfaces 22*, 1. American Airlines Decision Technologies, http://www.sabre.com/home/about/sabre_history/, February 2012.

IBM'S Journey into Analytics

IBM started life as a hardware company and began writing software as the early tabulating machines developed into mainframe computers in the 1960s. The company played a pivotal role in the development of the personal computer (PC), but allowed Microsoft to come to dominate the PC software market. IBM sold off its PC hardware business to Chinese manufacturer Lenovo in 2005.

IBM's research labs employed an impressive group of scientists and engineers (IBM scientists have won four Nobel prizes), and this group has increasingly become involved in business analytics. IBM had a long history of fabricating semiconductors ("fab") for its own use and, in the early 1990s, decided to expand into producing a range of products for diverse internal and external customers. This required an overhaul of all its semiconductor supply chains, and analytics was used extensively to drive this overhaul. IBM scientists developed analytical models to match production capacity to demand to determine manufacturing schedules and delivery dates. From 1994 on, a series of models integrating linear programming with traditional material resource planning algorithms and other heuristics were developed and deployed. The analytics work improved capacity utilization and customer response times, with benefits estimated at $80 million at launch in 1999, increasing to $200 million a year with further use. Average order response time was reduced to less than one day, with on-time delivery increasing from 90% in 1998 to 97% in 1999, while customer satisfaction increased 20% (*Source*: P. Lyon et al., "Matching Assets with Demand in Supply-Chain Management at IBM Microelectronics," *Interfaces 31*, 1; and S. Bermon & S. Hood, "Capacity Optimization Planning System (CAPS)," *Interfaces 29*, 5).

From this beginning, IBM scientists have published many articles applying advanced analytics to IBM fab supply chains (for example: L. Demeester & C. S. Tang, "Reducing Cycle Time at an IBM Wafer Fabrication Facility," *Interfaces 26*, 2; and B. T. Denton et al., "IBM Solves a Mixed-Integer Program to Optimize Its Semiconductor Supply Chain," *Interfaces 36*, 5). Other examples of advanced analytics applied to IBM internal operations have appeared. For example: Purchasing (P. S. Bender et al., "Improving Purchasing Productivity at IBM with a Normative Decision Support System," *Interfaces 15*, 3); services logistics (M. Cohen et al., "Optimizer: IBM's Multi-Echelon Inventory System for Managing Service Logistics," *Interfaces 20*, 1); and sales force management (R. Lawrence et al., "Operations Research Improves Sales Force Productivity at IBM," *Interfaces 40*, 1).

Multiple successes at applying analytics internally lead to IBM emerging as an important supplier of analytics services to outside clients. Notable among these was a system to optimize tax collections for the city of New York, which must collect more than $1 billion annually in delinquent taxes. IBM scientists developed an analytics-based approach to optimize the collection actions of agents in order to maximizing long-term returns, while taking into account the complex dependencies among business needs, resources, and legal constraints. "The system became operational in December 2009; from then through 2010, New York State increased its collections from delinquent revenue by $83 million (8 per cent) using the same set of resources. Given a typical annual increase of 2 to 4 per cent, the system's expected benefit is approximately $120 to $150 million over a period of three years" (*Source*: G. Miller et al., "Tax Collections Optimization for New York State," *Interfaces 42*, 1).

Another highly visible and successful large-scale IBM analytics project was the collaboration between the Industrial and Commercial Bank of China (ICBC) and IBM Research to develop a data-based methodology for siting bank branches (more under ICBC below).

In July 2008, IBM announced the acquisition of ILOG® at a cost $340 million. ILOG® owned two major analytics software products: a business rules management system and CPLEX®, the market leading large-scale optimization engine. This acquisition enabled IBM to combine its business process management, business optimization, and rules management technologies, to enhance customers' ability to collect all relevant information in real-time to make faster business decisions. A survey of 3,000 CIOs found that 83% reported that applying analytics to their IT operations was the most important element of their three- to five-year strategic growth plan.

"Over the past five years, IBM has invested more than $14 billion in 24 analytics acquisitions. Today, more than 8,000 IBM business consultants are dedicated to analytics and over

200 mathematicians are developing breakthrough algorithms inside IBM Research" (*Source*: http://www.analyticbridge.com/profiles/blogs/ibm-commits-100-million-to).

Industrial and Commercial Bank of China (ICBC)

ICBC has some 16,000 branches throughout China and is by many measures (market capitalization, deposits) the world's largest bank. The branch network is a key strategic asset of any retail bank and managing the branch network is a core banking competency. Branches were seen as ICBC's most important service and marketing channel, since they were the most effective means of customer acquisition.

As China's economy expanded and modernized, the centers of business and customer activity moved around, with new urban districts and satellite cities emerging, and personal wealth increasing. These fast-changing conditions and the competitiveness of the Chinese banking market, makes it essential for ICBC to quickly identify new high-potential locations in which to open branches, as well as moving or reconfiguring existing branches. ICBC needed to determine how many branches should be in each city and their locations, identify new high-potential regions for expansion, and improve branch location decision making in order to minimize costs and avoid poor location choices.

In 2006, ICBC partnered with IBM to begin development of ICBC's branch network optimization system. This system was driven by a market potential model where each city was divided into tens of thousands of 100-meter-square cells, and the business activity and demographic data for each cell was identified from Geographic Information System databases. This data was used to calculate a base market potential value for each cell, which was then refined using human opinion and optimization models to a final market potential estimate.

Finally, large-scale optimization coupled with expert judgment was used to find the cells that offered the best locations for branches taking into account market potential, competitor's locations, and other ICBC branches in the neighborhood.

This process has been implemented in over 40 major cities in China to great effect. For Suzhou, ICBC attributed US$1.04 billion in deposit increases to use of this system to improve branch locations. ICBC has trained 500+ employees to use the system and now sees branch locations as a strategic problem that is ongoing and needs constant attention.

The massive data requirement to address the bank branch location problem for ICBC, and the ability to acquire, maintain, and process this rapidly changing data using complex large-scale optimization makes this difficult analytics for a competing bank to quickly replicate. Consequently, this appears to be a good example of strategic analytics that should provide a competitive advantage to ICBC for some time (Xiquan Wang et al., "Branch Reconfiguration Practice Through Operations Research in Industrial and Commercial Bank of China," *Interfaces 42*, 2012).

Winning Analytics at ABB Electric

ABB Electric was founded in 1970 with the objective of manufacturing a range of medium-power electrical transformers for the North American market. In 1974, just as ABB Electric was approaching a break-even position, the "oil crisis" that followed the formation of OPEC precipitated an industry-wide shock that cut industry sales in half. Stalled from further growth, the industry became tremendously competitive almost overnight. ABB was left to compete with established giants such as Westinghouse, McGraw-Edison, and General Electric in this shrinking industry. The only way that ABB could survive was to take customers from the established competitors.

The first market action taken by ABB management was to offer a five-year warranty on all ABB's products. Since each item cost $300,000, and the industry standard warranty was one year, this offer gave ABB instant credibility in the marketplace, but required ABB to vastly improve its manufacturing to support the warranty. ABB developed and applied analytics models throughout manufacturing in order develop the extremely high standard of quality control required. The result was a highly sophisticated concept of manufacturing management that gave ABB the highest quality products in the industry. Remarkably, at the same time ABB became the low-cost producer.

Following success in manufacturing, the use of analytics at ABB spread to many other areas, including marketing decision models, design and manufacturing applications, and in research and development for new products:

> A strength of ABB Electric is that [analytical' techniques have been applied and developed throughout the entire organization, often integrating various functional areas. (*Source*: Gensch et al. *op. cit.*)

ABB has utilized analytics very effectively to support product marketing. Two published applications that have been very successful are modeling customer choice, and identifying "switchable" customers.

ABB went to a considerable effort to build a database of transformer purchasers, and to try to determine which transformer features were most important to their customers. Multi-attribute choice models were developed in order to predict future customer purchase decisions from knowledge of past decisions and customer preferences. From these models, ABB was able to predict, with 60–70 percent accuracy, the chosen supplier for each sale of major equipment. ABB could now target its marketing efforts to those sales where it had the best chance of gaining a new customer, or holding on to one of its own customers that was likely to switch to a different supplier. ABB also gained a competitive advantage in product design, since it knew which product attributes were most important to its customers, and could decide on where it could best compete. The models also helped ABB to better understand its competition; a necessary success factor in most competitive environments.

In 1974, ABB started developing a customer database by mailing out surveys asking customers to rank product attributes. ABB then conducted a statistical analysis to determine those product attributes customers thought were most important. In one market segment, the three most important attributes were found to be warranty, performance ("energy losses"), and appearance in that order. ABB addressed the warranty issue head-on by offering the best warranty in the industry, but the importance of the appearance of the industrial transformer (more important than price, the availability of spares, or maintenance requirements) proved to a be a surprise. ABB exploited this knowledge through the relatively costless innovation of offering transformers in several different colors.

The initial model proved tremendously successful, and ABB was able to improve the model over time. The concept of the "switchable customers" became important, allowing ABB to focus its marketing efforts and eliminate wasted time. ABB identified customers, both its own and competitors, who were unlikely to switch supplier no matter the amount of persuasion used. ABB's strategy was to "essentially . . . reduce the marketing effort to ABB's and the competitors brand loyal segments and to expand it to consumers for whom ABB was competitive." The model achieved this differentiation by estimating choice probabilities and determining the statistical significance of the differences in these choice probabilities.

Daniel Elwing, CEO of ABB Electric, has attributed the company's survival to these models, and to analytics in general. Elwing created an environment and a management style where analytics flourished. Through the use of these models, ABB had captured market share steadily and by 1988 had 40% of the industrial transformer market. ABB was both the lowest-cost producer, and the highest-quality producer in the industry.

Elwing observed in a statement at the 1988 Board of Directors meeting at which time sales had grown to exceed $100 million:

> Without the insights from our marketing models, it is unlikely we would have current sales of $25 million; in fact, without the use of these models, it is unlikely we would be here at all. (*Source*: Gensch et al. *op. cit.*)

Following the success of ABB in gaining market share in a much smaller market, Westinghouse and McGraw-Edison ceased transformer production. This boosted ABB's share even higher, to a point where the Federal Trade Commission was concerned about monopolization of the transformer market leading ABB to divest its transformer business in 1990 as Waukesha Electric Systems with Dan Elwing as president (*Source*: Gensch et al. *op cit.*).

Tackling the Cost of Health Care

The costs of providing adequate health care are escalating, in part as a result of differences in service levels, lack of measurement and evaluation, and the fact that consumers often do not pay directly for the products. In many cases, these costs are born by national or regional (state or provincial) governments. All of these issues contributed to the need for a system of product definitions to allow for measurement and evaluation, thus promoting consistency between services from different health service providers. Diagnosis Related Groups (DRGs) were developed by Professor Bob Feller of Yale University in an effort to begin to control the growing cost of health care in the United States.

A DRG is a classification of a patient according to illness and the bundle of services received during hospitalization for that specific diagnosis. In determining a DRG, a patient is first classified into one of 23 Major Diagnostic Categories (MDC). Every illness can be classified into one, and only one, MDC, including diagnoses that involve surgical procedures (Surgical Group) and non-surgical treatment (Diagnosis Group). Using the International Classification of Diseases (ICD) system of coding, each MDC category, Diagnosis Group, and Surgical Group is broken into more groups based upon factors such as:

- comorbidities/complications
- age
- discharge status
- non-surgical procedures

This system creates a tree structure having at least four levels:

- MDC
- OR Procedure (Diagnosis Group or Surgical Group)
- ICD classification
- Further class differences (as listed above)

When developing this classification system, three characteristics were deemed important: the classifications should be based on information routinely collected by hospitals; the number of MDCs (classes) should be simple enough to be manageable but specific enough to be useful; and within each MDC there should be both a similar pattern of resource intensity, and similar types of patients from a clinical perspective.

Before the analysis of data to establish DRGs could begin, two years were needed to develop the technology required. A panel of physicians was established and asked to explain processes and assist with functional and clinical information. Information from the Uniform Hospital Discharge Data Set (completed for each patient discharged from a hospital in the United States) was analyzed to find similar patterns of care for illnesses, and to aggregate patients into coherent groups according to the services received.

DRGs met initial success when used in conjunction with Medicare's Prospective Payment System (PPS). Patients qualifying for health care paid by the U.S. government under Medicare were classified into one of the DRG codes upon discharge and, except for a small number of extreme cases, the hospital was paid a fixed rate based on the classification. The PPS rates were set nationally but were adjusted for local wage rates, even though hospital costs to provide service for each DRG could still differ based upon the cost of inputs (labor, materials), the number of cases and facility utilization, the case mix (numbers of each type of different cases), and variations in physicians' practice.

The combination of the use of PPS rates and DRGs was successful in making hospitals more accountable for costs. DRGs:

> were adopted by Medicare in 1983 to serve as a basis for a prospective payment system for US hospitals. This system has resulted in savings of more than $50 billion in Medicare hospital payments through 1990 and extended the solvency of the Medical Hospital Trust Fund well into the next century. More than 20 countries are currently developing or have adopted DRG-based systems for managing and financing hospital care. (*Source*: R. B. Fetter, "Diagnosis Related Groups: Understanding Hospital Performance," *Interfaces 21*, 1, 1991)

Some of the benefits realized include:

- a decrease in the number of admissions,
- a decrease in length of stay,
- a decrease in Medicare Program Costs, and
- an increase in profit margins of hospitals.

Although the severity of the illnesses of admitted patients has increased, this may simply be due to better coding of illnesses. A search of the internet for DRGs will provide a sense of the importance of this classification scheme in today's health care management, and also a host of actual or proposed modifications/additions/revisions to Feller's original list of DRGs (*Source*: Fetter *op cit.*).

Summary

There are a many examples of firms where analytics activities appear to have created a competitive advantage sustained over a period of time. In the not-for-profit sector, where a competitive advantage is not usually an objective, there are many examples where senior decision makers have been informed by advanced analytics, and where analytics is used to address complex problems on a regular basis.

The strategic use of analytics by several firms has produced cost and revenue advantages maintained over many years and this has prompted competitive reaction and firm and industry restructuring. Firms have been forced out of business because they could not find a way to compete against competitors using analytics strategically.

There exists an industry of suppliers of analytics and analytics solutions populated by many individuals who have previously worked in firms that have achieved competitive success with analytics and who now make this expertise broadly available.

What the Manager Must Know

Analytics can be used and is being used to create a competitive advantage and to improve not-for-profit decision making. Managers must know enough about analytics to be able to recognize the source of this advantage and the kinds of skills and knowledge required to sustain the advantage.

If the advantage is being created internally, the manager must understand how to nurture and maintain the strategic analytics and its likely future direction. If the advantage is being created by a competitor, the manger must be able to recognize the source of the advantage, and to understand what needs to be done to try to replicate the work and counteract the competitive advantage.

Strategic analytics is not easily purchased. Rather, it requires investment over time to accumulate data and develop the understanding and skills required to arrive at useful solutions to very complex and difficult problems.

The manager must understand what steps are required to grow an analytics capability internally and to develop this to the point where it can be seen as having strategic value.

Recommended Cases

Tallink: Connecting Estonia To Finland, Sweden, and Russia (Ivey)

Columbus-America Discovery Group and the SS Central America (INFORMS)

Merit Brass Company (INFORMS)

Procter and Gamble: North American Supply Chain Restructuring (INFORMS)

South African National Defense Force (INFORMS)

Vilpac Truck Company (INFORMS)

Decommissioning Nuclear Power Stations

Stephen B. Roman (Ivey)

L.L. Bean, Inc. (Harvard)

Online Low-Price Guarantees—Dollar.com (A) (Ivey)

AT&T Telemarketing Site Selection (A) and (B) (INFORMS)

Harris/IMPRESS (INFORMS)

Ohio Polymer/Probut Hydrocarbon (Ivey)

INDEX